GOLDEN STAGES

GOLDEN STAGES

edited by

Richard Allchin and Adrian Bell

For Audrey, Marilyn, Patti and Amanda

GOLDEN STAGES

Copyright: © Richard Allchin and Adrian Bell, 2013

First published in 2003 by Mousehold Press

Revised edition published in 2013
by
Sport and Publicity
75 Fitzjohns Avenue
Hampstead
London, NW3 6PD
www.sportandpublicity.co.uk
email: sport_publicity@hotmail.com

in association with

Mousehold Press
6, Constitution Opening
Norwich, NR3 4BD
www.mousehold-press.co.uk

Cover Design – Terry Batsford (El Tel Designs)
Cover photograph – Andy Jones
Back cover paintings – Jeff Platten

ISBN 978-0-9531395-1-4

Printed by Mimeo, Huntingdon

CONTENTS

Editors' Acknowledgements:
The editors and publishers would like to thank the following: Terry Batsford, Emma Felton Andy Jones, Jeff Platten, John Pierce, Joe Scherrer and, last but not least, Dave Reed for their wonderful pictures and in helping us with the production of the book. We are also grateful to Carlton Kirby, David Harmon, Frank Quinn and Sean Kelly for all their help and encouragement. We also owe a debt of considerable debt of gratitude Phil Liggett for once again providing us with such an appropriately revised foreword, which was not an easy task considering the many years Phil had worked closely with Lance Armstrong. Whatever mistakes there are in the text are, of course, our responsibility.
Richard Allchin, Adrian Bell and Mike Clark

FOREWORD

All the great cyclists have, since 1903, ridden at least one Tour de France. You simply cannot retire without having attempted the toughest cycle race of them all, even if, for some, it has ended in tears. But, as in any sport, there have always been those who have dominated and, during 100 years of Le Tour, eight names spring to mind – their exploits highlighted in this beautiful book so timely produced to coincide with the 100th edition of this great race. Bartali, Coppi, Bobet, Anquetil, Merckx, Hinault, Induráin and Armstrong have become known as the giants of *La Grande Boucle*.

Like many sports, in the first decade of the 21st Century, cycling has been put under the microscope in relation to how it has been tainted by the use of performance enhancing drugs. In the course of this examination Lance Armstrong's reputation has been torn to shreds, despite the fact that many of his beaten rivals in the Tour de France have also admitting to institutionalised doping. Either they had been caught out by the sport's anti-doping programs (however badly run and disorganised they have sometimes been) or they have finally succumbed to pressure and come clean. Lance Armstrong was by far the worst of these cheats, not so much for his doping practices but for the arrogance, abuse and bullying of his regime and for his total disregard for honesty until all was lost.

The fact remains, however, that Armstrong rode in an era when doping was prevalent – most of his main rivals were cheating as well – and in that context he has to be considered a great Tour rider. On a level playing field he may well have won his seven Tours legitimately. That is the dreadful irony when hugely talented athletes convince themselves that they 'need' to resort to doping themselves. It doesn't obviate the need for dedicated training and hard work; it does, however, show a total disregard for the damage their illegal practices bring to the sport they confessed to love.

Fortunately these days our sport is getting very much cleaner, as Bradley Wiggins who, along with so many others, were able to prove in the 2012 Tour and many other races in the last few years. If there is a athlete more vehemently opposed to doping than Sir Brad, I have yet to meet him.

It is no coincidence that all of those eight man named above were giants of the sport in that they also won world titles, single-day Classics and other major tours. While remembering their exploits with fondness and now sometimes with despair, the one occasion that has stayed with me throughout my commentating career is undoubtedly the battle of La Plagne in 1987.

If I am to be remembered, it has to be for this. It was the one occasion when it seems I brought households to a standstill. To this day, it remains my most remarked upon piece of television commentary. 'Roche,' I shouted. 'That is Stephen Roche.' That was all I said. But on that day every cycling enthusiast the world over became an admirer of the Irishman Stephen Roche – the man who refused to lose the Tour de France in the Alps and went on to win it in Paris.

Let me set the scene. On the twenty-first day of the 1987 race, Roche, already the first Irish winner of the Tour of Italy a month earlier, had lost one minute and 44 seconds to Spain's Pedro Delgado on the fabled climb of Alpe d'Huez. Roche had gone from being the race's yellow jersey to second, 25 seconds behind Delgado, who was one of the best climbers of the period.

The next day – a stage of 186 kilometres from the base of Alpe d'Huez to the dizzy heights of the ski-station at La Plagne – started with Roche saying he could win the Tour providing he didn't lose two minutes to Delgado before the final time-trial at Dijon.

We had a new French director of the television pictures that year and when French idol, Laurent Fignon, joined a breakaway on La Plagne with Anselmo Fuerte and Fabio Parra, he conveniently forgot to show us the pictures of the drama unfolding behind. He said at the time that the Tour was a French race, and that Fignon should have pride of place.

Roche had started the climb of La Plagne two minutes behind Delgado, his words still ringing in my ears. Surely he had lost the Tour now after failing on Alpe d'Huez only the previous day?

Oh, ye of little faith! While television was showing pictures of Fignon winning the stage for France and moving up the overall standings to seventh, Roche – fourteen minutes behind – was pulling off the recovery of a lifetime.

Delgado knew he had to beat Roche by a big margin before the final time-trial and, with no pictures and scant radio reports, it seemed that the great Spaniard had put in the killer blow as the hairpin bends carried him up the mountain in fourth place. Roche was still, reportedly, two minutes behind. As I sat looking at the monitor, commentating for British television, I saw Delgado finish, and then, in the top of the picture, were two legs – nothing more could be seen. That's when I shouted into the microphone – 'Roche. That is Stephen Roche.'

The Irishman had pulled off the ride of the century, bridging two minutes to finish just four seconds after Delgado. Delgado was devastated and announced that evening that he had lost the Tour, although he was still its leader by 39 seconds. Roche collapsed at the foot of my commentary position where I remained passing comment on him until the ambulance took him away with an oxygen mask in place.

Next morning the Dubliner was all smiles and looking as fresh as a daisy. He had partly feigned the oxygen-debt to avoid the after-race scrum from journalists and allowed himself precious extra moments of recovery. Three days later he had won the Tour de France by 40 seconds from Delgado, who had to wait another year before winning the great race for himself.

Of course in 2012 my dream that a British cyclist would one day win the Tour came to fruition when Bradley Wiggins won the final yellow jersey in Paris. His eventual, some say remarkable, transformation from one of the finest track riders ever to grace the boards and cement finally lived up to his true potential on the road and won our sport's greatest prize – the Tour de France. Brad certainly took his time. He has always done things one way … his way , but once he really made up his mind to win the Tour he did exactly that. It was a fantastic feeling to be British in Paris that day, just as it must have been to be Irish in 1987. A truly historic ending to the ninety-ninth edition.

These great riders personify the power of the greatest race on earth. To have been touched by the *maillot jaune* makes you special; but to have put on the final jersey in Paris – that means you are one of only a tiny handful of all those riders who have completed a Tour de France in its ninety–nine editions.

Roll on July; the hundredth event should certainly live up to its potential. And I hope there will be many more Golden Stages to come.

Phil Liggett, MBE
Hertfordshire. May, 2013

INTRODUCTION

This revised publication of *Golden Stages* celebrates the 100th edition of the Tour de France, the world's greatest cycling race. Over twenty leading cycling writers and broadcasters have explored what it is that makes the Tour such a majestic and moving event. They have each selected and told · the story of a particular Stage. Together, their accounts (one or more from each decade) add up to a history of the Tour, and they show how much the race has changed in the 109 years up until this year, 2013 – the bicycles, the roads, tactics, organization and the world-wide commercialism now so evident. But they also show what has not changed – the extravagant scale of the race; the mystique of the *maillot jaune*; and the courage of all who compete. Those things have remained the same – and they are vividly portrayed here.

However the Tour, and cycle racing generally, have gone though a very dark period in the ten years since we published the first edition of Golden Stages. There can be little doubt that powerful performance-enhancing doping practices have been widespread. This has been true of other international sports, but cycling has had the most exposure and perhaps unfairly taken the brunt of public criticism. The fact that the final result of major races have been overturned, with the 'winner' subsequently disqualified days (sometimes even years) after the finish, has at times rendered the sport almost farcical.

We published the first edition five years after the 1988 'Festina' scandal' which, it was hoped at the time, would signal a radical change. We now know that was not to be. The following year saw the first of seven consecutive Tour 'victories' by the man who came to symbolise the very worst of that period, the man at the heart of what the US Anti-Doping Agency described as 'the most sophisticated and professional doping program in recent sports history'. Nothing, perhaps, indicates the bleakness of that period so much as the fact that when Lance Armstrong was stripped of his Tour titles, the Tour de France authorities felt unable to award the race to any other rider who finished near the top of the General Classification. The re-written history of the Tour has no official winners between 1999 and 2005.

And yet, cycle racing has changed very much for the better in the last few years. Cycling has done more than other sports in seeking to eliminate drug use. The peloton is a far cleaner place, and Sir Bradley Wiggins proved this in 2012 when he became the first British winner of the Tour de France. Brad's hate of doping is only matched by his love of cycling and the unbelievable workload of his training programs. Sure he takes short cuts, but they are always around corners on his bike, not with his body's blood-work.

One minor aspect of the Lance Armstrong revelations is that we were taxed in preparing a second edition of this book: should we include the chapter from the first edition which described his win in the Prologue time trial of 1999 – the first step in his seven year domination of the Tour? My co-editor Adrian wanted to exclude it, arguing that in the light of what we now know, it could no longer be regarded as a 'golden stage', but I fought for its inclusion. For me it has value as an historical document, and possibly as a warning that 'all things must pass' – some in oblivion, some in controversy – but you can't escape the fact that they have happened and should be regarded as part of the history.

I hope you enjoy the book for what it is: reflections on some great cyclists and their wonderful feats which, year after year, make the Tour de France so enthralling.

Richard Allchin
May, 2013

STAGE 1, 1903: PARIS–LYON, 467kms.

Les Woodland

Not much has changed. The café is still there, and the traffic island to one side. And a plaque beneath the awning records:

ICI
devant le RÉVEIL MATIN
le 1er JUILLET 1903
fut donné le départ du
1er TOUR DE FRANCE
organisé par HENRI DESGRANGE

A guide to Montgeron in that same year called it a pleasant enough place 'but spoiled by all the cyclists that get there'.

The place is a pricey restaurant these days. Not the sort of place cyclists would eat. Further plaques announce the Tour's fiftieth visit, and another in 1979, the sixty-sixth Tour. A lot of cyclists got there on those days as well. The villagers must have been hopping mad.

Bikies, in 1903 as now, loved a good café. The one they found in Montgeron was the Réveil Matin. French bars go in for unusual names, and this one means Alarm Clock or Morning Call. It had been there for ages, even at the start of the twentieth century. The mail-coach from Lyon used to change horses there before going on to Paris, and there were stables for horses and rooms for horsemen. There'd been a scandal when a couple of them were murdered in the hope their pockets were full of gold.

That sort of hustle and bustle meant sweaty and noisy cyclists could come and go without comment – other than the guidebooks, of course – and before long they started organising races there. Among those who turned up to watch was Henri Desgrange, who'd become a bit of a celebrity because he'd set the world's first ratified hour record.

Maybe that's why he picked it for the first Tour de France. It wasn't *The* Tour in 1903, remember; it had no reputation other than being a dotty idea dreamed up by a rugby writer called Géo Lefèvre to save Desgrange's reputation. His boss had become editor of a new paper called *L'Auto* and, frankly, he wasn't much good at it. Adolphe Clément, the bike-factory man, had wanted to do down the rival paper, Le Vélo, and picked Desgrange because he'd worked for him as his PR man. Desgrange had also written a training book, *La Tête et les Jambes* (which urged riders in training to have no more need of women than yesterday's socks, and also spoke of doping in cycling), so he knew what he was talking about. A lot of money had gone into the sports-paper idea; it hadn't worked, and Clément was demanding Desgrange justify the investment.

The result was a publicity stunt too big to trump. The Tour de France. And it started outside the Réveil Matin on a warm afternoon on 1st July 1903, and it's still well known. There's even a sign to it from the main road. You leave Paris by the Porte Dorée on the *périphérique*, the Paris ring road, and go down by the Bois de Vincennes where Jan Janssen became the first Dutchman to win the Tour in 1968, and then on to the Route Nationale 19 to Montgeron. You follow the white signs from there.

The Réveil Matin stands at the junction of the Melun and Corbeil roads, little changed from the sepia 1903 photograph on its restaurant menu. The Montgeron sign is across the road, the main village to the right. To the left is a small island in the junction of the road from Paris. Trees still grow along the opposite pavement.

Legend says Desgrange himself dropped the flag. He didn't. Desgrange never lacked confidence in later years – 'justifiably called a despot,' said the legendary French journalist Pierre Chany – but in 1903 he was too scared. He hadn't had the wit to think up the Tour and he feared for his job if he linked himself with a flop. He stayed in the office and sent Lefèvre and a flamboyant, moustachioed man called Georges Abran instead. Lefèvre followed the whole race by bike and train – the route and start times were decided by train timetables – and Abran's role was to wave the flag and spend much of the rest of the day in cafés, 'seated behind a Pernod' according to Lefèvre.

Street singers and mandolin players turned up on that first day of the first Tour, and salesmen selling Coco, the Coca Cola of its day. A collection of *types*, as the French would call them, changed in the bar cellars and emerged if not as butterflies than as apprehensive heroes. *L'Auto* reported:

> At 3.16 p.m. the men waved their hats, the ladies their umbrellas. One felt they would have liked to touch the steel muscles of the most courageous champions since antiquity. Who will carry off the

first prize, entering the pantheon where only supermen may go? I do not hesitate to make Maurice Garin, the white bulldog, my favourite.

Nobody ever called Garin the white bulldog. That was just Desgrange's invention. A lot of early racers used made-up names, including the first woman in Paris–Rouen, who called herself 'Miss America'. There was even a rider styled 'Samson' in this first Tour. No, Desgrange knew most of his riders were unknown to almost everyone and he gave them nicknames to win them affection. Others now long forgotten became the 'champion of the carpenters', the 'heel pedaller', and the 'prince of miners'.

Garin was a tiny man who'd been born in Italy, just across from the French border. For some reason his family thought they'd do better on the Belgian border instead and they moved right across France to Roubaix, and then to Lens, the coal-mining town where he is now buried. He was a dapper man, often pictured with a ciggie on his lips, and enough of a wow with the girls that he married three times. A wow on a bike, too, because he won Paris–Roubaix in 1897 and 1898, and came third in 1900.

The other favourite was Hippolyte Aucouturier, built like a wrestler, and a spectacular giant in a red and blue jersey. His moustache was wider than his face. He too had won Paris–Roubaix, and also Bordeaux–Paris and Paris–Brest–Paris. The German champion, Josef Fischer, was also there, and a ragbag of others, including a southern blacksmith called Jean Dargassies whose first bike ride had been only two months earlier. He'd never heard of the Tour until the bike-shop man told him he looked strong enough to ride.

'Don't worry about me,' he said when he turned up to enter. 'I'm a blacksmith and I know what physical effort is all about.'

A man called Jean Desvages rode only because he wanted to see more of France, but he still came 20th.

They rode in little more than their working clothes and certainly not in shorts. Some were linked with bike factories, like Peugeot, but clothes were valuable and the sport too new and poor to waste money on anything special, even if it existed. Which it didn't. And so in street clothes they set off in mid-afternoon with a long way to go. A very long way. The shortest daily stint was 268 kilometres, and the longest, the first stage from Paris to Lyon, a startling 467. The officials set off in pursuit. As for the Tour's management: 'The controls and the organisation of the race?' Lefèvre wrote. 'No car for me, just my bike.'

15

I was 26 years old and I was the champion of the cyclists' section at the Stade Français. So every stage I rode, I did my best to monitor the race. I followed the riders as far as the nearest station where the timetable would let me catch an express which would get me to the finish before the riders.

On that first day he took his first train to Moulins to watch the race pass, then another to Lyon.

So Abran waved the flag and doffed his boater and downed Pernods, Lefèvre chased along with riders who to him were little short of gods, often teasing gods – 'Shouldn't you be home in bed?' they chided at night – and a Fernand Mercier travelled ahead to arrange each stage's finish with *L'Auto*'s local correspondent.

Nobody had done it before, a race from place to place, and on again a day or so later, seemingly ceaselessly. Nobody knew how fast they'd go. In fact, Garin nipped along so sharpish – 26 k.p.h – that he reached the finish before Lefèvre and Mercier got there. Knowing the hyperbole that Desgrange would want, and doubtless keen to put the best possible shine on a personal cock-up, Lefèvre enthused, 'They are going faster than the train'.

Fragile organisation? Well, yes. But it didn't stop the Tour timing riders down to a tenth of a second.

These days they're timed to a thousandth, of course. What made decimals so odd in 1903 was that margins were so much greater. You have to think of early Tours not like the modern race but perhaps as an Audax, a *randonnée*. Riders started together; they rode at their own pace; they stopped at controls; they found most of their own meals and drinks; and they got separated by hours. They were all racing but they were more like marathon runners than cyclists: the best set a pace, and it was for the rest to keep up or fade. Desgrange liked it that way.

The roads were appalling. There were only a hundred or so miles of surfaced road in all France. The rest were compacted earth held in place by scattered rocks. The state of the road-making art was cobbles. You didn't need anything better for a farm cart.

Imagine that, 260 kilometres as a minimum, more than 450 as a maximum. In the night, and with no light, because you can't race 450 kilometres without starting one night and finishing the next. The stint from Lyon to Marseille began at 2.30 a.m. Marseille–Toulouse (10.30 p.m.) and Bordeaux–Nantes (11.30 p.m.) actually started the previous day. Desgrange soon said his ideal Tour was one that only one rider would finish. Or rather, *could* finish. When, years later, Jacques Goddet said the

Tour must have an inhuman face, that excess was necessary, he was only echoing his predecessor.

Riders complained, campaigned. Henri Pélissier in the 1920s repeatedly fell out with Desgrange in blazing arguments about whether races were meant to be fast or exhausting. You can guess Desgrange's view. He was torn in 1903 between a race of stupendous size and exhaustion, and the horror of having everyone drop out half-way through.

He made his riders race, therefore, not every day, but every few days. There was a humane aspect to it, but cynics also pointed out that the race rode only when it suited *L'Auto*'s deadlines, and not when Lefèvre and his colleague, Olivier Margot, couldn't get their reports back to Paris, or reach the next stage-town in time.

The night rides and long breaks between them became shorter as the years went on. Even so, Desgrange, who wanted a race so debilitating that even supermen would fall to their beds, was horrified that his poor bloody infantry were accepting contracts to ride track races on their days off. The Tour had made them celebrities and there was cash in hand for riding before a paying audience.

Predictably, Desgrange stopped such larking about. He couldn't stamp out the rest days, though, so riders were obliged to do just that – rest. Not always with the best consequences. The Frenchman Adolphe Helière went swimming on the rest day in Nice in 1910 and drowned after being stung by a jellyfish. His was the first death during the Tour de France. And, since you're now wondering, the first to die on, rather than off, a bike was the little Spanish climber, Francisco Cepeda. His front tyre rolled off the rim on 14th July in 1935, and he fell down a cliff on the Galibier. Helpers pulled him out half-conscious, and with blood streaming down his face, but he slipped into a coma and died three days later in hospital in Grenoble.

Other than the judges not reaching the finish on time, that first stage, and the rest of the first Tour, were a success even though riders and organisers were making it up as they went along. Garin won the first stage, Aucouturier the next two. By Toulouse, Aucouturier had an easy lead. But then he faded and Garin won, occasionally favoured by officials who illegally passed him food knowing their boss wanted him to win. Suspicions rose and the row proper broke next year. Desgrange denied collusion and offered to open his account books, but his critics maintained, accurately, that there was a link between Garin, his bike factory, and the men who had financed *L'Auto*.

Was it not reasonable, the cynics said, to suppose that all had an interest?

The row passed but it did show that hints of scandal, corruption and skulduggery were nothing new in cycling even then. But the race was already a success for *L'Auto*. It printed 14,178,474 papers in 1903. It had an edition on the streets within seven minutes of the finish in Paris and they sold instantly.

Crowds turned out at Ville d'Avray, the official finish. Of that morning, before returning to the capital Lefèvre wrote:

> For the final time, the peloton has forced itself into the night, the controls lit up and blinding, and soon the giants of the road will reach the goal that lay 2,500 kilometres ahead of them when they first climbed into the saddle.

The Tour had worked. Clément was satisfied.

His paper, *L'Auto*, began in the heat of an extraordinary business called the Dreyfus Scandal. Alfred Dreyfus was the highest non Catholic in the army, and had been accused of selling secrets to the Germans. Frankly, it was a stumped-up case to get rid of a Jew. There was a rigged trial and then a second hearing that was little better. Dreyfus was shipped off to a penal colony on Devil's Island, for life, in the hope everyone would forget him.

But they didn't. The first trial had been in 1894 and people were still arguing about it almost a decade later. Dreyfus became a rabbit to be tugged between pedigrees who liked the *status quo* and who supported a Catholic hierarchy and a sense of order, and a more mongrel element who wanted to do away with old stuffiness and to bring in a modern, liberal state. They were never likely to agree, and Dreyfus was less a cause than a symbol.

The Tour started because the existing big paper, *Le Vélo*, insisted Dreyfus was innocent. Clément and the others, on the other hand, said he dunnit. Things came to a head at a protest meeting on the horse-racing circuit at Auteuil, and the plot to set up *L'Auto* as a rival was started. The Tour made it work. On 20th November 1904 *Le Vélo* went out of business, and its bad-tempered editor, Pierre Giffard, was out of a job.

Desgrange had said at that crisis meeting in the rue du Faubourg Montmartre that he wanted an idea 'to nail Giffard's beak shut'. Well, he'd done it, and with the idea of Lefèvre – a man he'd poached from Giffard in the first place. Rather uncharacteristically, or with the magnanimity of the victor, Desgrange gave Giffard a job.

The Tour, of course, continued despite a hiccup next year when riders were towed by cars, the leaders were disqualified and shots were fired outside St Étienne to scare off thugs. Desgrange wanted to call it all off there and then, writing off a race that he said was wrecked by blind emotions. Once more – and again, later, when he was persuaded to take the Tour through the mountains, but refused to turn out to watch – the 'Father of the Tour' displayed his lack of confidence.

Father of the Tour? No, not really. That was Lefèvre. He'd thought of it, he'd followed it, judged it and reported on it. But even Desgrange could recognise a good idea when he eventually saw one, given enough time and yes-men. And either he styled himself 'Father of the Tour', or he didn't object when someone else did.

Maybe he wanted Lefèvre out of the way, somewhere he wouldn't challenge his own version of history. He took him off bike-race reporting and steered him towards rugby, boxing and aviation the moment the Tour became a success and the paper's sales began to rise. He took the glory for himself. Lefèvre described his boss as 'a hard man, in the good sense of the word'. A generous gesture.

Beside the pink bankings of the Parc des Princes in 1953, though, there were some old enough to know what Lefèvre had achieved. It was the Tour's fiftieth anniversary and Lefèvre was there with Maurice Garin and Hippolyte Aucouturier to see Louison Bobet take the first of his three victories.

And then? Well, Lefèvre stayed in the trade and became head of the French sportswriters' association and an authority and pioneer of car racing. Garin is in his grave at Lens, where he lay unnoticed for decades until Italian television found him there. He has no memorial anywhere in the world, a hero for winning in 1903, shamed for being disqualified in 1904. The Garin family has died out, its last heartbeats chronicled on the gravestone he shares with his wives.

Desgrange left his race in 1936 after a hospital operation and died on the Mediterranean coast in 1940. The initials H. D. appeared on, and only recently disappeared from, the yellow jersey. The Réveil Matin, as we've seen, still stands and trades to a rather posher clientele. But there's no point looking for souvenirs; they've all long been stolen.

And Captain Dreyfus? Well, the man who actually did it, Marie-Charles Esterhazy, fled to Britain and owned up. Dreyfus was finally declared innocent in 1906, three years after the Tour – to which he had unknowingly given birth – began. He was made a major and given back his old job. He died in 1935 – although not until 1998 did France say sorry.

And the Tour? Oh well, you know ... it struggles on somehow, doesn't it?

TOUR OF RENEWAL: 1919

Graeme Fife

28th June 1914, 3 a.m.

A total of 145 riders, including two Australians (a Tour first), left Paris for the twelfth edition of the Tour de France. Later that day, the Serbian student Princip, of the secret 'Black Hand' organisation, shot and killed the heir to the throne of the Austro-Hungarian empire, the Archduke Franz Ferdinand, and his wife, in Sarajevo. Two days after the Tour finished in Paris, Austria–Hungary declared war on Serbia; a week later, France was at war with Germany.

In the ensuing carnage France lost 1.3 million men, the highest proportion of any of the combatant nations. Of her 38,000 communes only one did not lose someone to the War. There were, in addition, three million men disabled or crippled, over a third of them made permanent invalids. Two hundred thousand civilians died from shellfire, bombs, the stray violence of combat. Although illegitimate births soared, the fertility rates within marriage plummeted. A contemporary wit remarked: 'French men were mean with their sperm but not with their blood.' The franc, solid as a rock since 1801, taking even Waterloo and the revolutionary Paris Commune in its stride, had maintained four-fifths of its value during the War, propped up by the Government. By 1919 it was worth only half its true value, and France was on its knees, riven by social and industrial unrest, the country impoverished, in ruins; then, during the winter of 1918–19, another 166,000 of its citizens died in a virulent epidemic of Spanish influenza.

In the office of his newspaper *L'Auto*, at 10 rue du Faubourg Montmartre, Henri Desgrange was wondering how to launch a thirteenth edition of his great bike race. On 3rd January Rutherford had split the atom for the first time; the task of reshaping La Grand Boucle after so devastating an interim must have seemed quite as improbable a task. With severe rationing in force Desgrange would need to secure exemptions for petrol, food and other commodities. The roads of north and eastern France were in ruins, bridges destroyed, signposts disappeared; the roads in the interior were dilapidated after five years of neglect. Moreover, European cycling had been bled dry – except in Italy, where, largely unaffected by the conflict taking place north across the Alps, save in the Alps where the

Italians fought – and defeated – the Austro–Hungarian army, racing had continued.

Many prominent riders had been maimed and would never ride a bike again; many had lost their lives – promising men like Engel, tenth in the 1913 Tour, and stalwarts like Wattelier, winner of the 1902 Bordeaux–Paris, veteran of the first Tour and those of 1905–9; and Georges Cadolle, who rode the 1910 race. Most telling of the losses were the three greats of the pre-War tours: Faber, Lapize and Petit-Breton. François Faber, 'the Giant of Colombes', winner in 1909, had set a record for the 1913 Paris–Roubaix at 35.333 k.p.h., which stood for 18 years. Octavio 'Curly' Lapize, winner in 1910, beating Faber in a bitter elbow-to-elbow tussle on the very last stage, won three each of Paris–Roubaix, Championship of France, Paris–Bruxelles, plus Paris–Tours, and took second in the 1911 Paris–Brest–Paris. Lucien 'Quicksilver' Petit-Breton, first double-winner, 1907 and '08, had been famous for his devastating accelerations.

> When you're feeling good on the flat, it's the best time for finding out how the others are going and to get them rattled: that's when I launch my sudden attacks, what they call my nervous fits. Not many of them can counteract what they take to be a disorganised waste of effort. They're thinking, 'If we all tried to match that, hardly any of us would get to the finish.'

Lapize, a pilot, had been shot down over the killing fields of Verdun where some 400,000 French soldiers died in 'heroic defence' of the massive network of fortifications on the Meuse. Petit-Breton was killed on a military mission when the motor he was in crashed. Faber had strode out alone and unarmed into no man's land, to rescue a gravely wounded comrade crying out for help, very close to the German line. Faber heaved the stricken man across his shoulders and was on the point of climbing down into the safety of his company communication trench when a German bullet hit him in the head.

Their loss was bitter, emblematic of the terrible waste the war inflicted, but Desgrange could not, *would* not, give way to sentiment. If anything could speak of France's redemption, inspiring her to heave herself like a phoenix out of the ashes of war, then it was his Tour. Unprepared the riders might be, but they would have to shoulder this crucial burden of *renewal*. Men like the French aces – Jean Alavoine, Henri and Francis Pélissier, and the one they called the 'Old Man', 34-year-old Eugène Christophe who'd ridden his first Tour in 1906; and the Belgians – Philippe Thys (already twice winner, 1913 and '14), Lambot, Marcel and Lucien Buysse.

Some twenty of the greats of the peloton were still around; and there were classy new men like Honoré Barthélemy, protégé of Henri Pélissier, eager to ride for the future and to re-establish the great race.

In the 1914 Tour, Thys and Pélissier, riding for the same Peugeot-Wolber team, had fought right to the finish. Unlucky in the Pyrenees, Pélissier – who'd begun his career under the wing of Petit-Breton – launched an imperious attack on the col d'Allos, then hammered them again over the Ballon d'Alsace in the Vosges and, nearing Paris, he trailed Thys by 23 minutes. But, on the stage between Longwy and Dunkerque, Thys' forks snapped. The 23 minutes began to leak away. He hefted the broken machine into a cycle shop and bullied the owner into helping him mend the forks.

'But you'll get penalised,' said the man.

'I know, but if I do the job myself, it'll take me an hour at least; if you give me a hand, I'm still in with a chance and it depends what time they dock me.'

In 20 minutes he was back on the road and chasing furiously. He came in third, behind the winner, Pélissier, now only 1min 49secs down, though he must surely have taken more, had it not been for the dense crowds of patriotic fans barring his way, cheering, clamouring to pat him on the back. Shades of Guerini, 1999, another Tour they saddled with the heavy task of renewal.

But Pélissier wasn't finished. On the final stage, he even had the effrontery to attack his boss on a climb no more than fifteen kilometres from the Parc des Princes and rode into the stadium 200 metres ahead of the pursuit: it wasn't enough. Thys took the overall by 1min 40secs. after over 200 hours of riding. 'Pélissier the blackleg,' wisecracked the papers.

So, he returned, ready for revenge: 30 years old, hypersensitive, yet with an iron control, given to no waste of words, or gesture, he was a class rider, an instinctive racer. Two Tours of Lombardy (1911 and 1913) and Milan–San Remo 1912, he had signalled his promise with third in a Tour de France for Independents run in August 1910. He and his 23-year-old younger brother Francis lined up for the start of the 1919 race, which set out from Paris on 29th June, the day after the Peace Treaty of Versailles was signed and Alsace-Lorraine returned to French ownership. That had been on the cards for a long time and, for the first time, Desgrange's route took the riders to Strasbourg, the administrative capital of what, since 1870, had been the German-occupied region. There had been sorties into the area, over the Ballon d'Alsace, but this was a grand gesture – the

Tour de France reasserting national pride over the return of sovereign territory: the soil of *La Patrie* hallowed by bicycle wheels.

There were new rules: the race would be on a strictly individual basis, no help to be given to or accepted from other riders. (This always had been the strict rule but abuse had crept in.) Further, any rider sacrificing his own chances for another rider or gaining an advantage by another's sacrifice, would be fined heavily. The severest fine was 500 francs, for accepting a lift in a car, even when incapable – through injury, exhaustion or a broken machine – of riding the bike. (A stage victory was worth 350 francs.)

For the first time, the organisation provided official feed stations – a necessity enforced by rationing. Riders were enjoined not to hurl themselves like madmen at the food bags – each marked with the rider's number – and to remember to collect a fresh bidon at each stop. If they refilled the bidons at a pump, they had to work the pump themselves. They were also required to keep receipts for any food bought in between the feed stops – two per stage – and if they failed to produce them (against reimbursement of expenses by the Tour organisation) they would be fined. This supplementary food could not be ordered in advance. In fact, the riders had to function as tourists: quaint notion.

Another probable side-effect of the War, belligerence and technological advance going hand in glove as ever, meant that the bikes had improved: each rear hub now carried two freewheel cogs either side, which gave the riders a choice of four gears where hitherto they had had only two. Change still necessitated dismounting and shifting the chain or turning the wheel round; nevertheless, it was progress. Every rider had to start and finish on the same machine, stamped by the Tour officials – including one secret mark.

There were only 69 starters: two Italians; the rest, French and Belgian evenly split; how many of them had kept some kind of contact with the bike by riding with the Cycle Regiments of the French army, I cannot tell. I do have a postcard showing a platoon of French Bike Infantry overtaking a regiment of artillery on a muddy road somewhere near the Western Front, and a picture of François Faber on a road in eastern France slip-streaming a soldier in kepi, sash and puttees; presumably a fan. It became commonplace to compare the laden Tour riders, festooned with gear, food bags, tool kits, spare tyres, spare clothing, slung over their shoulders, to the *poilus*, 'shaggies', French for Tommies, staggering along with full packs.

Before the War, the team-men had ridden for rival bike manufacturers: Peugeot–Wolber had dominated the 1914 race, taking twelve of the fifteen stages. Commercial throat-cutting had led to intense salary bargaining – not so new a phenomenon, indeed. The star riders, *cracks* as the French call them, had demanded higher and higher retainers and bonuses. So, a new combine of the leading French cycle manufacturers, La Sportive, collared most of the peloton, expressly to eliminate spiralling competition over money as well as to reduce the overall costs of sponsoring the continental racing season. The reduced number of *cracks* in the ranks and the fact that many of the younger riders had not had a chance to prove themselves yet, put La Sportive in a very strong position to enforce signature on an extremely restrictive contract. At the head of this consortium was the martinet they called 'Marshall His Nibs', Alphonse Baugé, who took delight in badgering and cajoling the riders to more effort.

The Pélissier brothers refused to sign up. They were men of some pride, some self-esteem, and not in the way of crawling to cynical businessmen and abiding by *diktats*.

'So much the worse for you,' scoffed Baugé, 'if you want to play at revolutionaries. No independent sponsor is going to sign you up.'

In fact the *directeur sportif* of J. B. Louvet, independent of the Sportive cartel, offered the Pélissier tandem contracts *if* they won Paris–Roubaix; if *not*, the deal was off and he would call in his money. Facing a hostile opposition of 120 contract riders, the two brothers attacked not far from the start, raced like demons and came into Roubaix Henri first, Francis second. A few weeks later Francis won a legendary Paris–Tours victory, in driving snow, to beat the famously impervious Christophe and, to cap their defiance, shortly after that Henri took Bordeaux–Paris. On the eve of the Tour, Baugé was haranguing his demoralised troops, urging them to bloody well do something about this pathetic state of affairs. The Pélissiers were running them ragged.

29th June 1919, Paris

On the ride from La Place de la Concorde, via a stop to pay homage to Faber at the café he'd frequented in Colombes, Francis Pélissier took a heavy fall and eventually reached the start on the bridge over the Seine at Argenteuil two hours after the race had set off. He buried himself all night, seeing nothing, as they said, beyond his front wheel or his handlebars, and reached Le Havre some four hours after the winner, Rossius, who'd beaten Henri by a minute; 388 kilometres in 15hrs 50mins. Rossius, however, was disqualified from the victory for handing his patron, Thys, a bidon. A futile sacrifice, as it turned out: Thys had had no intention of finishing the stage; he'd come to the line under protest, arguing money with La Sportive, and was hell bent on going home to Belgium. He abandoned just before noon. Desgrange was furious. Thys, he said, had made a pile during the War and had gone bourgeois (a shaming insult from a Frenchman): he would never get to the top again. (Thys won in 1920, the first triple victor.)

Henri Pélissier was in the lead; he rode everyone off his wheel to victory in the second stage, Le Havre to Cherbourg, 364 kilometres in 15hrs 51mins 13secs and Francis scorched into Brest on Stage 3, Henri just behind, 405 kilometres in 16 hrs. 30 mins. 5 secs. On those first three stages it had been carnage. The rain fell relentlessly and turned the roads – badly rutted, pitted, ill-surfaced – into quagmires. On Stage 1 no fewer than 28 riders had abandoned, victims of endless punctures, falls and crushing fatigue: the worst casualty rate on record. The papers reported that it was 'the first time that a first stage of the Tour de France is accused of murdering our riders.' Stage 2 accounted for a further fourteen: only 27 riders set out from Brest. They were about to ride down the entire length of the French west coast to the Spanish border, 900 kilometres, in two stages.

At this point, the Sportive riders offered the Pélissiers a deal: the rivalry would finish them all off; there was no point in such demonic racing with the Pyrenees *and* the Alps to come. Henri gave them short shrift: 'The race will go to the strongest ,' he said. 'This Pélissier, drunk on his wins,' muttered the others.

They left Brest at 2 a.m. in fog so thick that the car headlights – their only illumination – penetrated no more than ten metres. By Châteaulin, 45 kms, the fog had lifted but the recent storms had left not so much a road as an endless series of mud lakes. There was, too, a head wind blowing, 'strong enough to wrench a bull's horns off'.

Coming out of Quimperle, at 72 kilometres, Henri Pélissier stopped to tighten his headset which had shaken loose in the non-stop racketing over the dreadful roads. The Sportive riders – already accused of riding in covert relays – saw their chance and attacked, Francis with them. The rules forbade him to stay with his brother; riding with the conspiracy might give him at least an opportunity of limiting the damage. It was a forlorn hope. Henri faced a probable solo ride of 300 kms in pursuit of men who were set on humiliating him, all of them riding in a passion, openly relaying, bit and bit like any modern bunch. By L'Orient, 145 kms, seven riders had been shelled out and Henri Pélissier was beginning to pick up the exhausted stragglers, one by one, as they peeled off, drained by the wicked pace, waifs and strays scattered along the route, will-power smashed, drained of any desire to go on.

Outside Nantes, 314 kms, he picked up and dropped Goethals (later a stage-win specialist but destined not to finish this, his first, Tour) then Barthélemy. But, he punctured and they overtook him; alone again. He caught them a second time, Goethals weaving – parched and desperate for water, Barthélemy going strongly. They rode together. At this point, Desgrange drove up and harangued them.

'You're not allowed to relay.'

'And the others in front, they're *not* relaying ?'

'If Barthélemy helps you, you're out, both of you.'

(Incidentally, relaying was common practice in the long-distance races, where crack riders regularly took tows from pacemakers along the route. Desgrange wanted his Tour to be different.)

The next straggler was Francis, a giant of a man, now sprawled at the side of the road, sobbing with fatigue: 'the Tour is an abomination … I'll never ride it again.' He couldn't even get back on the bike, let alone follow his brother. Henri, tiring, forged on, reeling in the field, but, five kms from Sables d'Olonne, he clambered off at a peasant's thatched hovel, slumped to the ground and begged a drink, fumbling in his pocket for some money. The peasant refused the money. 'This Tour de France is for mercenaries,' the mud-caked wild man explained in his posh Parisian accent, 'but the Pélissiers are free men.' He remounted, and went through the motions into Sables, a mere 28 minutes down on Alavoine. It was a staggering feat which Desgrange praised extravagantly: as magnificent as Terront's celebrated Paris–Brest–Paris victory in 1891. Yet, when the rest, only 21 of them now, left Sables for the 482-kilometre ride to Bayonne, Henri and Francis took the train back to Paris.

'The Pélissier tandem won't last long,' wrote one of those journalists better suited to reporting croquet, 'and courage, which certainly isn't one of their defining qualities, failed them completely today.'

There was a general truce on the next mammoth stage, 482 kms to Bayonne, the longest stage ever, where they arrived, many of them, 'as limp and weak as rag dolls'. After 24 hours rest, they rode into the Pyrenees: the entire chain, 649 kilometres, every major col, into Perpignan, in two stages. To put that into current perspective: what the 1999 Tour did in two days, they did in one.

Christophe, who'd taken the overall lead after the departure of Henri Pélissier, held on; Alavoine, who had been riding majestically on the flat – two stage wins – and was tipped to win overall , lost ground on the first day of the climbs. He was a fly customer, though. He'd ride up to

Desgrange's car and say: 'Mr Director, Sir, about this regulation number 35 ...' and conversation would proceed. And then: 'Thank you, Sir, now about this regulation number 36...' all the while hanging on to the car up the gradient.

But the neophyte Barthélemy was the revelation: he took the stage to Luchon (cols d'Osquich, Soulor, Aubisque, Tourmalet, Aspin, Peyresourde) handsomely. Alavoine came back, however: he flew over the next procession of monsters then added a fourth stage win into Marseille. The effort sapped him; Barthélemy took the next three stages and, a born climber, liberated by the access of gradient, dipping almost casually into the depths of his strength, he soared into and over the Alps: 333 kms, Nice to Grenoble; 325 kms Grenoble to Geneva; crossing every massive rock pile in the way – Grande Chartreuse, Galibier and the rest. But, Christophe wouldn't be shaken off: he held onto the overall and, in Grenoble, on 18 July, he made history by pulling on the first official *maillot jaune*, yellow to match the paper on which *L'Auto* was printed. (There was an unofficial yellow jersey worn by Thys in 1913.)

While the French riders were hogging the main show, Lambot, the Belgian, third overall, was biding his time. Alavoine said of him 'he's collecting corpses'; every abandon had yielded him a higher placing and, in truth, he was not a brilliant rider; simply a very efficient one in parcelling out his effort. He stoked himself on hard-boiled eggs and jam sandwiches, drank very little and never filled his bidons at fountains. 'You can tell who's drunk too much,' he said, 'they're the ones on the sick list.' Big eater, Lambot: always cleared his plate *and* the rest of the table when the other riders were tottering off to bed.

'The best trenchermen make the best riders.'

He'd moved up to second, 28 mins down on Christophe; and, on the penultimate stage, the 'Witch with Green Teeth', as they called the spirit of bad luck, struck Cri-Cri once again as it had clobbered him on the Tourmalet in 1913. They were riding from Metz to Dunkerque, through the shattered landscape of the Western Front battlefields, 468 kms, and as if the roads weren't in a parlous state anyway, long stretches of the course were cobbled, the old cart tracks, Hell of the North. Clattering over the pavé out of Valenciennes, at 336 kilometres, Cri-Cri's forks started to wobble; he managed to scramble off before they snapped and as he did so, a voice in the peloton rang out:

'The Old Man's dropped – Go.'

Lambot saw his chance: he went, rode into Dunkerque after 21hrs. 4mins. in the saddle, and took yellow. Christophe, alas no stranger to this misfortune of broken forks, effected a repair in a bike shop and rode on, over three hours down on the Belgian. Next day, shattered by his ordeal, he trailed in last of the mere eleven survivors of this thirteenth Tour de France. The sole Independent – unsponsored – rider to finish, Nempon, the man from Calais, was escorted most of the way into the Parc des Princes by none other than Henri Desgrange himself, cheered and applauded by the crowds, a heroic lone effort to complete one of the toughest races to date, proud bearer of the *lanterne rouge*, 21 hours behind Lambot. Alavoine was second at 1hr 32mins 54secs; Cri-Cri third at 2hrs 16mins 31secs.

The Tour was restored; Desgrange had been nervous – how would the public react? At one point even he voiced qualms about the appalling ordeal *his* riders were going through.

We must conclude that not only is the Tour de France a frightful challenge in itself, but that this year it is more frightful than ever. Let us not forget that after five years of war, our riders have not been used to such gigantic effort, an effort aggravated by a whole train of factors which have taxed and stiffened their muscles and tested their resolution to the limit. It will be a rare breed of man who makes it to the finish in the vélodrome.

Not for nothing did they call the Tour the True World Championship of the Road.

Well, as he put it, the roads made their pitiless selection; supplies of his newspaper L'Auto were snapped up every day within minutes; even the legendary timekeeper, Bazin, was on regimental form. Asked to wake him at 6 a.m. precisely, Desgrange knocked on his door, only to see it open and there was Bazin, watch in hand, exasperated. 'It is now one minute and ten seconds past 6 o'clock.'

Firmin Lambot, winner in 1919 of the 'Tour of Renewal', seven months after the Armistace. He won again in 1922.

STAGE 10, 1926: BAYONNE–LUCHON, 323kms.

Adrian Bell

Continental road-racing was once described by Geoffrey Nicholson as a sport in which each minute of excitement demanded its price: 'an hour of pure drudgery, back bent under the sun, shoulders hunched against the wind and rain'. It was this, he said, which explained why so many professional riders were recruited from the peasant smallholdings: 'they are used to the toil and monotony of jobs which have to be completed whatever the weather'. He was talking at the time about Bernard Thévenet, double-Tour winner in the 1970s, but he might just as easily have had in mind a rider from half a century earlier – Lucien Buysse. He, too, fitted that description to a tee.

Buysse came from a cycling family in a small village in Flanders. His elder brother, Marcel, perhaps the most naturally gifted of all of the brothers, had won six stages in the 1913 Tour and finished third overall that year. By 1926 he had retired, and rumour had it that he was now off to Ghent to open a restaurant – no small feat, at that time, for a country boy. Lucien, by contrast, had no such upwardly mobile, urban aspirations: he was a countryman, through and through.

His initiation into the Tour had been peculiar. He was essentially a track rider, and although he had ridden the Tour with brother Marcel in 1914 and again in 1919, he had abandoned both times. A succession of six-day races had been his only preparation for his third attempt in 1923, and on that occasion he did finish, in eighth place overall. More to the point, he won a stage – the 411-kilometre stage from Perpignan into Toulon – ahead of race-leader Ottavio Bottecchia and the eventual Tour winner Henri Pélissier. That was to be the turning point. From then on he rejected the vélodromes and devoted himself entirely to the Tour.

In 1924 he had finished third and, the following year, in a scrupulous display of the *domestique* role, he was second behind his Automoto teamleader, Bottecchia. But at the Parc des Princes he had confided to his friends:

> I am happy that Bottecchia is first; yet it is not the best man who won … I raced this year according to the orders of my *directeur*

sportif, Monsieur Pierrard, and to earn money. Next year I will race to win, and I will win.

Over the winter it had seemed unlikely that he would even make the 1926 start-line. His 11-year-old daughter had died and Lucien, in his grief, had no interest in riding a bicycle. Perhaps it was his younger brother, Jules, who lived under his roof, who helped him through his bereavement because in the spring they were out on the roads training together. Lucien took third place in the Bordeaux–Paris, but that was merely a training ride – preparation towards a greater ambition. All seemed to be going well, he reported.

The Tour began at Evian (the first ever start outside Paris) and, at 5,795 kilometres, it remains the longest on record. The first week produced mixed fortunes for the Buysse brothers. Young Jules claimed the yellow jersey after a long, solo break on Stage 1, from Evian to Mulhouse, and held it until the 433-kilometre third stage. Here Gustaaf Van Slembrouck and Albert Dejonghe broke clear to ride into Dunkerque more than ten minutes ahead of all their rivals. These two Belgians, both from the J. B. Louvet team, now headed the general classification.

But Lucien, meanwhile, was suffering. The hot dry weather had turned the roads of northern France into a veritable dust bowl. Churned up by the wheels of the cars, and even the bicycle tyres, the dust reduced visibility in places to some ten metres. It penetrated everywhere – 'the odious dust' as Gabriel Hanot, correspondent for *Le Miroir des Sports* described it:

> The dust attacked your eyes, filled up your nose, blocked your ears, got into your mouth and cracked under your teeth, infiltrated your clothes and got into even the most hermetically sealed luggage.

This was a perennial problem on those unmade roads, but this was the worst in years, and Lucien's eyes were badly affected throughout the first week.

The next six stages took the riders 2,000 kilometres across the north of France, into and out of Brittany and then down the whole of the western seaboard. And very little happened. Interminable stages of 400 kilometres and more, ridden at a snail's pace, often arriving two hours behind schedule, produced just the brief flurry of a bunch sprint. The journalists grumbled: only a leading rider puncturing and perhaps the hour-long chase to get back to the group gave them anything to write about. Desgrange was exasperated at the riders' lack of enterprise.

So, finally, we arrive at Bayonne, with the the overall classification exactly as it had been on the morning the riders had left Dunkerque. What immediately awaited them was the tenth stage which would take them the 326 kilometres up over the heights of the Aubisque, the Tourmalet, the Aspin, and the Peyresourde before the final descent into Luchon. It was to prove the decisive stage in this twentieth edition of the Tour, just as it has done on so many occasions.

When Desgrange, in his restless search for an ever bigger, ever higher Tour, announced that the route of the 1910 race would include this excursion into the western Pyrenees, with its quartet of fearsome climbs, 26 riders, already signed-up, promptly quit. 'It is a circle of death,' they protested. And Octave Lapize (allegedly fearful of the wild bears that roamed the mountains) who won that first Pyrenean adventure, hissing 'Assassins' as he wearily pushed his bike past the organisers assembled at the top of the Aubisque – that is engraved in the legends. By 1926 this stage had become thoroughly embedded in the Tour's normal route. In fact, the Tourmalet has figured more often than any other of the Tour's great climbs.

Soon after the 76 riders (out of the original 126) left Bayonne, at midnight on 6th July 1926, to ride this 'circle of death', a light rain began to fall. It was still raining long after the finish-control at Luchon was finally closed, 24 hours later. As they made their steady upward journey through the foothills the temperature dropped, and silver needles of icy rain, glistening momentarily in the headlamps of the following cars, began to fall more heavily. There was no odious dust to trouble them, now, for the road was turning to mud.

At Eaux Bonnes, 180 kilometres into the stage, the peloton was still huddled together, as if these cold, soaked *coureurs* hoped to gain some semblance of warmth from each other's proximity. Then, as soon as they left the little spa town to face their first test on the lower slopes of the 1,709-metre Aubisque, Lucien Buysse made his move.

His tactic was simplicity itself – grip the handlebars tighter and press harder on the pedals. He made no appeal to his domestiques for help; he threw no enquiring glance to an already suffering Bottecchia for permission; he just went away. His was not the violent acceleration of a true *grimpeur* – he was not that kind of rider – but the steady, gathering speed of a strong, resilient man in the peak of condition. He was 33 years old and a veteran of five Tours; in all probability, this would be his last chance or, rather, his only chance. He meant to take it.

Once he was 50 metres clear, climbing into the clouds that had streamed in from the Bay of Biscay and were spilling down the face of the mountain, he was out of sight of the peloton. Except that there was no longer any peloton to speak of; already fragile in this continuously atrocious weather, it had splintered under the impact of his attack. From the moment they left Eaux Bonnes, at the foot of the first col, almost all those riders who finally reached Luchon struggled on alone or, at best, with just one other companion.

Buysse crested the summit of the Aubisque 1min 48secs ahead of Omer Huyse and Léon Parmentier. Dejonghe was at two minutes and the Italian climber, Bartolomeo Aymo, at five minutes. On the narrow, twisting descent towards Argelès, perilous at the best of times but now made treacherous by mud and mist, and frozen hands scarcely able to operate the brakes, Dejonghe caught and dropped the two in front of him and bridged the gap to Buysse. Together they rode towards the bottom of the Tourmalet through the valley of the Gorge de Luz.

Soaked to the skin, mud-spattered and still shivering from the descent, here, at least, they found some brief respite from the numbing cold on the col. Here their bloodshot eyes could make out the contours of the valley road somewhat better. But Gorge de Luz? It was certainly no Gorge of Light. So consistently bad was the visibility throughout that entire day, that Hanot described it to his *Miroir des Sports* readers as a 'stage without landscape'. In the valleys you could snatch glimpses of green meadows stretching up towards the scree shed from the peaks, or fresh torrents pouring down the mountainsides, but on the cols towards which the leaders were now speeding …

On the roads of the cols, drowned in the clouds or the fog, visibility never went beyond 50 metres and sometimes just 30 metres. The riders and even the cars came out of the shadows or disappeared like ghosts. There was, on this stage, something ethereal and unreal.

So, out on to the Col du Tourmalet goes the Buysse/Dejonghe tandem. 'A nasty detour' as so many riders have defined the climb, eighteen kilometres and a rise of 1,400 metres will take them to its 2,115-metre summit. Buysse leads, Dejonghe content to ride a length behind and to one side of his wheel tracks. Second overall in Bayonne, 1 min. 9 secs. down on his team-mate, Van Slembrouck, he is now the leader on the road, and he has no interest in forcing the pace. Even in this gloom, the contrast in their styles is strikingly apparent. Buysse is down on the shallow hooks of his handlebars, his body flat across the top tube, and every thrust on the pedals is accompanied by an exaggerated movement of his head and shoulders; there is not a muscle in his body that seems not to be engaged in the fight. Dejonghe is all elegance: he sits bolt upright, hands on the tops, his upper body motionless and betraying nothing of the effort his legs are making. It is brute strength versus suppleness. If Buysse looks as if the next thrust might be his last, Dejonghe looks poised to take flight.

Just beyond Barège, half-way up the col and with the issue between them still unresolved, they are unexpectedly joined by a third man. Silently out of the mist, like one of Hanot's ghostly apparitions, comes Odille Tailleu. This is his first Tour, his first encounter with the giant mountains of the Tour, and he rides for the J. B. Louvet team. Reinforcements for Dejonghe, perhaps? Not today, for this is a day when the trade-team tactics that Desgrange so despised will count for nothing: today is the kind of Darwinian struggle of the fittest that he always envisaged his Tour should be.

Tailleu goes through and takes up the challenge; the attack is repulsed. He tries again, and this time he is successful. Slowly the gap grows until he is out of sight – no ghost but a flesh and blood *coureur* enveloped once more in the clouds. Behind him, it is Dejonghe, the temporary race leader, who cracks: he dismounts, takes a sodden sandwich from his bag, and begins the solitary uphill trudge through the mud that slops into and over his cycling shoes. Suppleness has had to give way to brute strength: deprived of Buysse's back wheel he is destined to lose more than an hour over the next two cols. This will be his final Tour.

Up ahead, first Buysse then Tailleu dismount to continue on foot. The last four kilometres on the Col du Tourmalet turn into a high-altitude cyclo-cross duel – sometimes in the saddle; sometimes pushing their bikes upwards in the soft mud to the side of the tracks left by the cars, where their light cycling shoes might gain a better purchase against gravity. Occasionally they catch sight of each other; more often they are rendered invisible through the mist and ice-cold rain that has never let up. Tailleu crosses first, a good minute ahead of Buysse, to begin the freezing, slithering descent.

Aymo is next to the top, five minutes back: the Italian has climbed strongly and conceded no further time to Buysse on the Tourmalet. Then comes Devos at eight minutes, followed, two minutes later, by a dispirited Dejonghe, joined now by his French team-mate, Bellenger. Behind this élite group, those who have not yet relinquished their struggle against the cruel mountain elements are scattered over the full length of the col.

Bottecchia, winner of the two previous Tours, and Van Slembrouck, his proud yellow jersey hidden beneath a black oilskin jacket, are nowhere to be seen.

Even before the leading pair had reached the brief, but welcome, respite of the valley floor, Tailleu was in serious trouble. The iced water he had repeatedly drunk on the climb of the Tourmalet was already exacting its toll – gripping his stomach in vicious, spasmodic cramps and involuntarily opening his bowels. At the foot of the Col d'Aspin his one-minute advantage over Buysse had been reversed.

Now the Flandrian was truly on his own as he set about the third brutal climb of the day with his strength undiminished. Many of those who made it to Luchon that day, and many who didn't, complained of the debilitating cold, and of hands so numbed that on the cols they couldn't pull effectively on the handlebars. They spoke of chest pains, and of rheumatism. Buysse, however, seemed unaffected by any of these handicaps.

Below him, the ailing Tailleu was caught and passed, first by Aymo, and then by Devos. But the gap which they had succeeded in holding at manageable proportions on the Tourmalet was, on the third col of the day, growing with every ungainly thrust of Buysse's pedals. On the top of the Aspin his lead over the Italian had been extended to eleven minutes. Clearly the stage was his, and only the size of his winning margin was at stake, and that matter was resolved on the final climb. Between the top of the Aspin and the 1,569-metre summit of the Peyresourde he doubled his advantage over Aymo and, even in the final few kilometres, descending into Luchon, he added a further two minutes. It wasn't so much that he accelerated – he had the acceleration of a six-ton lorry, according to one French journalist – but that every one of his rivals weakened. On a day made exclusively for strong men, strong in body and heart, and schooled in the business of completing the job whatever the weather, the countryman from the lowlands of Flanders had no serious rival.

It was after five o'clock in the afternoon when Lucien Buysse (with a 'superb complexion and a radiant face', according to one report) arrived at the finish. He had spent 17hrs 12mins 4secs in the saddle, or occasionally out of it, covering the 326 kilometres. At an average speed of 18.9 k.p.h. it remains the slowest stage in the entire 100-year history of the Tour de France. Yet, a full hour after Buysse had completed his epic, only nine other riders had limped into Luchon. Aymo was second, 25mins 48secs down, Devos third, a further four minutes back; and poor Tailleu, the débutante, was eighth, 48 minutes behind the man he had led over the Tourmalet. By nine o'clock in the evening still only 21 of the original 76 who had set out from Bayonne the previous midnight had reached the finish.

Behind them, the shattered remnants of the peloton were spread-eagled across two mountain cols. Exhausted men, frozen to the marrow, were in tears, while spectators poured cognac down their throats, and tried to rub and beat some warmth into their shivering legs, or some flexibility into hooked, rigid fingers. In the midst of this havoc Ottavio Bottecchia, winner in the previous two years, abandoned the race. And what nobody could have known at that moment was that this would be his last encounter with the Tour. The following spring, he was found mysteriously dead beside the road in Italy – most probably the victim of a real assassin, a Fascist hit-man.

What of Desgrange? He could hardly have been blamed for the weather, but was he concerned about this carnage? If he was, he would surely have been reticent about showing it: hadn't he said that the perfect Tour de France would be one in which only one man proved himself strong enough to reach the finish? Just one solitary coureur riding in stoical isolation into Paris. Be that as it may, at nine o'clock he and his officials decreed that the finish control in Luchon would remain open till midnight, not close at 10.30 p.m., as the rules demanded; furthermore, cars were to be dispatched from the town, as far back as the Col d'Aspin, to shepherd home the lost sheep. Of course, the Tour's organisers have always reserved for themselves the right to interpret their rules with some leniency according to circumstances – French pragmatism that is invariably cloaked beneath a rhetoric that speaks of 'heroic exploits'. So it was on this occasion – a humane gesture that allowed a number of those who had stubbornly refused to abandon to get down off the Peyresourde long after 11 o'clock, and yet remain in the race. Some had walked for miles in the rain and the dark, like Raymond Decorte, who was still able to laugh and pronounce 'everything is fine'. Others undoubtedly received various forms of help from the cars, illicit assistance to which the organisers turned a sensibly blind eye. As Hanot diplomatically explained:

> It seems that the riders were only to be assisted by the light from the cars' headlamps, but nobody demanded much precision on that point.

Even with that degree of laxity, however, only 47 finished within the extended time-limit. Others were still being ferried down to Luchon into the small hours. And it was still raining.

One of those who lived to fight another day was Benoit Faure, riding his first Tour. 'Never again will I ride this Tour de France,' he vowed at Luchon. 'I'm a tough country boy. I can suffer, but this work is not fit for human beings. If a farmer treated his horses like that he would be thrown into jail for cruelty.' After the Tour (in which he finished 23rd) he pursued his general complaint about the life of a *touriste-routier* in an article for *Match*. Desgrange fined him 4,000 francs for his literary effort.

x   x   x   x   x

During the rest day in Luchon Buysse was fêted. Journalists waxed lyrical about a solo performance that had been truly *formidable*. He had the yellow jersey and a lead of 36 minutes over second-man, Tailleu. 'Now I am going to live on my advantage,' he announced, before adding the scarcely veiled threat: '...unless I am attacked.'

Tailleu, by contrast, was more openly menacing. Disconsolate at having lost out so heavily in the second half of the stage, he promised that he would do his utmost on the next stage, to Perpignan, to repeat the attack he had made on the Tourmalet. How often we have heard that, after a disappointment on the first stage in the high mountains – 'The Tour begins tomorrow'. For Tailleu, the Tour did not begin the following day: on the road to Perpignan it ended. He lost a further 37 minutes to Buysse. But what induced Buysse to return to the offensive during that second day in the Pyrenees?

Comfortable though his lead was, he must have realised that on current form he was capable of putting his yellow jersey further beyond anyone's reach. What's more, there would be good money to be gained from another stage-win. Perhaps, also, his mind drifted back to 1913, for it was on that very same stage that year, that his older brother, Marcel, had attacked on the Col de Puymorens to arrive first into Perpignan. Whatever the reason, as the much reduced string of riders passed through Ax-les-Thermes, with the col rising up before them and 150 kilometres still to go to Perpignan, Buysse went to the front and again challenged anyone to stay with him.

Nobody had the strength, or the stomach, for it and immediately he was clear. Seven kilometres into the 28-kilometre climb his lead was already two and a half minutes; at 13 kilometres it was 3mins 50secs; at 17 kilometres it had stretched to 7mins 20secs and now on good, dry roads, with the sun warming the back of his yellow jersey, he passed over the 1,920-metre summit fully ten minutes ahead. This was not a solitary battle of survival against the elements, but a purely athletic triumph over all his rivals. And this normally taciturn man responded to the applause and the shouts of 'Allez' that greeted him at the top with a beaming smile.

To complete the Buysse family festival, young Jules broke clear on the descent of the Puymorens and closed to within four and a half minutes of Lucien, before slowing down for fear that he might encourage others to follow suit. In reality, it was a somewhat groundless fear. When he crossed the line seven minutes down and into the tearful roadside embrace of his brother, the nearest challengers were still some ten minutes further back down the road. Lucien now had a lead of over an hour and, barring an accident, his jersey was secure.

In fact, he did have an accident. On Stage 14, having led over the Col d'Allos, he crashed on the descent and broke his front brake. As resourceful in the Alps as he had been resilient in the Pyrenees, he used the sole of his shoe, pressed hard against the front tyre, as a makeshift brake. By the stage-finish in Briançon the sole was worn right through, but Nicolas Frantz, closest to him now on overall classification, was himself too worn out to take any advantage. Besides, the gap at this point had grown to an hour and twenty minutes. All that remained were three final stages that would carry the race the 965 kilometres to Paris!

So, the longest Tour ever and, incidentally, the first one in which there was not a single French stage-win, ended as it had begun – slow, interminable promenades enlivened only by the final bunch sprint. Not only was it the longest, it was almost the slowest on record – slower even than Garin's win in 1903. And, but for that one cataclysmic stage in the Pyrenees, it would have been one of the most boring Tours ever. For Desgrange, who had been complaining for years about the riders' lackadaisical approach to the long flat stages, this was the final straw. The following year he would put into effect the remedial action he had been threatening: only the mountain stages would be raced *en ligne*; all the flat stages would be run off as team time trials.

The riders wouldn't call him an 'assassin'; they would do what they had always done – bend their backs under the hot sun or against the wind and rain, and get on with the job – but they were going to detest it.

STAGE 15, 1934: PERPIGNAN–AX-les-THERMES, 158kms

Richard Yates

By 1934 Henri Desgrange's formula of national teams, introduced in 1930, had made the event a huge success: French riders had won the event for four consecutive years – a far cry from their single victory in the 1920s; newspaper sales had rocketed while up-to-the-minute news was transmitted by radio; sponsors were increasingly being drawn into the event, and local councils were willingly paying the required fee to have a Tour stage start and finish in their town.

Road conditions were better than a decade earlier, and the stages were shorter, too – riders had refused to race flat-out over the huge distances that Desgrange had previously demanded. So, at the stage finish, riders no longer looked as if they had just come up from a coal mine – indeed, the stars of the Tour, men such as André Leducq who had won in 1930 and 1932, were beginning to achieve the same status as the stars of the cinema.

Equipment had also improved and, although Desgrange continued to insist that the Tour organisers supplied the riders' cycles – finished in anonymous yellow with the words L'Auto exhibited on the downtube – he did allow them to fit their own handlebars and saddles as the bikes were assembled at the Velodrome d'Hiver a couple of days before the start of the event. With typical, self opinionated stubbornness, however, he refused to permit the use of any sort of derailleur gears despite the fact that they were now allowed in the Giro d'Italia. Serious riders, he claimed, would never consider such devices; they were merely for weekend riders and tourists.

To be fair to him, derailleur mechanisms were still unreliable and poorly made, and many riders were inclined to agree with Desgrange, arguing that being able to change gear at will would have an adverse effect on their rhythm. Their machines were fitted with a double freewheel on each side of the rear hub, and to climb the hills they had to stop, release the back wheel, move the chain on to another sprocket, and then retighten the wheel. It was not really a process that demanded a lot of skill, but those who knew the route, and exactly where to change gear, were at a considerable advantage. Perhaps of even more importance was the fact that when a rider punctured he could, at the same time as he replaced the tyre, engage a bigger gear in order to get back to the safety of the bunch. Another effect was that the best sprinters were those who could turn small gears quickly rather than the big, muscular sprinters of the present day.

By the mid-1930s the quality of race photography had also improved in leaps and bounds, and now even included aerial shots. For the *Grande Boucle* of 1934 the richly illustrated sports weekly, *Le Miroir des Sports*, was planning to bring out three editions per week. This was to prove significant for not only did the 1934 event produce one of the greatest of all Tour de France images, it is fair to say that the story of that year's Tour really revolved around that one single photograph or, more accurately, how the Press interpreted that picture.

Although the ever popular Leducq was not riding the 1934 Tour, the French team was very strong. It was led by Antonin Magne who had won three years previously, and included René Vietto, a very young rider from the Côte d'Azur. This twenty year old was a last-minute selection who had gained entry by travelling up to Paris and duly winning a selection race. It was rumoured that he was a good climber, despite his strange position on the bike, and that he'd ridden the Giro d'Italia the previous year, at the age of 19, which, if true, only demonstrated his lack of judgement. Few people took him seriously, but thought he might possibly be of some help to his team-mates – if he could survive the punishment.

All the same, the journalists were somewhat hard on young René when they interviewed him. 'Do you really think you can last three weeks in the saddle at your age?' they challenged him. 'And what experience have you had of the Alps and the Pyrenees? Don't you think it's all going to be too hard for you?' The happy-go-lucky debutante smiled at them all and said, 'We'll have to wait and see, won't we?'

Against a background of growing political unease the race began, with everyone still talking about the events of the previous weekend when, across the Rhine in Germany, large scale political assassinations had taken place during what was later to be called the 'Night of the Long Knives'. And in Paris, itself, only four months previously, there had been serious anti government riots which led to many people being injured and no less than fifteen dying from police bullets. In short, there were any number of worries for the future, but the national fête of the Tour de France meant 27 days of excitement and distraction when political concerns could be temporarily forgotten.

The 1934 Tour started with a bang and it was a dream finish when the previous year's winner Georges Speicher crossed the line first in his World Champion's jersey. Vietto lost eleven minutes but so did another dozen riders. The next day was even harder when a big group stayed away all day and at the finish were no less than fifteen minutes in front of the bunch. Vietto came in another eighteen minutes later, thus, in just two days he had lost 44 minutes. In fact, on that second day young René had punctured four times. Tyres were enormous by today's standards and stuck on to wooden rims (aluminium rims were not to appear for another three years) and such was the problem of punctures that all riders carried two spare tyres – one behind their saddle and another folded round their shoulders. René had run out of spares and had sat at the side of the road in tears. However, the spectators would not tolerate that kind of behaviour – nobody retired from the Tour just because of a mere puncture. They cadged a tyre from a passing journalist and another from an Italian rider who was on the point of retiring, put the tyres on the wheels, and René back on his bike.

On the fifth stage to Evian he was in trouble again. On this stage, the longest in the race at 293 kilometres, he got tar in his eyes and was crying with pain at the finish. They had all been nearly ten hours in the saddle but it had been a slow stage and he'd only lost eight minutes. The rest day put things right and René proved that he was at home in the mountains by finishing with the leading group on the leg to Aix-les-Bains. The race stayed in the Alps for the next three stages. On the first Vietto led over all the mountain passes and held off a chasing group for over 50 kilometres of flat roads to win at Grenoble. In one day the young man from Cannes had silenced all his critics by proving that he was a first-rate climber, an excellent descender, and could ride strongly on the flat.

But there was more to come because the next day he finished just behind the race leader, Antonin Magne, and Giuseppe Martano, the main challenger for the yellow jersey. And the following day, after being away by himself for 150 kilometres, he pocketed all the mountain-top time bonuses and won his second stage.

Offering time bonuses for the leading riders over the summits of the cols was a device Desgrange had introduced so that the pure climbers would not be too disadvantaged against the skilled descenders. With the exception of Briançon, there were no towns large enough in the mountains to qualify as a stage town, so there was always a descent to the finish and, thus, a rider's skill as a descender was almost as important as his skill as a climber: Leducq and Speicher and later Lapébie were mediocre climbers but won Tours largely through their ability to go downhill faster than the others. It was only after the second world war, and the appearance of ski resorts and mountain-top finishes, that Desgrange's time bonuses were gradually reduced until they disappeared altogether. In 1934, however, they were sufficient to move René up into sixth place on general classification.

Overnight René Vietto had become a household name. It was all quite sensational and he was immediately dubbed the best French climber ever. He climbed in a big gear, but always in the saddle; on the descent he was an artist, and he rode powerfully and impressively on the flat. But above all he was innocent and charming, with the most captivating smile. In short, he was the sort of rider that Henri Desgrange always dreamed of. As the race stopped at Nice for a rest day, the people of his home town of Cannes excitedly prepared a hero's welcome for him: the race was due to arrive there the following day.

When the news came through that Vietto was away with Martano the mood of the spectators at the finish in Cannes reached fever pitch. Eventually René arrived and outsprinted the Italian to win the stage, and the cheers were even more enthusiastic when it was announced that, after all the time bonuses had been deducted, he had moved into third spot overall. Cannes had never seen anything like it, the crowd was completely out of control and one burly fan lifted René on to his shoulders to carry him to his hotel in triumph. Jacques Godet, Desgrange's chief assistant, tried to restrain this over exuberance but was knocked out cold by the fan in question.

Poor Vietto was very worried about the whole thing but it all had a happy ending. Those who were present at the arrival of this incredible stage to Cannes would never be able to forget it, and a large number of his newly acquired fans managed to convince themselves that, with the Pyrenees still to come, he was a main contender for overall victory. A nickname was found for him – 'Le Roi René' – after the king who had reigned benevolently over the South of France in the Middle Ages. Vietto was certainly the king in the mountains.

After the traditional promenade beside the Mediterranean the race arrived at the foot of the Pyrenees in Perpignan. Vietto had slipped to fourth place and, more significantly, he was 41 minutes behind the Yellow Jersey, his team-leader, Magne. But that mattered little to most of his fans, many of whom argued that he would no doubt pick up most of the time bonuses in the next four mountain stages, just as he had done in the Alps. But the Pyrenees were to be even more dramatic than anybody could have imagined.

The first of the Pyrenean stages was not very animated but ten kilometres from the finish at Ax-les-Thermes there was a minor drama when Magne broke his front wheel. Almost without thinking Vietto, who was riding with him, stopped, gave him his own wheel, and waited for the lorry to arrive with a replacement. It was all part of the day's racing – Magne was, after all, leader of the French team and currently heading the race. Even Desgrange, who had always insisted that the Tour was essentially a struggle between individuals, had been forced to recognise the reality of team tactics. 'The race will be individual, but team spirit will be tolerated,' he had famously conceded.

So, René's gesture was such an unremarkable event that none of the team thought of mentioning it that evening over dinner. But a photographer had been on hand to record it, and then the Press had a field day. The caption to one photo claimed that Vietto was crying 'hot tears' while he waited 'long minutes' to get going. The minutes may well have seemed long but there were not many of them: the simple fact is that he'd lost only three and a half minutes by the time they reached the finish of the stage.

Nevertheless, 'Vietto sitting on the wall in tears' has gone down in history as one of the most famous of all Tour photographs. René's 'generous and sporting sacrifice' had ruined his chances of overall victory, or so it was claimed, and later the story was to be further embellished to the point where most people came to believe that the only reason Vietto had lost the Tour was because of his act of generosity on that first day in the Pyrenees. The power of the Press was such that they had not only turned a previously unknown provincial rider into a national hero overnight, they had also imposed their own interpretation of the overall result of the Tour.

René himself was highly amused at the whole thing – aware, perhaps, of the considerable financial rewards this popularity would bring him – and later jokingly claimed that it had been a 'hold up', pure theft, and that at one stage he'd even considered calling the police.

Ironically, on the second stage in the Pyrenees the story was repeated: Magne broke some spokes in his wheel and once again Vietto handed him his wheel. It was an act with slightly more significance as this time René lost a full four and a half minutes on the race leader and dropped down to sixth place. But this time there was no photographer on hand to sensationalise the incident.

René may have lost time but he had not lost his form as was proved on the stage from Luchon to Tarbes. Magne had grown tired of the constant attacks of his nearest challenger, the Italian Martano, and when he saw his rival weakening he went on the attack himself over the Col d'Aspin and the Peyresourde. The stage may well have been only 91 kilometres long, but the yellow jersey proved beyond all doubt that he was the complete master, and by far the strongest rider in the race. At the finish Vietto rode in a splendid fourth but, nevertheless, nine minutes behind his team leader, while Martano lost thirteen minutes.

The final day in the Pyrenees was spent crossing the mighty Tourmalet and the Aubisque. René attacked on the first climb and stayed away all day to pick up the maximum possible time bonuses which enabled him to move back into third place, but he was still a full 43 minutes down on the leader and 27 minutes behind Martano. The French public loved it all: here was the incontrovertible proof that Vietto was the moral winner of the 1934 Tour. After this, his fourth stage win, he could not possibly have been more popular: by now everyone knew that his parents had a grocer's shop and that he had worked as a page boy in a large luxurious hotel in Cannes. Everyone wanted to see him and were more than willing to pay for the privilege, so there would be some very lucrative contracts awaiting him when the race arrived in Paris.

With the mountains behind them there was little hope of René making up time on the six stages that took the race to Paris. With the Tour almost invariably decided in the mountains, Desgrange had always been worried that the race would lose its interest in the final few as it wound its way back to the French capital, and in 1934 he introduced yet another experiment. It was to prove very successful and now plays a major role in all the main Tours. It was a long, individual time trial. These were not new as previously French Championships, and even one World Championship, had been decided by this formula, but they were still comparatively rare events and many riders were worried at the amount of time they could lose.

On the 90 kilometres between La Roche-sur-Yon and Nantes, Magne again proved he was the strongest, just as he had done in the mountains, and that he was a worthy winner of the race overall. As a small, lightweight climber, Vietto could not hope to compete with the best of them and finished in seventh place, nine minutes down. It was his inability to ride well against the watch which was to cost him dear throughout his career.

It mattered little that Vietto had slipped to fifth place when they reached Paris. He had won the King of the Mountains prize, four stages, and if there had been a prize for the most popular rider he would have won it by a mile. At the Parc des Princes track most of the cheers were for René and the crowd insisted that he rode the lap of honour alongside Antonin Magne, the overall winner. The contrast between the two men could hardly have been greater. 'Tonin' was cold, sombre, serious and a man of few words, and every inch the battle-hardened professional. René was talkative, happy-go-lucky, spoke with the charming accent of the south and was very much the innocent debutante.

The Press continued to play on 'René's sacrifice' in the mountains and the letter of thanks that Magne wrote to him remained one of his most treasured possessions. The young man from Cannes really needed a guide to help him through the jungle of professionalism. Antonin Magne willingly took on this role and accompanied him on most of his post-Tour appearances. He taught him to stop being so generous with his money, not to give too large tips and not to place his trust in all and sundry. But René remained impressionable and had complete faith in his trade-team manager, André Trialoux. The latter offered to look after his money for him – an offer that René readily accepted. Later he admitted that 'Trialoux looked after my money so well that I never saw it again.'

Unfortunately success really had come too soon to the former page boy and he found it difficult to handle. After a reasonably good season in 1935 (in which he won the Paris–Nice and finished eighth overall in the Tour de France with two stage wins), he then spent two years in the wilderness as he succumbed to the temptations of the high life. Late nights, expensive cars and a life of luxury led to poor results, and a loss of public esteem. The myth of his sacrifice of the '34 Tour to Magne had been virtually forgotten until he bounced back in the 1939 Tour. Not being considered for the national team he started with the regional South-East formation and quickly regained his place as the darling of the crowds after spending fifteen days in yellow. But his lead was always very tenuous and he finally lost it on one disastrous day in the Alps when his closest rival, the Belgian Sylvère Maes, put seventeen minutes into him. It was the year that saw no less than five individual time trials in which René was to relinquish a further fifteen minutes to the Belgian, finally arriving in Paris in second place, half an hour adrift.

By now, however, René had changed: he was no longer the charming innocent debutante of 1934: a racing accident in Brussels had turned him into an argumentative and difficult rider, a man of few words and a short temper. Yet, such was the enduring power of that single black-and-white image, he remained a mythical figure, and was everyone's favourite for the first post-war Tour in 1947. To the delight of all, especially the Tour organisers, he won two stages and spent fourteen days in the leader's jersey. With three days to go his final victory looked inevitable, but once again he failed miserably in the time trial. He lost over fourteen minutes that day, and all hope of an overall win. He finished his Tour career as he had started it some thirteen years earlier – in fifth place. If his performances prove one thing, it is the fact that to win the Tour de France a rider must have no obvious weakness: he must be able to do well in the mountains and against the watch. And above all he must never have a really bad day.

Along with Raymond Poulidor, René Vietto remains the most popular man never to have won the Tour. They were both the eternal bridesmaid, several times losing the Tour through one bad day in the saddle, or on a day in which fate conspired against them. It was their human frailty which made both men so popular. Of Poulidor, it was said, 'he wore his malediction like a virtual coat of shining armour'. Of Vietto, nothing needed to be said: that famous photograph of him sitting on the wall minus his front wheel said it all.

'The Sacrifice of René Vietto' – one of the most celebrated images of the Tour. Vietto sits waiting for the team lorry after giving up his front wheel to team-leader Antonin Magne on Stage 15 of the 1934 Tour.

STAGE 20, 1949: COLMAR–NANCY, 137kms.

Richard Yates

Saturday 23rd July 1949 was to witness one of the most amazing and memorable stages of the Tour de France – almost the longest time trial stage in the history of the Tour – no less than 137 kilometres. The route, between Colmar and Nancy, included a feeding zone and crossed the Col de Bonhomme, a major climb of 3,000 feet. The penultimate stage of what had already been an eventful and exciting race, it was a clash between two of the greatest riders ever – Fausto Coppi and Gino Bartali.

Both Coppi and Bartali were *Campionissimi* – a rare title given to super-champions of Italian cycling. There is no established definition of what it takes to qualify for this unofficial title but probably it requires a rider to have won five major tours and five Classic races. Of course the title is reserved for Italians but if it were granted to foreigners then Merckx and Hinault would qualify; but Anquetil and Induráin would not.

Some three weeks previously when the riders had lined up in Paris for the start, much was expected of the Italian team with their two supermen. There was even a second Italian team (the Cadetti) with their own star, the bald Fiorenzo Magni, who had won the Tour of Italy the previous year after Coppi's morale had cracked and he'd retired from the race. Three Italian stars in one team would have been unimaginable. As it was, journalists had always claimed that Coppi and Bartali were so jealous of each other, and such bitter rivals, that there was no likelihood of any sort of co-operation between them.

This rivalry was a gift to journalists, who were able to produce an enormous amount of copy to fill their pages and sell their newspapers. It reached such alarming proportions during the 1948 World Championships, when they spent all their time marking each other so tightly that both eventually retired. Shocked by their behaviour, the Italian Cycle Union had been obliged to step in. Both men were publicly reprimanded, given a two-month suspension, and told that this nonsense had to stop: there was plenty of money and enough prizes for each of them. This seemed to work, although the Press, of course, preferred the rivalry. When it came to the 1949 Tour de France, the younger Coppi had comprehensively proved in the Giro of that year that he was the stronger, but, even so, the ageing Bartali was way above the rest of the Italians. Furthermore, he had won the Tour the previous year, picking up the climbers' prize and seven stages in the process, including the extraordinary feat of winning three consecutive stages in the Alps.

The Italian team was managed by Alfredo Binda who had been a *Campionissimo* in his day; he won the Giro five times between 1925 and 1933. Very experienced and astute, he had very quickly helped his two stars to reach an agreement: each man would have five team-mates at his disposal and, providing the circumstances were right, Bartali would help Coppi to win. The agreement was not made public and journalists continued to look for any sign of their long standing rivalry.

Such was the prestige of these two *Campionissimi* that they overawed most of the French riders. Bartali was always somewhat aloof in public, but even Coppi's gentle simplicity did not make riders feel they could approach him. Bartali, with his broken nose that made him look more like a boxer had a cast iron morale. The sensitive Coppi – he looked wonderful and delicate on the bike – had always been presented as a superman without any weaknesses, apart from the fragility of his bones.

This was Fausto's first Tour de France and he was in for a shock in those opening stages. For sure, he had ridden the Giro five times (and already won it three times) but the long, flat stages of that race were always slow, controlled processions with the racing reserved until the final 30 kilometres. In the mountains, of course, it was every man for himself, but none of the minor Italian riders would ever have dreamed of breaking the unwritten rules and attacked him. In France, however, the racing was go-all-the-way from the gun, often over those terrible cobblestones of the North and, in that July, it was far hotter than in Italy during May. Only a few weeks earlier Coppi had destroyed everyone, Bartali included, in the Giro d'Italia, but racing in Italy was never like this and he was simply not used to it.

After four stages his morale had fallen to such a low point that he was beginning to say to Bartali that it was pointless to go through such suffering when he could be at home relaxing and enjoying his riches. But Gino knew the Tour de France – he had ridden it three times and won it twice – and was scornful of Coppi's complaints: 'And where did you get your luxury villa from?' he asked. 'And your cars and everything you possess? From racing, of course, by your own efforts and suffering.' Fausto knew he was right and, in an effort to show who was the boss, went away in a break on the fifth stage to St Malo with the new Yellow Jersey, the tiny young Parisian, Jacques Marinelli.

He'd picked a bad day, however, and found himself suffering more than ever in the heat. He complained to Marinelli that he was really going through a bad patch but Jacques vaguely assumed that this was some sort of joke. The little naturalised Frenchman (both his parents were Italian) looked closely at this living legend, this superman, this god that so many people worshipped. He watched his legs go round smoothly and seemingly without any effort, the shoulders not rocking at all and his hands resting delicately on the bars as if he were caressing them. He looked wonderful, simply wonderful, but when Marinelli saw the champion's face contorted with pain he realised he was not joking.

Much has been written about this stage to St Malo and it has become one of the legends of Tour history. The simple facts are that Coppi crashed, bent his forks and was obliged to wait six minutes before the main bunch, and a replacement bike, arrived. His morale was now at an all time low and he wanted to retire. Bartali tried to help him as did Magni, but they both lost patience and finally set about chasing the break. His other team-mates did not abandon him and he finished the day in the bunch, but totally demoralised. 'Coppi loses 18 minutes and all hope of winning the Tour,' the headlines screamed.

This was somewhat misleading as many other top riders had finished alongside him, eighteen minutes behind the break and thirteen minutes behind the Bartali/Magni group. It had been a very long stage of 293 kilometres on a scorching hot day and no less than eleven riders retired, including most of the Spanish team. Nevertheless, Coppi's morale was destroyed; it wasn't only his bones that were brittle. Manager, team-mates, journalists, and even the Tour organisers all tried to persuade him to continue, but all he would promise was just to 'give it another day'.

A rest day and then a win in the time trial to La Rochelle helped a lot, and his spirits finally started to return. Binda persuaded his two stars to play the waiting game, arguing that the race would certainly be decided in the Alps. The two men were only too happy to comply and the young Marinelli, who'd worn the yellow jersey for four days, was to continue to bask in its glory for a further two days.

Just before the Pyrenees he was robbed of his precious tunic by Magni, the leader of the Cadetti team. Fiorenzo went away early on the stage to Pau with the little known Italian, Biagoni; the promising young Belgian, Impanis; and the strong Frenchman, Fachleitner, riding for the South-East regional team, who had finished second in the 1947 Tour. Although the route did not cross any major climbs, the intense heat made it a very hard day indeed, and caused another eleven riders to retire. The break finished twenty minutes in front of the bunch, but this time nobody spoke of Coppi collapsing. The delighted Magni was to wear the yellow jersey for six days.

Those who were looking forward to the prospect of Coppi and Bartali living up to their reputations in the Pyrenees were largely disappointed: following Binda's advice, both men refused to show their hand and some people started to wonder whether they really deserved their reputation. So the results of the racing under the hot sun of the Pyrenees were inconclusive except for the facts that Magni lost a little time (but not his yellow jersey); Marinelli, now in the bright green jersey of his Paris team, proved that he could climb, and Fachleitner moved into second place. A mere two minutes down, there was speculation that he could take over the lead as the race approached his part of France and perhaps even keep it to Paris. But Fachleitner had a huge boil on his foot and even the rest day at Cannes gave him insufficient time to recover, and he was forced to retire in the Alps.

The Tour finally lived up to its promise on Stage 16 when the race left Cannes *en route* for Briançon, the highest town in Europe. It was the only stage finish at altitude where Magni's considerable skill as a descender would not help him to keep his yellow jersey. After 275 largely uphill kilometres, and ten and half hours in the saddle, Coppi allowed Bartali to cross the line first and capture the yellow jersey in the process, as it was the older man's birthday. Third man, Jean Robic, riding for the West France regional team, was five minutes down and, on this surprisingly cold day, the rest of the field was spread out over an hour. Magni lost his yellow jersey, of course, but in yet another magnificent ride Marinelli held on to his third place overall, which he would keep to Paris.

On the second day in the Alps Coppi converted his one-minute deficit on Bartali into a three-minute advantage. With Coppi now in yellow and Bartali second on the stage, and second overall, it was a crushing demonstration of their superiority and everything was falling nicely into place. Exactly as Binda had predicted, the Alps were proving decisive.

However, all was not well. This second Alpine stage had crossed the frontier into Italy and finished at Aosta. The ardent Italian supporters of that region had always been somewhat anti-French, but their dislike of their transalpine neighbours had been accentuated by what they had read in the newspapers. Some Italian journalists had claimed that both Coppi and Bartali had been badly treated in France: they had been allocated to inferior hotels and not treated with sufficient respect by the French organisers. This was probably quite untrue, but the over excitable Italian fans did not need much to provoke them.

Coppi arrived alone at Aosta to win the stage with Bartali at five minutes and Robic, again third on the stage, at ten minutes. After their two heroes had gone through, the spectators turned on the following cars and riders, the French ones in particular. Abuse was hurled and stones were thrown. It was all really quite shameful. Coppi apologised publicly for their behaviour as did Binda, Bartali and the rest of the Italians. But the damage had been done; the events were reported in the French Press and reprisals were expected. Although the two *Campionissimi* were special, the French had no great love for a people who had declared war on them some nine years previously, after the German army had defeated them so decisively. Up to this point it had been a fabulous Tour, but the immediate situation was worrying, especially in view of how isolated the riders would be in the long time trial.

The next day's stage finished in Switzerland where two other members of the Italian team were allowed to take the honours. The following day, however, the race returned to France finishing at Colmar, and the French reprisals began. Binda had stopped at the feeding zone at Belfort to pass the musettes up to his riders. With his red, white and green armband, he was easily recognisable as Italian, so the crowd started to insult him: 'Hey Macaroni! What a bunch of clowns you are.'

The Italian team manager took the bull by the horns and crossed the road to the crowd. 'It's Binda,' said one of them reverently and the crowd fell silent.

'I am ashamed of my countrymen and what they did at Aosta,' he said. 'I apologise sincerely, but please do not take it out on my riders; they've done nothing wrong.'

'He's right,' shouted someone. 'Coppi and Bartali are still the best.' The Italian manager was applauded and there, at least, the affair was settled. However, other Italians were less fortunate and certainly suffered from the insults of the French spectators. The last four riders to cross the finish line at Colmar were all members of the Italian team, disheartened and discouraged by their reception. Two of them finished outside the time limit.

That night, on the eve of the time trial, there was a conference between the Tour organisers and the Italian team manager. On no account would the time trial be cancelled, but, in order to protect the Italian riders, it was suggested that they should wear plain jerseys. Binda rejected this proposal: his riders were proud to wear their Italian colours, he said.

And, in any case, he claimed he had total confidence in the French public. So, by way of a compromise, it was decided that the starting order would be changed and the names of the Italian riders would not be displayed on their following cars. Coppi would be the last man off, four minutes behind Marinelli, eight minutes behind Robic and twelve minutes behind Bartali. Furthermore, the two Italian riders who had finished outside the time limit at Colmar would be reinstated. On the day, Binda was right: apart from a few whistles the Italians encountered no problems from the thousands of French spectators.

At stake on the day of Stage 20 of the 1949 Tour de France was the biggest prize in the sport of cycle racing.

Coppi was an all-rounder and an excellent time trialist, and by now wearing the yellow jersey, his morale had largely returned even if he remained somewhat anxious. Bartali was that very rare combination of climber and sprinter. Unlike Coppi his style was erratic, but effective, and he had the habit of surprising and demoralising his opponents by changing up a gear just before the top of a climb. Gino did not like time trials but few riders did. In the 1948 Tour he'd finished 28th in the race against the watch, some twelve minutes down on the winner, but it hardly mattered – he still won the race by the huge margin of some 26 minutes. Before the war, when Coppi was still a junior, he'd won time trials but he did not like making the effort unless it was really necessary.

Today, it would be necessary. A gap of three minutes and three seconds was not insurmountable over a distance of 137 kilometres. Coppi was human and could not always be counted on to produce the goods as had been shown in the early part of the Tour. If he snatched victory from Fausto in this 'moment of truth' neither Binda nor Coppi could complain that he had broken his agreement. After Coppi, Bartali was the second best rider in the world, but how Gino would just love to prove, perhaps for one last time, that it was he who was the master.

As the riders assembled in Colmar it was yet another hot, sunny morning. The town had been battered and destroyed some four years previously in what was known as the 'Battle of the Colmar Pocket'. The town was to witness the start of another fierce, if less destructive, contest between the two Italian idols.

Bartali was riding his own make of cycle equipped with his own 'Cervina' derailleur. It was in the pre-war style of what was known in Britain as an 'Osgear' – it had a very long tension arm mounted directly below the bottom bracket. Some years previously Coppi had refused to use the difficult twin-rod Campagnolo derailleur which was mounted on one of the backstays. Like most of the other riders in the Tour, he preferred the more modern double-roller Simplex which, though French, was made under licence in Italy. Virtually all riders from Italy were obliged to use Italian equipment which was no great disadvantage: their quick release hubs were far in advance of the French with their wing nuts; and, in general, Italian frames were more rigid than French ones, if also heavier.

As the top riders left Colmar it was evident that Bartali started in a very determined way. The prickly little Frenchman, Jean Robic, followed him; not really known for his ability against the watch he nevertheless finished second in the time trial two years previously when he went on to win the Tour on the very last day. If he was unpopular with the riders, the journalists loved him, and he will always be remembered for his claim that 'I go uphill so fast that I have to put my brakes on to get round the corners.'

Marinelli started four minutes later. He had been convinced by his team manager that it was an advantage to have Coppi behind him. The yellow jersey was sure to catch him, but if he could stay with him for long enough then he would be assured of a good time and be guaranteed to arrive in Paris in third place. Marinelli was finally being taken seriously. He had proved that he could climb the high mountains and it was now up to him to show that he could ride well against the watch, but it never occurred to him that he could catch his danger man Robic for four minutes. The Tour had been like a dream come true for Jacques and by now he was a household name in France. He had already signed several contracts for post-Tour appearances and in his mind he was adding up his future gains. The big climb up the Col de Bonhomme came about a third of the way along the course, and Jacques knew that if Coppi caught him before the top of the climb he would not be able to stay with him. But on the descent it would be a different matter.

Meanwhile, Bartali was riding his own race. Powerful and efficient, he caught several riders including Apo Lazarides, the best rider in the French national team, and showed no sign at all of weakening. But Coppi's class was evident from the very start. He was the fastest on the long climb, but still he was unable to catch Marinelli before the top. After the climb Jacques caught Robic, but shortly after that Coppi caught them both. It was a measure of the great man's class that he caught his eight-minute man, who was to finish the Tour in fourth place overall, before even half the course had been covered. But perhaps this was not too surprising for those privileged enough to watch Fausto closely. Smooth and beautiful in his action, he made it all look so effortless. If many claim that he was the greatest of all time that is largely due to his superb style.

Both Marinelli and Robic managed to hang on to the flying Fausto – but not for long since to maintain his incredible pace would have meant them 'blowing up'. After 100 kilometres Coppi eased up as he was in danger of catching Bartali – he had no wish to humiliate him. Yet this same Bartali was comfortably faster than anyone else. If Bartali's performance was superb, Coppi's was beyond words.

At the finish Coppi beat Bartali by seven minutes and two seconds and Marinelli by eleven minutes and fifteen seconds to prove beyond doubt that he was the master. If he had not eased up he would have won by ten minutes, or even more. Never again would the Tour see such proof of superiority on one stage. Bartali may well have been past his best at 34 years of age, but even so he was in a class above the rest of the field.

Today most of the key riders of the 1949 Tour are dead, apart from Magni who lives in retirement beside one of the beautiful Italian lakes, and Marinelli who is the Mayor of Melun, near Paris. But the memory of the 1949 Tour and its fabulous twentieth stage will never die. It was, perhaps, the high point of the 'Golden Era'.

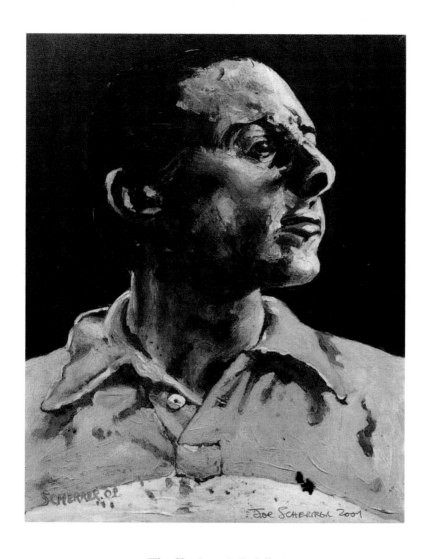

'The Charismatic Pedaller'

*From an original painting of Fausto Coppi, reproduced
by kind permission of Joe Scherrer*

STAGE 13, 1951, DAX-TARBES, 201kms

'TOUCHING THE VOID'

Herbie Sykes

Willem ('Wim) van Est was a big, garrulous, barrel-chested sort of a man. The second of sixteen kids born into North Brabant farming stock, he'd left school aged twelve to help his dad, a farm labourer. When, however, his draft papers arrived Wim, like many others, went underground. Having disappeared off the radar, he followed the lead of Theo Middelkamp, one of his idols. Middelkamp, the first Dutchman to win the World Championship, had become a full-time smuggler, using the toptube of his bicycle to secrete falsified documents and tobacco. Like Middelkamp, Wim's contribution to the war effort would involve stealing across the Dutch-Belgian border in the small hours, lubricating the wheels of two grateful border communities.

By the cessation, however, Brabant was pretty well in tatters. With little prospect of legitimate paying work, Wim saw no choice but to carry on his 'import-export' activities, his twin specialties cigarettes and (bizarrely) dairy products. When, however he was arrested trying to haul – of all things – live cattle across the frontier, his rustling career was brought to an abrupt end. Released from prison six months later, he began contemplating how best to earn a legitimate crust.

Wim van Est was a very fine cyclist, as hard as nails and formidably strong. No wonder; prior to his incarceration his stock-in-trade had been lugging 80-kilogram sacks of butter and cheese across the border. Though Dutch racing wasn't all that marvellous, Wim had learned through his previous profession that the Belgians were crazy for cycling. He knew there was money to be made there, and so he'd nip across and clean up at the kermesses, then do likewise in the local stuff of a weekend. A professional contract (or, more specifically, a jersey, a bike and his expenses) promptly followed, and he celebrated by winning the time trial at the Tour of Holland. Later that summer he took a train to Paris, borrowed a beat-up old bike and came second in the Grand Prix des Nations, the unofficial World TT championship. A late developer perhaps, but 26-year-old 'Iron William' was a beast of a rider, as strong as the ox he'd been daft enough to try to smuggle into Belgium. He was on his way.

Dutch cycling, unlike the Flemish variety, had traditionally been track oriented. However van Est's performances, and his hugely likeable personality, made him a star in his homeland. He wasn't particularly quick, but he could churn massive gears over long distances, and had the strength of two men. The fast guys would pay him to eat wind, and he'd spend hour after gleeful hour doing just that.

His big break came in June 1950. Sent to ride the insane 586-km motor-paced Bordeaux–Paris (twice the length of Milan–San Remo), he went and won the thing. In so doing he confirmed himself as his country's most popular rider. The contracts duly rolled in, and the following summer they invited him to the biggest potential bonanza of all: he was to ride the Tour as part of the national team.

Wim knew – everybody knew – that an exploit at the Tour would earn him untold riches come August. Aside from the GC bunch, the *Grand Boucle*'s stage winners, her *lanterne rouge*, her larger than life characters and heroic failures could all expect to be selected for the lucrative post-Tour criteriums, the amphetamine fuelled jamboree of the cycling season. The Tour was the race as regards prestige, but for most it represented a means to an end. Its protagonists recognized that failure to perform there – and by extension to earn contracts for the crits – rendered it an exercise in futility, just a month of horrific, futile sufferance. In the unending fight for survival which was the lot of cycling's great unwashed, it was the high-octane 'racing' of August which put food on the table through the winter months. Most riders had contracts only for the months during which they raced, their winters spent grafting on the farm or the factory floor. A good showing in July was therefore imperative in that it offered a chance to earn (relative) fortunes, up to two years' salary for some.

July without August, then, was the cycling equivalent of meat without potatoes. All of which explained the frantic early morning breakaways, but also why during the Tour even the most sober amongst them would morph into comedians and showmen. They behaved like clowns not because the July sunshine frazzled their brains, but because they were trying to get themselves on the radio and in the papers. The more airtime and column inches they garnered, the more people would want to see them, and the more people wanted to see them the more chance they had of getting rides in August. That on occasion the Tour resembled a pantomime, then, was entirely predictable. It was a circus, with the cyclists cast as the clowns.

With the Pyrenees not due for two weeks, the 1951 edition was characterized by long, successful breakaways – lots of them. Stage six to

Rennes saw Wim initiate the perfect move, a group of five GC nobodies taking a punt. Sadly, however, the Frenchman, Edouard Muller, was the fastest, and Iron William settled for third; close, but no cigar, and no criteriums.

Following Hugo Koblet's astonishing, race-winning solo effort on stage eleven, the 38th Tour de France convened in pretty little Agen, destination Dax. Undeterred by his near miss, Wim once more got in the move. As the best placed of the riders on GC, he took it upon himself to drive the break. He did so in the hope that, though fifteen minutes adrift himself, the bosses of the peloton might see fit to give them an easy ride. The following day would see the Tour reach the Pyrenees, and Wim figured that nobody amongst the players would have much stomach for a big chase on this clay-hot afternoon. He was right; he and team-mate Gerrit Voorting manfully forged an eighteen minute advantage. Better still, in Dax's cinder-tracked little stadium, he outgunned them all to claim both the stage and the yellow jersey – the stuff of dreams.

The following morning a French journalist asked the new *maillot jaune* how he fancied his chances of keeping the jersey on the monstrous Aubisque. Wim confessed that not only had he had quite a late night, but that he'd never actually seen a real mountain before. As such he'd not the faintest idea, though he wasn't about to relinquish the jersey without a fight. He was ready to give everything in trying to hang with Koblet, Luison Bobet, Fausto Coppi and their like. He might not wear yellow in Paris, but he figured that if he honoured the jersey with a brave showing in the high mountains, his contract value would nicely reflect his elevated status.

With Tourmalet, Aspin and Peyresourde on the menu the next day, the favourites kept their powder dry on Aubisque. However two kilometres from the top Gino Bartali, here celebrating his 38th birthday, decided to light the blue touch paper, and Wim found himself losing ground. At the pass, though, he found the perfect ally – Fiorenzo Magni. The Tuscan was the best descender in cycling, and so Wim decided to attach himself to his wheel, get a free tow back to the rest of the hitters. Smart move. In principle.

The descent of the Aubisque was lethal. Narrow, extremely tight, and wretched with craters and sharp little stones, it was made more perilous still by the fact that the surface was damp. Trying to follow the genius Magni was a foolhardy undertaking by anybody's standards, and Wim immediately overcooked it. But for a low retaining wall he'd have fallen into a ravine, but he climbed back on and once more set to, desperate to extend his fifteen minutes of fame. Though terrifying for those who witnessed it, it was little more than the precursor to one of the most incredible incidents in the history of the Tour.

Rejoined now by a group of three, he once more misjudged his braking distance, only this time with horrifying consequences. One second the Spaniard, Francesco Massip, was following his wheel and the next, Wim van Est was... flying. Where previously the wall had saved him, this time it acted as a catapult. Sickeningly for those who witnessed it, the yellow jersey disappeared into a 300-metre ravine, into an abyss.

As the mortified cyclists of the Tour de France dismounted in cardiac horror, it seemed utterly hopeless; there was no way van Est could survive a plunge like that. The shell-shocked Dutch manager, Kees Pellenaers, peered over the precipice. He sighted a small figure (he'd later state that it 'looked like a daffodil') down below, and began to yell balefully, desperately, after it. Wim van Est, however, didn't respond – just a shocking, eerie silence.

Then, just as all seemed irredeemably lost, Pellenaers' daffodil started to stir. At first it was a tiny, barely perceptible movement, but then Wim van Est was seen to be crawling towards his bicycle. Despite overwhelming odds to the contrary, his fall had been broken by a tiny patch of flat, which he'd managed to cling on to. A foot or so either side and Wim would have tumbled to his death but somehow – and in some miraculous way – he had survived.

The rest is the stuff of legend. Iron William had fallen so far (accounts vary between 30 and 70 metres) that the tow rope they had in the commissar's car wasn't long enough to reach him. They therefore extended it using the entire Dutch stock of forty tubulars, and sent a man down to rescue him.

Blooded and bruised and in deep shock, an overwrought Wim van Est was hauled back up the Col d'Aubisque. Like all warriors of the road he told them he wanted to go on, but quite rightly they gave him cognac and carted him off to hospital instead, thus confirming his place in cycling legend. The Dutch team, their tubs so swollen as to be useless, abandoned en masse, but returned to a hero's welcome all the same. One of their number, Willem van Est, had been reprieved by the cycling Gods. Unwittingly, the former smuggler from Brabant had been the author of one of the most incredible stories in the history of the Tour de France.

Wim van Est would dine out on his outrageous escape act for years, but arguably the biggest winner of all was one of his sponsors. The watchmaker, Pontiac, had patronized bike racing in Holland and Belgium for years, and sales were brisk off the back of the sport's pre-eminence. The trick, such as it was, was straightforward enough. Another kind of Pontiac (the huge, gas-guzzling American automotive variety) would precede the peloton, with a giant sized replica watch attached to its roof. Inside a guy would scream 'Tic-tac-Pontiac' into a microphone, and the crowd would thus be informed that the group was on its way.

Iron William's extraordinary Tour de France would prove manna from Heaven for the marketing department, who promptly devised another corker. They had Wim, newly installed as his nation's sporting talisman, liberally sprinkle gold dust on the watches by informing the Dutch public that; 'Zeventig meter viel ik diep, mijn hart stond stil maar mijn Pontiac liep.' [Seventy metres did I drop, my heart stood still but my Pontiac didn't stop.] And that, you have to admit, is a pretty good line.

STAGE 22, 1957, TOURS–PARIS, 227 kms

'A MOVEABLE FEAST'

Mike Breckon

'If you are lucky enough to have visited Paris as a young man, then wherever you go for the rest of your life it stays with you. For Paris is a moveable feast.' (Ernest Hemingway)

In the nineteen fifties British families celebrated discreetly, by today's standards, a son's twenty-first birthday – when he achieved what was known as his 'majority'. It was usually recognised with the gift from parents of a suitably engraved wristwatch, an accessory then much sought after. My older brother had received his in 1954 and my mother, I am sure, was planning a repeat of the gesture for me three years later. She was shocked when I told her that I didn't want any such thing. I told her I was much more interested in *experience* than material items, and that the experience I wanted was that of watching the finish of the Tour de France in Paris. And of Paris itself.

I had begun to follow Le Tour as soon as I became drawn to the sport of cycling at the age of thirteen. I tracked the action in the sepia-tone pages of the French magazines *Miroir Sprint* and *Miroir des Sports*, which works of art I purchased from Ron Kitching's famous bike shop in Yorkshire. The dramatic photography and creative page layouts of these magazines told stories of courage and drama: fragile human beings pitting themselves against nature's elements and the geological challenges of the French countryside. The pictures were inspiring and fascinating, and I dreamed of one day at least seeing, if not participating, in the greatest race on earth. My opportunity would come, I realised, when I became twenty-one years of age and could break free of the shackles of a middle class British upbringing.

In the early 1950s I had admired Louison Bobet in Le Tour. He was elegant and stylish ... and very fast. But by 1956 Bobet's domination of the Tour de France had come to an end.   That year it was unexpectedly won by a French regional rider, Roger Walkowiak, allegedly aided by numerous lumps of sugar dipped in alcohol, as cycling writer René de Latour later told me. The next year heralded the dawn of a new era. It was also the year of my 21st birthday

Le Tour was contested then almost exclusively by continental European professionals, brought together for the event into national squads of riders from different commercial teams but from the same country: France, Belgium, Italy, Spain, Holland and Switzerland. And a 'mixed' Luxembourg team which usually didn't have sufficient pros available at home, so included promising 'foreign' riders from outside cycling's heartland. Five French regional teams made up the field of 120 riders.

In 1955 the race entry had increased to thirteen teams and British enthusiasts like myself had been thrilled when a national squad, mainly made up of Hercules-sponsored riders and including a Yorkshire lad called Brian Robinson, was invited to participate. Brian did well, finishing a promising 29th in his first Tour de France. My excitement was further heightened in 1957 when Robinson, now a seasoned and respected professional who had finished in 14th place overall the previous year, was included in the make-shift, Luxembourg-based International squad. Also, because I would actually be able to see him race in the Tour, as Britain's cyclesport publication, Cycling, now organised a special annual trip to Paris to see the finish: a weekend in the City of Light for which the cost of trains, ferries, hotel and stadium seat were included, all for fourteen guineas (about the price of a decent watch).

Meanwhile, I had finally convinced my doubting mother that such a weekend would be a lot more exciting than the traditional birthday gift, certain as I was that it would remain with me for the rest of my life. The trip would also allow me to explore a city which had become the destination of my dreams through my reading of the novels of Ernest Hemingway. Required for my English examinations at school, I had been drawn to his prose and to his favourite city … his 'moveable feast'.

The Cycling party – there were about forty of us – gathered at Victoria railway station in London on Friday evening. We were typical of 1950s British cycling at its most idiosyncratic: some were dressed in tweedy plus fours, others wore waxed rain jackets. Some secreted small camping stoves in their luggage to 'brew up' tea in their Paris hotel rooms rather than drink 'that filthy stuff they call coffee'. We looked like a party of intrepid adventurers off on expedition rather than a group of sports fans going to Paris for the weekend. As for me, I had every intention of going my own way in Hemingway's Paris. Drinking tea was the last thing on my mind!

After taking the boat-train to Dover and transferring to the ferry for the midnight crossing to Calais it was on to Paris by train, where we arrived early on Saturday morning after much excited talk on our journey about the Tour so far. The race had been wide open at the outset with Bobet absent, and the young French star, Jacques Anquetil, was only one of six possible winners who had been featured in *Miroir Sprint* magazine. But Anquetil then won the third stage and took the overall lead after the fifth. He lost it, but then won another stage and took back yellow in the Alps. 'Does he climb?' asked the magazine's headline. 'Oh Yes' was its printed response to its own question. The French nation drew a collective sigh of relief.

It was going to be Anquetil's year, of that there was little doubt. Jacques, still only 23 years old, came to the race in great form and high spirits: his main rival, Bobet, had withdrawn (some say he didn't want to risk being beaten); he had ended his period of conscription in the army in March then had immediately started to win races ... and he had just begun an affair with the wife of his doctor – the glamorous Jeanine Boeda, who was to become his companion for life. The world, it seemed, was becoming his oyster!

Anquetil started the Tour with an early win, taking the third day's stage to his home town of Rouen (where he presented his winner's bouquet to Jeanine). On the stage before the Alps he followed the advice of his experienced team-mate, André Darrigade, and took more than ten minutes out of his rivals. In the Alps he rode well, finishing with stage-winner Nencini on the Galibier stage, but then lost time to some of his rivals through inattention before the Pyrenees. The awesomely difficult range of mountains in the south-west of France came towards the end of the race and here Anquetil finally stamped his authority on the 1957 Tour de France.

On Stage 17 Anquetil finished with the leaders after three major climbs. The next day on the Col de Tourmalet stage Jacques launched an audacious attack. He paid for it later in the day, yet managed to retain the *maillot jaune*, still leading the race by nine minutes. Then finally, Anquetil did what he did best, and captured the undying admiration of our motley group of British cycling fans in the process, by winning the 20th stage time trial by four minutes. He now had an unassailable lead of almost quarter of an hour. But what, we wondered, would Jacques do in the quintessential 1950s British bike race – the 25-mile time trial?

It was generally agreed that he would have problems beating the current British champion, Billy Holmes from Hull, who had gone below

56 minutes for 25 miles in a classic British time trial on roads near Bristol to set a new national record. Surprisingly, we were probably right!

If one makes a comparison between Holmes's effort and Jacques Anquetil in full flight in the Tour de France, they are extremely close. Overall conditions for the two rides were, of course, very different. But they both took place on flattish courses, close to the coast so likely to be assisted by tail winds. There was a difference in distances – Anquetil rode 66 kilometres, Bill rode 40 – but Jacques' ride was 'straight out' while Bill's was the traditional British time trial's 'out-and-back' with a dead turn in the road at the halfway point. The Frenchman also had a following car to urge him on and crowds at the roadside to cheer him to victory. Bill's audience consisted of a few cows in a field!

Then there was the matter of gears – the Tour leader was on his time trial bike with multiple gears selected for the day, the British record holder on a single 50x16T fixed-wheel gear. In addition, Anquetil had a rival to chase – the Tour runner-up with only two days to go to the finish in Paris, Dutchman Wim Van Est. had started three minutes ahead of him and Jacques caught him in the closing kilometres of the time trial.

Finally, there was one more advantage probably held by Anquetil. He later openly admitted to taking amphetamines during races and particularly, it is very likely, in such an important stage as the time trial which would seal his first victory in the Tour de France. Yet despite all of this, the average speed of the two riders was virtually identical – only 0.043 kph separated the two, with Holmes the slightly slower at 42.998 kph. So the British fans' view was probably right, that Bomber Billy as he was known, would have given the new French star a run for his money if they ever met face-to-face on a level playing field!

Before checking in at our hotel on arrival in Paris early on Saturday morning, I left my compatriots to brew up their tea. I headed for Les Halles and, though activities in the old food market were quieter than usual, it being a Saturday, I thoroughly absorbed the Gallic atmosphere. I had my first ever bowl of onion soup encrusted with cheese, together with numerous cups of 'that filthy stuff' which the French call café. It kept me going for the rest of the day … and the rest of the weekend!

I saw all the sights and did all the things a tourist should do that day, losing myself in the Paris of Hemingway, returning to the hotel only to change before setting out again for the Left Bank and dinner at one of the unique Parisian restaurants of which I had read. I wandered along the Boulevard St. Michel studying the menus. At La Coupole, on the Boulevard Montparnasse, I ate snails, and *bifteck bleu* (bloody and rare, as I knew racing cyclists ate their beef) together with *frits* and a green salad with oil and vinegar dressing, my favourite meal to this day. It was washed down with substantial carafes of *vin rouge de la maison*. I then adjourned to Café de Flore on the nearby Boulevard St. Germain for more café and a large cognac. I watched the world go by, feeling that I was at the very heart of civilization.

But while Saturday was for Paris, Sunday was – as it always was (paraphrasing Hemingway writing of bullfighting) for cycling. I rejoined my fellow travellers – some of whom had not even left the hotel – for our date at the iconic Parc des Princes, which had witnessed the arrival of every Tour de France for more than half a century (and would go on doing so until 1967), joining 40,000 other fans for the greatest moment of the year in cycle sport.

We weren't treated just to the arrival of Le Tour; there was to be a full afternoon of racing before the new champion arrived for his coronation. There was a full omnium programme – a series of different track races including sprints and pursuits, time trials and miss-and-outs (devil-take-the-hindmost as we called them in England), all designed to entertain. And to showcase the participants: all the top stars who for some reason or other had not started, or had dropped out of the Tour during its three-week marathon trek round France.

To my delight they included British track star Reg Harris and Brian Robinson, who had damaged his wrist in a fall on Stage 5 of the Tour nearly three weeks earlier, but was now back in competition. Other contestants included Irish star Shay Elliott, Belgian champions Rick Van Steenbergen and Fred DeBruyne. And none other than my ultimate hero of all time, the *Campionissimo* himself, Fausto Coppi. It was to be the only time I ever saw him, but he remains to this day, my champion of all cycling champions. What an aperitif it all was to the main course.

The cycle track at the old Parc des Princes (which has since been torn down and rebuilt elsewhere – though without a cycle track) was one of the classic locations of Paris, which Hemingway himself had often visited. Built where once the French royal family hunted in the forest, the velodrome seated 40,000 and was rented by the same people who owned and ran the Tour de France. By 1957 the actual track had been reduced in length to 454 metres, but still long enough to encircle a football/rugby pitch, its bankings steep enough to host races behind the giant motor pacers of that era.

On this particular afternoon those bankings were on fire, first with the spinning wheels of the stars who entertained us, then literally, as there was a shower of rain and the bankings were doused with petrol and set alight to dry them off. Like the omnium races we had watched, the result was a close run thing. Workmen were still trying to extinguish the flames with blankets as the fifty-six surviving members of the peloton swept on to the track from the tunnel under the stands!

A group of professional racing cyclists, who had just spent three weeks negotiating 2,928 miles through the hottest summer in living memory – across the plains, battered by the cobblestones of the north, and climbing what were then little more than gravel tracks over the giant summits of the Alps and Pyrenees were not going to be stopped by a mere fire! As officials desperately tried to douse the flames, the riders charged along the home straight. There was no sign of slowing down as they launched their final efforts, crossing the line with a lap to go. Miraculously, the flames were out when they arrived at full speed at the transition into the steep angles of the banking.

Three days earlier, in Bordeaux, the great French sprinter, André Darrigade, had been beaten into second place on his home track. There had been furious jersey-tugging and fist-waving as Darrigade took a bunch sprint for second place in front of Italian riders Padovan and Baroni. Two days later there was more of the same in the sprint at Tours with Darrigade the winner over Padovan. In Paris we witnessed yet another tempestuous sprint, the Frenchman again finishing ahead of Padovan and taking the stage to the roar of the crowd appreciating another French victory. This was the seventh Tour stage win for the rider from the Landes region, who went on to win 22 stages in the Tour, as well as a world championship and the Milan-San Remo classic.

Jacques Anquetil then crossed the line, safe in the leading part of the peloton and so took his first of what were to become a record-breaking five wins in *La Grande Boucle*, the beginning of a new era in Tour history and of French domination of the race. Watching from our seats near the finish line, the British party had a superb view of the finish … and the aftermath.

Today, everyone disappears into a heaving crush of people after the Champs-Elysées sprint, then climbs into the team coaches. At the Parc des Princes we observed the riders after they had crossed the line – each individual in his own little world, finishing the race and absorbing its meaning. Some riders cruised on round the track before dismounting in its grassy centre, which was filled only by a relatively small number of journalists and photographers, team and race officials. Others slumped onto the grass, thankful that the endless pedalling had stopped after three weeks, or continued to circle the track looking for family in the stands.

Many climbed off and just sat on their crossbars, sipping a Perrier water handed out by the sponsors, with a dazed look on their faces and finding it difficult to believe that it was finally all over. The star riders, meanwhile, were deep in conversation with suited gentlemen carrying battered leather briefcases, who were doubtless their business agents.

Whatever they did, the sight of it was like being backstage after the curtain comes down on a great performance. It was a privilege to be there, to pay them all respect, just to be part of it. After a solemn podium ceremony in the Gallic style and the tours d'honneur of the stage winner, the various jersey winners and finally the new champion, Jacques Anquetil, splendid in his golden fleece, the final act of this amazing annual three-week drama gradually dissolved before my eyes. The 44th Tour de France was over. I headed most reluctantly for the Gare du Nord.

Since 1957 I have seen the Tour de France on a number of occasions: climbing the Col de la Madeleine in a snowstorm and finishing in the sunshine on the Champs Elysées; racing past on the country roads of Brittany and by an English pub in Hampshire. But you never forget the first meeting with the passion of your life. And I have help with mine. A British cycling magazine recently published an extraordinary black and white panoramic photograph of the Parc des Princes on that memorable day in 1957.

It shows Anquetil on his lap of honour, almost smothered by a huge bouquet, pedalling along the home straight towards the finish-line. He is waving to the crowd, which can be seen quite clearly, smart in their Sunday best, applauding their hero. Somewhere amongst them is a group of British cyclists, including a Yorkshire lad, who had just been provided with the inspiration to ride his bike for the rest of his life and who would remain a fan of the world's greatest annual sports event, through its ups and downs, for more than half a century.

Vive le Tour!

STAGE 21, 1958: BRIANÇON–AIX-LES-BAINS, 219kms.

Charlie Woods

Charly Gaul was a wild throw by the almighty genetic gambler, a world-class athlete in the guise of a small, lightly built youth hardly out of puberty.

Though he tends to shrink from the limelight, he is still one of Luxembourg's favourite sons, especially during the month of July. Who are the others, you might ask. Only Tour historians can readily furnish the answer: François Faber who won in 1909, and Nicholas Frantz in 1927 and '28. Charly caught up with them in 1958 with a final-week offensive which added a brilliant page to the legend of *La Grande Boucle*.

Gaul burst upon the general consciousness on Bastille Day in the 1955 Tour when he soared over the historic Alpine climbs of the Aravis, Télégraph, Galibier and Vars arriving in Briançon nearly fifteen minutes ahead of the favourites. Those ancient prominences might almost have bowed their peaks in deference to this serene-faced kid and his dauntless twiddling. For his *coup de pédale* was as distinctive as his boyishness, a smooth but rapid twirl of the chainwheel on a rear sprocket of *cyclo-touriste* proportions. Here was a demonstration of class at its purest; his day-long break immediately gained recognition as a classic Tour exploit. Louison Bobet, the home favourite, obviously wasn't going to have it all his own way in his quest for that third victory in a row. The Continent held its breath and began to fall in love with this youthful revelation.

Because Charly had other assets besides sporting prowess: he was a blue-eyed heart-throb after the fashion of his contemporary, James Dean; but eager newshounds were to find that he was equally uncommunicative. His eloquence and assurance seemed reserved for the bike, and the bike alone.

Bobet took up the gauntlet on the next key stage which tackled Mont Ventoux, winning alone with great authority. Against all expectations, the newly christened 'Angel of the Mountains' was completely eclipsed, which was probably the first sign of his vulnerability to intense heat. The show-down between the two came in the Pyrenees, with Gaul breaking early, Bobet chasing to rejoin him and the tandem working together to amass a comfortable margin on all the others. Louison was home and dry despite a late charge from Jean Brankart. But for all the Belgian's best efforts, the defining image of the Tour was of Bobet and Gaul. Their David and Goliath struggle confirmed Charly's rise from rank outsider to the select heights of possible winner. On the bottom step in the Parc des Princes he twinkled as brightly as a newly discovered star.

In 1956 he confirmed his promise by winning the Giro in a snowstorm at the top of Monte Bondone. It was one of those apocalyptic stages which sees the morning's general classification tossed into the air and fall, at the end of the day, into a completely new (and smaller) pattern. Once the heavens opened, the angelic climber astounded followers by turning into an irrepressible water sprite, revelling in conditions which washed away half the field.

It might be that he discovered this ability in 1951 when, at the tender age of eighteen, he was sent to ride the amateur Tour of Austria. The crucial stage took in the Grossglockner which is slightly higher than Mont Ventoux and just as formidable. One can imagine the youngster engaging rather sheepishly with such a monster. He knew that he could climb well on ordinary hills, but this was no man's land. At half distance, however, despite his manager's exhortations to caution, his class had told and he found himself alone in the lead. A few moments of giddy pleasure were soon dispatched by the ever present need to keep the pedals turning; he was, after all, still in no man's land.

This show of force was greeted by another, a thunderstorm and the first few squalls of rain probably cooled the fever of his labours and brought with it a lighter, freer atmosphere. He had always been at ease in rainfall, but in his already exalted state this must have seemed like a blessing from the mountain itself. The sudden drenching may even have released him from any further inhibition, prompting him to give free reign to his jubilation. Beginning to pedal now with an edge of fierce affirmation, he perhaps completely forgot himself for a long series of ramps and bends, lost in the rapture of unexpected powers fully realised for the first time; to such an extent that not only did he win the stage, but broke the existing record for the climb.

Amidst the celebrations on that finishing line in Austria, and though he had made other momentous discoveries during the day, he might still have felt the rain clinging to him through his jersey and the assurance that he could always depend upon its grace and inspiration.

Charly rode a creditable Tour of France in '56 after his triumph in Italy, winning a stage and taking the mountain's crown. But in 1957 his destiny revealed its harsher face. The Tour started in a heatwave and on the second stage he was ignominiously dropped on a little rise outside Cherbourg. All the big national teams took off, of course, and though he chased with his faithful lieutenants he fell further and further behind until he was forced to unpin his number.

So it was that he came to the start in 1958 with a good Giro in his back pocket – third behind Baldini and Brankart plus a stage – and surrounded by the strongest team he had ever been granted. The Luxemburgers were combined with the Dutch; solid *rouleurs* like Wim Van Est, Gerrit Voorting and Wout Wagtmans could be depended upon to look after him on the flat and, with his clout as an overall contender, he was able to bring in his compatriot Jean (Jo) Goldschmit as *directeur technique*. Everything seemed set fair for a successful campaign; he had the age and the experience now, but there was always a cloud of imponderables hovering over his candidacy. Was he serious enough, would his luck live up to his ability, would fate be with him? All the pundits broke into a chorus of that old refrain: 'Always the bridesmaid but never the bride,' half taunting and half in hope because Charly had a place in everyone's heart.

A row in the French camp further strengthened his hand. Marcel Bidot, the highly respected tiller-man of Bobet's hattrick had decided to build his team around Anquetil who had won the year before. Bobet, who hadn't ridden the Tour since '55 and making his return, was another automatic choice. But Anquetil drew the line at Raphaël Geminiani whom he feared might gang up with Bobet against him. After years of devoted service both to the national team and to Louison, *Le Grand Fusil* – The Big Gun, as he was called – found himself out on his ear. He must have reached some accommodation with Bobet because he blamed Bidot for the betrayal and, swearing revenge, fell into the welcoming arms of the *Sud-Ouest* regionals under Adolphe Deledda, another ex-national team man. With the host nation's teams at each other's throats there would be less likelihood of any combines forming against the little Luxemburger.

During the first week he kept his powder dry while the French skirmished between themselves. Bobet launched a big offensive on the fifth stage accompanied by Anquetil and Geminiani which left Gaul two minutes adrift. Geminiani counter-attacked the next day trumping the nationals to the extent of ten minutes and a further three on Charly. But by then Voorting was in yellow, having won the second stage, so morale was high. Charly had set his sights on the first time trial at Châteaulin in Brittany. A tricky circuit with lots of abrupt climbs and tight corners, it suited his abilities and he struck a resounding blow. Anquetil, the acknowledged master of the discipline, was relegated to second place at seven seconds. Charly's cap was well and truly in the ring.

The next test came in the Pyrenees, but there was no showdown. Bahamontes was allowed to pick up points for the King of the Mountains and a stage victory at Luchon. Charly had a little dig on the Aubisque and then on the Peyresourde, dropping all but Geminiani who thus revealed the level of his form and his commitment to overall victory. An effort which was rewarded by the receipt of his first yellow jersey in eleven Tours at Pau. Then there was the stage that everyone feared, Mont Ventoux *contre la montre*. Charly took every precaution against the heat, strapping an ice bag to the back of his neck and triumphed, taking four minutes out of Anquetil, and five each from Bobet and Geminiani. But the latter regained the yellow jersey which he had lost to the upstart Italian, Vito Favero, who, previously just a *gregario*, was riding the race of his life.

The day after, in the foothills of the Alps, Gem strengthened his grasp with the help of all the main contenders. Charly had to change bikes with Ernzer because of a loose chainring and the rest took off. There were accusations of sabotage but the end result was that he was left chasing on his own. He lost further ground by crashing on a descent and changing bikes again, ending the day fifteen minutes down on the Big Gun. The next stage offered the High Alps, but Charly was unable to rise to the occasion and even lost more time. It seemed that he had paid dearly for his efforts on the Ventoux, and that in spite of all precautions his old enemy, the sun, had had its way. Final victory, which had beckoned so tantalisingly at the summit of Ventoux, now appeared to have slipped irrevocably out of reach.

There was nothing left but the final mountain stage, Briançon–Aix-les-Bains, which took in the foothills of the Alps and the Jura. The profile didn't seem demanding enough for big gains, but he had to grasp his last chance. On the first of the five climbs, the Lautaret, the bunch stayed together until near the top. But on the next, the Luitel, a nasty little grind, steep and narrow, Charly took his cue. It was already raining but now a steady glacial downpour had set in. He danced away and only Bahamontes tried to stay with him; no one else budged. Who was he a threat to now? Not even the Spaniard whom he quickly dropped, when he saw the front runners coming back at him. Geminiani admitted afterwards that he just looked on complacently. 'There goes Charly,' I said to myself, 'off to do his little number.' All the main contenders had other scores to settle – between themselves – the Angel's wings had been clipped.

But Charly felt otherwise. The privileged members of the caravan who were closest were amazed at his power and grace in such terrible conditions. While behind, Anquetil was trying to out-distance Geminiani, threatening his yellow jersey. A battle royal had been engaged as Gaul's petulant sortie developed into an avenging raid. At the top of the Luitel he turned on to the Chamrousse, a further seven kilometres of ascent. He crossed beneath that banner with a lead of one minute on Bahamontes, three plus on Anquetil and nearly five ahead of Geminiani and Bobet. On the descent Jacques and Gem diced with death, one to stay away the other to close; but by Grenoble they had both slipped further behind Charly.

Next came the Col de Porte which led to the Cucheron and then the Granier – all of them lashed and buffeted by the storm. On the first slopes of the Porte, Anquetil began to crack; his legs turned wooden and his chest tightened. His flight was over. Geminiani, helped by Nencini and Favero, had brought him to heel. Up ahead Gaul carved through the mist to cross the summit with four and a half minutes in hand over Geminiani, six on Anquetil and thirteen plus on Bobet. As he began the descent, he punctured, but was quickly on his way again.

The Cucheron was short but murderously steep towards the top. With two kilometres to go he had augmented his lead to eight minutes over Gem and more than nine on Jacques. The sky darkened further and the weather worsened, but Charly blithely pursued his *échappée* with no sign of weakening. Behind him, in the open team car, Jo Goldschmit and his deputy stood upright taking the brunt of the elements layered with woollens beneath soaked macs, their berets pulled down over their ears. Back along the caravan a similar desperation was evident, everyone having donned whatever stitch of clothing lay to hand. All in stark contrast to the hero of the hour who forged on in the bare minimum of jersey, shorts and cap. With bare arms, bare legs and bare-faced determination he was riding the tempest into legend. This was the day for which all the others were a preparation and which thereafter would tint with splendour each one remaining to him – and, of course, he knew it. The rain told him, the rain pouring from the skies and swirling up from his wheels, the rain which eventually made any clothing redundant. It had long since transformed him into its own naked creature like a fish in a stream and just as naturally bore him along.

The Luitel and the Porte would have gained him the stage, but with the Cucheron and then the Granier he was setting himself up for something more momentous.

The Granier wasn't long, only 9.5 kilometres and gently sloped, but it was a col too far for most of the principle contenders. The weatherman, pleased with his champion's progress, threw in a thunderstorm for good measure. Tortured by this further natural insult, the hitherto indefatigable Gem blew up. No longer able to hold the wheel of his faithful team-mate Jean Dotto, and overwhelmed by despair, he began to cry. Further back along the road Anquetil was zigzagging wildly in between being pushed by Walkowiak.

Meanwhile, Charly, encouraged by the extra accolade from his presiding element, was going from strength to strength. His lead on the Big Gun had stretched to twelve minutes and seventeen on the Norman. After a ham sandwich at the summit of the Granier – he had survived thus far on sugar lumps – he hurled himself into the descent, covering the run-in, with five cols and 200 kilometres in his legs, at an average of 28 m.p.h.

It was dark as night in Aix-les-Bains beneath the same frigid downpour. Cars and motorcycles had turned on their headlights, but a substantial crowd was still gathered. Charly took the last corner carefully and then sprinted for the line without losing anything of his immaculate style. Jo Goldschmit threw a raincoat over his shoulders and the winged climber's first request was to be taken straight to the hotel. They wouldn't let him go, of course, and he was still there fulfilling the winner's protocol when his victims began to crawl in.

The fine Belgian Tour rider, Jean Adriaenssens, put in one of the best rides of his career to finish second at seven minutes, continuing his steady progress to a final fourth place overall. Favero was best of the favourites at nine minutes, crowning good teamwork by the Italians to regain the overall lead. Next came Geminiani crossing the line to collapse into the arms of Deledda and André Leducq. The former winner took pity on him and prevailed upon the driver of the *Le Parisien* car to give them a lift to the hotel. In the back seat the exhausted rider began to sob on Leducq's shoulder, but after a while pulled himself together. 'What about Favero?' he enquired. 'Thirty-nine seconds up,' came the ready reply. This cheered him; he might have lost the yellow jersey but he could get it back in the time trial. Victory was still possible. Emboldened, he enquired of Gaul,'how much did Charly pull back – was it five minutes?' There was an uneasy silence, everyone stared ahead. Eventually it fell to the photographer in the front seat to mutter the dreadful news out of the side of his mouth: 'Fourteen minutes, fifteen including the bonus…' A pitiful moan tore through the Big Gun's stricken frame and he buried his head once more in Leducq's shoulder. 'That's it then,' he said, sniffing pathetically, 'Charly's won the Tour.'

The car came alongside a gathering of journalists. Louison Bobet was giving an impromptu Press conference. 'Charly is a rider like no other,' he declared. 'Raphaël has lost fourteen minutes; I, myself, lost nineteen; and Jacques twenty-three. Margins like that don't occur nowadays, they hark back to the pre-war Tours which makes me think that Charly's one of those old style roadmen mysteriously reborn amongst us. Either that or he's not human at all, more of a supernatural being.'

Charly did indeed win the Tour. He ran away with the final time trial taking four minutes out of both Favero and Geminiani to put himself in yellow. The day after, he mounted the podium in the Parc des Princes with a hattrick of time trial victories and an historic mountain stage – a winner in the grand manner. It was his finest hour and richly deserved, but the radiance of victory which shone from his face only served to enhance his boyishness. It was as if some little third-cat. with a new licence had scooped the world's greatest race and been transformed in the process – he really had become a golden boy.

At 70, somewhat dumpier now, he still pops up when Luxembourg hosts the Tour. He was at the summit of Ventoux last year for Virenque's victory and he joined the line-up of past winners for the Centenary Tour presentation in the autumn. However, he still remains something of a shadowy figure, largely forgotten, but by one of those telling ironies of eternal recurrence his riding style has come back into fashion. Switch on any mountain stage these days and the screen fills with our contemporary *grimpeurs* earnestly twiddling upwards. Whether they realise it or not, they've all taken a crank out of Charly's chainwheel.

STAGE 20, 1959

ANNECY – CHALON-sur-SOÂNE, 202km

Graeme Fife

Overnight, after the 14th Stage, 219 undulating kilometres from Albi to Aurillac through the Massif Central in suffocating heat, Brian Robinson had suffered badly, once again his recalcitrant stomach.* To the misery of pain and bodily discomfort, the added nightmare spectre of another abandon.

An advertisement showed a smiling Darrigade attributing the secret of his superb form to relaxing nights on a Simmons mattress. As for Rivière, he wore the pyjamas of champions, made by Doncho, soft, warm, of health giving wool. If only...

I asked Robinson about this recurring gastric complaint. 'Was it ever diagnosed as anything more radical?'

'No. All I can think of is that when we got into Aurillac, we were absolutely famished and the guy gave us some *pain d'épices*, which we wolfed down. It may have been stale or something, I don't know. And, of course, our body temperature was that hot, I suppose drinking a lot of chilled water may have had something to do with it. You were discouraged from drinking too much during the race – that was the thinking in those days – so you always had a mouth like...like a French bog, if you like.'

Anquetil said that he rode ninety kilometres of this stage without eating or drinking. He admitted that all the bottles of liquid he saw were tempting but that this day he wanted to suffer and 'to hit the bull's eye'.

Diarrhoea is more often caused by dehydration and excess of sun than by tainted food so it may, simply, have been that Robinson's system, overstretched, desiccated and boiled, succumbed to the stress of the day rather than any immediate biophysical disorder. However, he had been

---

* Robinson, in the thick of the action all day, finish fourth in a four-man sprint on the track at Aurillac, behind Anglade, Anquetil and Bahamontes. Track stars, Forlini and Varnajo, told him afterwards that if he'd delayed his sprint another 50 metres he would have won.

forced to quit the Vuelta that year because of problems with his stomach and had been prescribed medication. After the stage finish in Bayonne, facing the Pyrenean stages, he stopped taking the tablets because he felt they were affecting his form. The strength of his ride into Aurillac suggested that he had made the right decision. Although it is impossible to say for sure whether pills could have prevented the recurrence of the stomach upset, it seems more likely that they would not. The swiftness of his recovery bears that out.

That evening, in Aurillac, Jean Bobet, a graduate in English, went to see Robinson and Shay Elliot in their hotel room. He fumbled for a pleasantry. Robinson reassured him, there was no need – 'We speak French here.' Bobet said that they had each, for some time, become continentals. Not much of an accolade in many English eyes, perhaps, but a sure sign of their professionalism as riders in the continental peloton competing in the Tour de France. He was, above all, impressed by the commitment of the two men to their career as professionals. 'They practise their trade with the same fervour that their compatriots reserve exclusively for cricket. Alas for them.' Bobet's reference to cricket may well be a cliché; the evident respect for the fervour of these two lone giants of the road was heartfelt.

x x x x x

The following morning Robinson came to the start feeling awful, sick, enfeebled. Elliott, singled out by a commissaire for some irregularity in his turnout, was fined 500fr for being ill-dressed. The field set off for Clermont-Ferrand on another day of torrid heat. Robinson managed to stay with the bunch until the first attack went at Puy Mary, 67km out, and from then on, the ride was torture.

For six hours, Elliott nursed, cajoled, pushed, encouraged, talked to, relayed and helped his ailing friend. He poured water over his head, splashed his face gently, when the commissaires weren't looking planted his hand in the Englishman's back – of course, the commissaires did eventually see him and the fine ensued, to both riders, 2,500 francs and 30 seconds penalty, Elliott for giving the aid, Robinson for accepting it. There were times, said Robinson, when he probably wished Elliott would just shut up, that the constant babble of his voice, *come on, keep going, stick to it, we'll make it, come on Brian, come on,* would stop, go away, leave him in peace. But, if the words underscored the torment of sitting on the bike near incapable of effort, they also served as a continuous reminder that his friend was there, at his side, sheltering him from buffets of wind, leaning across to cool him down with a refreshing douse from the water bottle, riding with him, nursing him along *comme une mère poule*, said the journalist, the same term, remember, used for the Derny men who shielded the riders in the Bordeaux-Paris. Dr Dumas supplied glucose tablets – a necessary supplement for a rider who had voided so much solid food and could ingest none, but its accumulated effect was to cause gripe in the guts and to leave a foul taste in the mouth.

Grinding along behind these two riders, like the Grim Reaper, came the broom wagon, the besom attached to it reinforcing its role as the sweeper-up of discarded and broken bits of the race. And, Elliott's stream of words, the exhortation, jarring as it sounded much of the time, a barrage in his ears, was also an echo of his own unshaken will, to keep going until he dropped, never to give up, to ride until he could ride no longer. Mountaineers looking after others suffering from hypothermia in extreme cold do the same, they talk and talk and talk to keep them awake, for if they go to sleep, death follows close behind.

At the feed station in Riom, Elliott took both musettes and loaded up with all the extra bidons he could carry. He pressed his friend to eat, to supply some of the energy he was dredging up from somewhere just to keep going.

Robinson en perdition…they said, the French (translatable as 'distress') having something of the force of the earlier English sense of utter destruction, complete ruin.

As he observed this melancholy affair from the pillion of a motorbike, Jean Bobet thought how the forefathers of these two men had fought: the one to annex and subjugate Ireland, the other to make it free. 'I was moved to see them so closely bound by distress. The solid strength of the one aiding the weakness of the other. They were not unaware of the futility of their persistence because they calculated the permissible time gaps all the way along their slow journey.' He concluded his account with an appeal to the fans who complain when the peloton goes too slowly. 'I have not told you everything but I am sure I have told you enough so that, from now on, you do not take potshots at cyclists.'

The riders called the *grupetto* at the back of the race in the mountains 'Darrigade's autobus', Darrigade the experienced pro who kept the slower moving bunch of non-climbers together at a speed which would just miss the time guillotine. 'If you stayed with them,' Robinson told me, 'you knew you were safe, it was an insurance policy.' No such indemnity for him or Elliott this day. They knew they were doomed. They came in forty-seven minutes down.

'To be honest,' said Robinson, 'I don't know how I got to the end. As to that rule that kept me in, I was as surprised as anyone.'

The rule, an ancient one invoked by his International team *Directeur Sportif*, Ducazeaux, gave a waiver to any man who had started the day in the top ten overall. Robinson was thus reinstated, Elliott, for all the selfless devotion he had shown, the sacrifice of his own race, was not. Robinson was mortified, even if Elliott insisted that he had come to the Tour to help Robinson and that he had done. There were alpine stages to come and he, unlike his friend, was no climber. Robinson had a chance to come back and do something. It was typically throwaway and unassuming in the genial Irishman, whatever grievous disappointment it glossed over. Although Elliott was definitely out, the discussion about Robinson continued for some time and, when the blackboard of names for the individual time trial was marked up next morning, beginning with the official *lanterne rouge,* the German Matthias Löder, Robinson was not, at first, included. Robinson, the actual *lanterne rouge,* nonetheless crept back up the overall classification. Setting off first, up the twelve kilometres of the Puy-de-Dôme's conical volcanic outcrop, he acquitted himself well, finishing in the middle order. Hassenforder, over eight minutes down on the winner, Bahamontes, was excluded on time. Bahamontes recorded 36–15, his nearest challengers: Gaul at 1–26 and Anglade at 3 minutes.

During the Rest Day in Saint-Etienne, after the time trial, Robinson had begun to recover his strength, thanks to the kindly attentions of the Tour doctor, Dr Dumas, and ample quantities of yoghurt. Now, boring into his mind, a determination to do something to repay Elliott's courageous help.

Annecy – Chalon-sur-Saône, 202kms

Robinson had finished the previous day, the last of the alpine stages, thirty-six minutes adrift, but looking fresh and in fizzy good spirits. That evening, the mechanics fitted a pair of very light Italian-made wheels to his pale blue Geminiani frame, carrying lightweight time trial tyres. Robinson spent the time before supper scrutinising, once more, the profile of the next day's stage to Chalon-sur-Saône – a drop to the foot of the third category Forêt d'Echallon 963m, a lumpy middle section and a steady descent into the old town, once residence of the kings of Burgundy.

Le tout pour le tout…going for broke.

Several factors persuaded him that this was a stage for a solo break: most of the riders were physically and mentally tired after the alps, their thoughts were on the time trial, the last stage into Paris and the scramble for points in the team competition; the hilly terrain of the Jura and the Saône-et-Loire suited him, 'his kind of country' and, foremost, he badly needed and wanted to have a go, to give Elliott's sacrifice meaning. He also needed to put on a show. Before the Tour started, in Mulhouse, Daniel Dousset, the criterium agent, had told him and Elliott that if they did not thrust themselves out of the anonymity of the Internations team, there would be no contracts. Robbed of the opportunity of a win in Aosta when his tyre rolled off, this stage it had to be. (After the birth of their second child, Robinson and his wife had decided to leave the site at Bry and Shirley and the two children, Michelle and Martin-Louis, took to the road, going where the racing took them. It greatly lessened the emotional strain of separation, a curious vagabondage, the family as one, pa earning the money on the move. In the amalgam of all that they were putting into success on the road as financial investment, there was much hanging on a stage win.)

The lightweight wheels and tyres made no great material difference, a few seconds advantage, maybe, but their effect on morale was potent. The tyres would be more prone to puncture and, if it rained, their silk walls would take in water and swell the tube. However, feeling good about riding a lighter machine had considerable psychological value and this was a day for focus, concentrated will and pointed ambition.

'One man alone had the courage to shake off his chains and set off on an adventure, the Englishman, Robinson, the reprieved man of Clermont,' wrote the *Équipe* reporter.

On the approach to Bellegarde, Robinson moved to the front of the bunch. He knew the town from having ridden a criterium there: a sharp bend in the road led onto the steep climb up through a stony gorge towards the Forêt d'Echallon. It was an ideal point to cut loose and disappear. This he did, followed at once by the climber, Jean Dotto, a former team-mate, riding for the French Centre-Midi regional team. 'Jean Dotto was screaming for me to wait for him as we climbed the Echallon.'

Dotto reached the summit ten seconds ahead of Robinson but was not very quick downhill. 'I decided to drop him as the French team would be chasing and he wasn't much of a descender. They caught him, but didn't bother about me. That descent was a bit hairy, mind you – I was on 8oz tyres and there was a lot of gravel about, so I was afraid of puncturing.'

On the descent through the trees into Oyonnax, riding at hectic pace, clipping corners, cutting a line as close to straight as he could, Robinson dropped Dotto. He pushed on alone, another 140km ahead of him – once the distance of the Grand Prix des Nations' individual time trial – tracked by Ducazeaux in the team Peugeot. When he reached a minute advance, he knew the gauntlet was down. Forty kilometres on, he had a lead of five minutes and eased off a little, to ride within himself. Even so and despite an intermittent headwind, he continued to gain time. 'After a while, you get into a sort of breathing rhythm which ties in well with things going through your head, such as *I'm going to win, I'm going to win…this is the day for Shay.* My mind was sharp, my legs were good and my morale was formidable, fully psyched up. With one hour to go, I knew the win was in the bag but I had to put that out of my head and just get on with the job. Even so, it was a real comfort to know that and I didn't let up till I crossed the line.'

Some way out from the finish, the motorbike with the slate drove up to show him the time advantage: *Pel 19' Reste 36km.*

Afterwards, in the euphoria of the win, he said, 'I still had a little left in hand'.

He rode down the long straight to the line in Chalon-sur-Saône, cheered all the way by a big crowd, the wooden fencing draped with a Martini banner, the Tour director Jean Goddet, in his trademark khaki bush shirt, shorts and knee-length socks, a motorcyclist and officer of the Garde Républicaine escort waiting to applaud the lone winner as he raised his arms and rolled in to victory, 20'–6" ahead of the second man. *Robinson le puncheur…* Robinson the hard-hitter.

x x x x x

The climb at Bellegarde played a significant role in another rider's fortunes that day. Robic was dropped and had to ride the remainder of the stage alone. The difference was that he was in the decline of his career and already weak, with little hope of beating the time limit. The more Robinson drew away from the peloton, the graver Robic's plight became. At the side of the road in towns and villages, eager children born after the days of his pomp – he won the Tour in 1947 – cheered him as he slogged past, hunched over the handlebars, hailing him Biquet… Kid, don't give up.

Antoine Blondin, the writer and perennial Tour follower, anxious to save Robic's day, had driven up alongside Robinson en route and reports the conversation thus:

'Hello, Brian, want you to stop. [in English]. Won't you stop? You're eliminating Robic. What's it to you if you win with only a slight advance? Let him catch up on the time gaps – it's you who's making them.'

'And if I get caught…?'

'Okay, listen: ride to the finish and stop short of the line, then cross it when you judge it the right moment to take your victory and to save the beaten innocent who's paying the price of it.'

Blondin seemed happy with the logic of this. It had no effect on Robinson, however. He merely pushed harder on the pedals, indifferent to the appeals and, as Blondin records, 'answered them in cruel terms evincing that other aspect of *fair play*: may the strongest on the day be wholly the strongest'. Robic came in forty-one minutes down on Robinson and, despite an impassioned plea laced with an acrimonious tirade to which Goddet remained impervious, he was eliminated.

For Robinson, honour, prizes – stage, team, combativity – contracts, a telling punch, indeed: 'It's difficult to describe the feelings of satisfaction, stimulation, pleasure, excitement, all these things and, of course, the public appreciation is so overwhelming it brings tears of joy, also the fact that the family back at home, friends and all share in that pleasure. Even today, when someone reminds me of those super moments, it stirs the blood.'

(adapted from *Brian Robinson: Pioneer* by Graeme Fife)

How the French press saw it

84

STAGE 3, 1963: JAMBES–ROUBAIX, 218 kms

Graham Healy and Richard Allchin

Jacques Anquetil's St Raphaël team was every bit as powerful as the year before and again the Irish star Shay Elliott was to be a very important part of the world's best team. However Shay had just an average start to the 1963 season and as 'vice-Champion du Monde', as much of the continental press at the time often used to call the Silver medal winner of the World Road Championship, the media thought he might start the year a little bit more emphatically. But with two major Tours on the horizon Shay knew he had to be more circumspect with his effort.

His early season performances more often than not would be very good. However, in retrospect it's easy to see that those main targets were the Vuelta again and the Tour de France. The previous year he, perhaps unfairly, hadn't been given the opportunity to ride due to new regulations in support of the French contingent. In riding the Tour de France this year he would have the chance of being the only English-speaking rider ever to win stages in all of the major Tours.

In a controversial Vuelta the previous year Anquetil didn't finish the race because of internal politics between him and team-mate Rudi Altig and an 'ambiguous' illness that he claimed he had suffered. That meant he didn't fulfill his abiding ambition of winning two grand Tours in the same year. However in 1962 Elliott had ridden brilliantly and had not only finished in an historic third place overall, but also won a stage and worn the leaders jersey for several days, again a totally unique performance by an English speaking rider in a Grand Tour. However he wasn't done yet he was also second in the Points Classification producing even more history in the world of professional cycling just as he had in his earlier career.

Elliott, although without any early personal glory this year, had strongly supported Anquetil to yet another overall win in Paris-Nice, and in the Vuelta he did the same for his French team leader which eventually led to his overall victory in the Spanish national Tour. Shay, despite his foremost dedication to Anquetil's overall success was given his freedom to go for stage wins and took a fine victory on the 13th stage to Valencia, the longest stage of the race covering over 250 kilometres. After another small win in France before the Tour he was eventually selected to ride the

Grand Boucle. He was there to support Anquetil, of course, but he would have the freedom to go for stage wins as in the Vuelta if the chance arose and didn't radically affect Anquetil's overall challenge.

On the opening 152.5-kilometre stage to Epernay Anquetil fell and cut his left hand, but without any really serious injury. Shay and the rest of the St. Raphaël team paced him back to the peloton without any major problems. One of Anquetil's main rivals, the great Spanish climber Federico Bahamontes, winner of the Tour in 1959, had shown his intentions were serious even at that early point in the race by getting into the winning break of four. The stage was won by the Belgian Eddy Pauwels from his compatriot, Edgard Sorgeloos, with Britain's Alan Ramsbottom a fine third and Bahamontes in fourth. Eddy Pauwels, now with the yellow jersey, was a possible outsider for the overall and Bahamontes had gained some valuable time on Anquetil. It had not been a good day for the St Raphaël team.

Rik Van Looy won stage 2A after 185 kilometres, which ended in a big bunch sprint. Stage 2B was a team time trial where, although it was known that Anquetil was off his game, St Raphaël were very disappointed to finish in only fourth place. Pelforth were dominant that day with Ramsbottom, still in excellent form, leading them over the line. The French 'super team' lost nearly a minute, and Pauwels kept the yellow jersey.

The third stage of 223 kilometres from Jambes to Roubaix included some very difficult roads, many over the cobbles of the infamous Paris-Roubaix classic and, not altogether surprisingly, a number of riders were to crash out of the race.

After 70 kilometres a group of 12 broke away, with two of Anquetil's team-mates, Shay and Stablinski, up in the break. Because they were in the team of the race favourite, and also because the break contained at least two obvious danger men – Henry Anglade, a previous Tour runner-up and the classy Belgian rider Gilbert Desmet (1) who could climb very well – neither of the St. Raphaël men were obliged to work. However, these two were not the only danger as the two Spaniards in the break Antonio Suarez and Luis Otaño had very good Grand Tour palmarés: Suarez had won the Vuelta in 1959 including two stage wins and the KOM title and had also finished third in the Giro in 1961 together with a stage win; Otaño had two top four placings at that time (and was to be runner-up the following year in the Vuelta) with a final total of three stage wins, and later in 1966 was a stage winner in the Tour itself. So, all in all, this break wasn't just a routine effort but had the credentials for making a major influence on the overall result.

The fact that it contained these four danger men, Anglade, Desmet, Otaño and Suarez, and that Elliott and Stablinski were not contributing to the workload, didn't stop the twelve-strong group from gaining a lead of nearly ten minute. Shay was to puncture twice over the cobbled roads, first after 150 kilometres and again 30 kilometres later, but each time, with Stablinski helping him by slowing the group down, he got back to the break. After one of his punctures Shay was so impatient for his team car to arrive that he had jumped off his bike and removed his back wheel, not realising it was actually his front that he had punctured. However, Shay had understood that this was a great chance of a stage win, after so many near misses in Tour stages. This day he had great legs to match his ambition and not only that, today it seemed he would have the total support of the current World Champion, Stablinski, who had already had his share of stage wins in the Tour and owed a debt to Shay for his World title.

The composition of the leading group in a stage of this type was somewhat unusual, especially with the two Spaniards whose countrymen hardly ever featured in a classic like Paris-Roubaix, although it was only towards the end of the stage that the difficult cobbled sections were to kick in. Anglade, who in the long run probably had the most to gain, worked like a demon to keep a good lead and some of the others did their bit. However, among the Belgian riders, Desmet had finished second in the Paris-Roubaix in 1959 and sprinter Michel Van Aerde had finished second in the Tour of Flanders the previous year. So their ambitions seemed to be clear – Van Aerde to win the sprint at the Roubaix stadium and Desmet to take the yellow jersey. So, despite having an 'easy' ride, Elliott and Stablinski couldn't be sure of the victory. The St.Raphael duo therefore had to hatch a plan for one or other of them to win, preferably on their own.

Six kilometres from Roubaix Stablinski led the group on to a cycle lane at the side of the road. Everybody followed, except Shay, who jumped clear on the cobbled stretch, while his team-mate helped the cause by again deliberately slowing the break. The narrow lane made it difficult for the others to get around Stablinski, and this was just the chance Shay needed. When he attacked he gave it his all, as he had done in many races before. This time the bad luck he had suffered so often, especially in the Tour, was not going to prevent him from gaining glory on this day. Shay was well clear, and arrived into the Vélodrome at Roubaix over half a minute ahead of his breakaway companions. Stablinski rubbed salt in the wound by finishing second, beating the top Belgian sprinter Van Aerde, to make it a one-two for St Raphael. Both Elliott and Stablinski took a lot of criticism from their rivals, especially Anglade who had worked so hard to gain time on Anquetil. But really he hadn't much to complain about; this was cycle racing at its most raw. Elliott had ridden magnificently; it was his day of glory in the Tour and so very well deserved after the disappointments of the past.

Shay not only won the stage, but also the yellow jersey. He was only the second native English speaker to wear the yellow jersey as Britain's Tom Simpson had worn it for a day the year previously. This stage win made him the first and only Irishman ever and the first English speaking rider to win stages in all three major Tours – an historic achievement in itself. Even the Irish greats, Sean Kelly and Stephen Roche, never managed that despite their fantastic records. The history Shay, as an Irishman, had made that day has never been equalled and fifty years later to the year his memory should be treasured and appreciated. It was only in the last decade that Shay's record has been equaled by anyone from an English speaking country. It was a truly unique record for one of cycling's first pioneers from outside mainland Europe.

After the finish Shay was, of course, mobbed by reporters just after he crossed the line, before setting out on a lap of honour around the Vélodrome. He said: 'I'm very happy to have won this stage. I hadn't done much in the stage until the Paris-Roubaix [cobbled] section. Today is a sort of revenge for me on this great classic route.' This was in reference to his Paris-Roubaix ride in 1958, when a broken saddle just a few kilometres from the finish denied him victory.

He went on to say that he'd been instructed by the team to go to the front. 'It was Anquetil, after seeing that I was strong in yesterday's stage, who told me to ride at the front today and control the breakaways, and that's how I managed to jump into the good break. Our mission was clear. We had to make sure that the break didn't take too much time, and then mark the most dangerous opponents in the finale. I was in perfect condition and I knew that I was going to do well, but I didn't think it would be such a victory…I am very happy, because it means something in the life of a cyclist to wear the yellow jersey, particularly for Ireland. Now people will realise that cycling also has its place elsewhere than on the continent. In those final kilometres I was thinking of my son Pascal. I wanted him to be proud of what I was doing.'

Whether he would try to defend the yellow jersey would depend on the course of the race he told the reporters. He was careful not to sound too ambitious, although it was very unlikely he would cause friction in the team since Anquetil would not feel the Irishman represented any real threat, although a number of very inexperienced or naive journalists suggested he might be.

In a scene reminiscent of what had happened to Harry Reynolds all those years ago in Copenhagen, the brass band at the Roubaix Vélodrome played 'God Save the Queen' during the prize presentation, instead of the Irish anthem 'Amhrán na bhFiann'. They obviously had not been expecting a win by Shay. It was not the first time that he'd encountered confusion over his nationality. In fact, throughout his career, many race commentators and journalists had described him as British. He never got overly upset by this, merely pointing out every time that actually, he was Irish!

After the stage Jean Stablinski said, 'Séamus was best placed on General Classification, and it was completely normal that he should attack and I should protect him. For my old friend Séamus, I am as happy as he is.' Then he added, somewhat ironically when the true account of that race came to light, 'I remember the World Championships in Salo last year.'

Anquetil was equally delighted to see his loyal team-mate take the win, but disappointed that he had lost time to Anglade and Desmet. Henry Anglade won the prize that day for most aggressive rider, and was not particularly happy with the passive role Shay and Stablinski had played in the break, although he later admitted that the two St Raphaël riders had been right to ride the way they did. The day after he had taken the yellow jersey a French cycling magazine tried to help readers to pronounce the name 'Séamus' by outlining the French phonetic spelling of it thus: 'Sé-a-musse'.

Shay was to hold on to yellow for the next two stages into Rouen and then into Rennes as the race continued westwards. The stage to Rouen was raced in appalling conditions with strong winds and rain, and misfortune struck him not long after the start. On the cobbles, six kilometres into the race, he was involved in a big crash, which also took down Henry Anglade. They both escaped unscathed. Shay attempted to break away after 60 kilometres and gained a minute on the peloton, but the audacious effort proved futile and he dropped back to the bunch. Only Shay would have attempted such a move, but whenever he was in this kind of form he was difficult to control.

His wife, Marguerite, prominent in a pink suede coat, appeared again at the stage end in Rouen to embrace Shay, after travelling with their son, Pascal, from Paris. 'I congratulated him by telephone yesterday,' she said. 'Today, I decided to do it in person.' At the stage end Shay spoke to reporters of his chances of winning overall: 'Naturally, I know my chances of winning the Tour are very slim, as I am not good in the mountains and there are still seventeen days left, but the nine minutes between me and Anquetil and Van Looy raises my hopes.' In retrospect, this comment surely has to be taken with a pinch of salt, with Shay throwing a scrap to the beguiled press.

The Irish media, again showing their naiveté about the sport of cycling, ran with the headline, 'SHAY CAN WIN THE TOUR'. They discussed his possibilities with Shay's father, Jim. 'At this stage I'm not sure what to do, but if but if Shay keeps this up, I'll be there.'

He remained upbeat even when asked to discuss the suggestion that Shay's climbing abilities would possibly let him down later in the race: 'When Séamus won a stage in the amateur Route de France, it was over the most mountainous course in the whole race. He might drop some time in the mountains, but I don't think it will seriously affect his chances. Besides, it's the descent I'm worried about rather than the climbing. It is during mountain descents that most accidents occur, especially when they are trying to make up time.'

But, as has been shown time and again, a great amateur climber does not necessarily make a dominating climber when he turns to the cash ranks. He relies more on his strengths and natural talent than he might exhibit later in his professional career. Shay was surely an outstanding professional rouleur, but neither mountain climbing nor time trialing were ever going to be his strongest attributes. His pretensions for the Overall were eventually left in the dust, just as Shay must have known very well they would be.

Father Jim, although not a French speaker, had been following the Tour on the French radio station, Europe 1 (there being no live radio coverage in English during the 60s). 'I do the best I can, and most of the time I can make out the position by listening to the names of the riders when they are read out,' he explained.

Stage 6b in Angers was a 24.5-kilometre time trial, and it was hoped that Shay, with over a minute advantage on both Anglade and Desmet, could put in a good enough ride to maintain his lead. 'I'll have a go,' Shay was to say on the start line of the stage, 'but how I hate time trials.'

Unfortunately, he lost nearly three minutes to Gilbert Desmet who took over the lead, as Shay slipped back to third. Disappointing though this was, he had several days of glory in the bank, and the assurance of more lucrative criterium contacts. And in any case, Shay was first and foremost a team player: the most important feature of the day, he said to journalists afterwards, was that Anquetil had won the stage convincingly:

'I never hoped to do more than hold the jersey for more than a few stages. Now I will be going all out to work as a team member for Anquetil, and try and place him on the winner's podium in Paris on July 14th.'

Shay had worn yellow for four stages, and that feat is all the more impressive if you consider that this was more than some great cyclists ever did , including some who actually went on to win the race outright, such as Charly Gaul, Jan Janssen, Jean Robic and Greg LeMond. Big stars amongst many others such as Rik Van Looy, Tom Simpson, Rik Van Steenbergen and his former mentor Charles Pélissier, and countrymen Sean Kelly and Stephen Roche as stated earlier wore the jersey for fewer days than Shay. His exploits were unique in Ireland's sporting history, yet they didn't make the impact they should have done. They were somewhat overshadowed by something momentous taking place in Ireland itself.

Following directly on from a European tour, which included a visit to Germany where he made his memorable 'Ich bin ein Berliner' speech, the American President, John F. Kennedy, was making an emotional journey to his ancestral homeland. Hundreds of thousands flocked to see JFK, the first American President to visit Ireland, and his visit occupied the headlines of every newspaper for days. This meant the greatest days of Shay's career were, unfortunately, generally confined to the sports pages – the four days of the President's visit virtually coinciding with Shay's four days in yellow. It was perhaps typical of Shay's often untimely bad luck that the presence of JFK would understandably displace almost everything else newsworthy from the headlines.

After four glorious days in the yellow jersey his more characteristic misfortune – on the road – hit him on the eighth stage, when he punctured three times. 'I finished very tired,' he said afterwards. 'It was a stage in which I wanted to take it rather easy in view of the big efforts when we begin climbing mountains, but puncture troubles forced me to make a big effort in catching up.'

On the stage to Grenoble Shay once again showed his worth as a team-mate. Louis Rostollan injured his hip in a fall and was struggling behind the peloton. As he was a strong climber, and therefore very important to Anquetil's overall chances, Shay dropped back to help him get back into the bunch. But Rostollan's injuries were slowing them to the point where they both faced the possibility of elimination, and 50 kilometres from the finish Géminiani instructed him to leave Rostollon to his fate and ensure he finished within the time limit. There would be no repetition of the incident with Brian Robinson in the 1959 Tour.

The following day St Raphaël would lose another rider when Stablinski dropped out (as did one of the pre-race favourites, Charly Gaul, and the great French sprinter, André Darrigade). Stablinski had crashed heavily during the stage, and once again, Shay had to drop back to nurse a stricken team-mate, again to no avail as it turned out.

Anquetil would go on to win the race, despite being put under some severe pressure by Bahamontes. After the departure of two of the team due to injury it was left mainly to Shay and Guy Ignolin to protect Anquetil and leave him in a position whereby he could take the *maillot jaune* from Gilbert Desmet on the 19th stage time trial to Besançon, which he duly did. If Shay had been thinking about another stage win his chances were now very slim; he had more than enough work on his hands simply protecting Anquetil.

The final stage finished in the Parc des Princes in Paris, and Shay completed the Tour in 61st place, nearly two hours behind the winner. 'I am not too disappointed with my placing,' he said. 'It doesn't make any difference if you finish 20th or 60th. You have to finish in the first ten or higher. After that, people are more likely to remember you because you have won a stage or worn the yellow jersey. And I did both.'

St Raphaël were to take the team prize and they also won the largest amount of prize money – the equivalent of £8,294 – which, following tradition, was divided amongst all the members of the team. The real money was not from the prizes, but from the lucrative contracts for the post-Tour criteriums, and here Shay stood to do well, thanks to his stint in the yellow jersey and the superb stage win.

(Adapted by Richard Allchin from *Shay Elliott; the life and death of Ireland's first yellow jersey*, by Graham Healy and Richard Allchin)

Shay Elliott in the yellow jersey during the 1963 Tour,
reproduced from an original painting by
kind permission of Jeff Platten

STAGE 17, 1963: VAL D'ISERE–CHAMONIX, 228kms.

John Wilcockson

Nineteen-sixty-three was a momentous year: it saw the assassination of American President John F. Kennedy in Dallas; Britain's Great Train Robbery; Martin Luther King's "I have a dream" civil-rights speech in Washington, DC; the death of Pope John XXIII in Rome; and the emergence of The Beatles. In cycling, it was the year of the 50th Tour de France, which the organisers commemorated by starting the race in Paris for the first time since 1950 and holding the event preliminaries in the historic Notre Dame Cathedral.

That 1963 Tour also happened to be the first I followed in person, not in a Press car, but on my bike, averaging 200 kilometres a day, starting from the Channel coast, and riding through Normandy, Brittany and the Gironde, over the Pyrenees, through the Massif Central, and into the Alps. Back then, cycling (and the Tour) was much simpler than it is today. Salaries were low, television coverage was in its infancy, and technology was barely a factor. Unlike today, most of the Tour riders rode the same bike every day, whether it was a flat stage, mountain stage or time trial. There were no disc wheels, tribars, skinsuits or outrageously high gears. So it was somewhat of a revolution when Frenchman Jacques Anquetil switched to a special, lighter, climbing bike to scale the infamous Col de la Forclaz on the seventeenth stage between Val d'Isère and Chamonix.

The Forclaz is a dramatic climb that rises more than 1000 metres (3300 feet) from the Rhône Valley through fruit orchards and into a forest of conifers. And that year, as in the only previous time the pass was used, in 1948, the Tour used the original 19th century route, which was more like a goat track – unsurfaced (it still is!), very steep and narrow, with extremely sharp hairpins. In 1948 many of the riders were forced to walk because they were over-geared. Among those who had to dismount was Frenchman Raphaël Geminiani, who in 1963 was the *directeur sportif* of Anquetil's St Raphaël–Gitane team.

Before this stage, and only four days before the finish in Paris, three-time Tour winner Anquetil was lying in second place, just three seconds down on 1959 Tour winner Federico 'The Eagle of Toledo' Bahamontes.

The wavy haired, bronzed Spaniard still climbed like a dream, even though he was nearing the end of a distinguished career that netted him a record six King of the Mountains titles at the Tour.

Forty-eight hours before this ultimate day in the Alps, 'Baha' scored a superb stage win at Grenoble, gaining two minutes (plus a one-minute time bonus) on the other race leaders, to move ahead of Anquetil on general classification. That put him in second place overall, ready to challenge the then race leader, Gilbert Desmet I of Belgium. (Desmet had a team-mate of the same name who was known as Gilbert Desmet II; they were not related.) Bahamontes then took over the yellow jersey, on his thirty-third birthday, when Desmet was dropped on the long climb over the Col de l'Iseran to Val d'Isère, so setting the scene for the Stage 17 confrontation between an exuberant Spanish climber and an inscrutable Frenchman.

x   x   x   x   x

To follow the 1963 Tour I rode a red and green, hand-built 'Frederick' that I inherited from my dad, who'd died unexpectedly two years earlier. That bike, built by former Claude Butler frame builder Fred Pratt, is what galvanised my interest in cycling. At first, the bike took me on long rides around England, followed by bike tours in Wales and Scotland during my school holidays. I began reading about events like the Milk Race and Tour de France; and, in preparation for my Tour trip, I followed a few stages of the 1963 Milk Race in the South West.

Earlier that year, through my college in London, I applied for a summer job in Europe; it would be my first trip to the Continent. The destination was Rorschach in north-east Switzerland, where employment in the building design office of a textile factory awaited me. I'd shipped a small suitcase of clothes and books to Rorschach, which left me with just a well filled saddlebag for my trek around France – although the long days on bumpy side-roads would soon batter my clip-on bag support, which I reinforced with a couple of bungee cords. In the bag, besides my spare clothing, maps, camera and a transistor radio, was a small bivouac tent, which I used several times, when there were no convenient youth hostels.

Besides all the great riding through the French countryside, the highlights of my first Tour had been seeing Irishman Shay Elliott, one of Anquetil's *domestiques*, wearing the yellow jersey on the stage from Roubaix to Rouen; watching Anquetil win the 24.5-kilometre time trial at

Angers, where I returned to my chained-up bike to find that the rear tyre had 'exploded' from sitting in the hot sunshine all afternoon; and packing up my tent before dawn at the foot of the Pyrenees, riding through the cold, early morning mist into the Luz gorge and then almost falling off my bike in awe as the mists parted and I looked up to see ice-crested peaks piercing the blue sky beyond the canyon's dark cliffs.

That day in the Pyrenees, over the Col du Tourmalet (my first ever mountain climb!), Anquetil managed to stay in touch with climbers Bahamontes, Raymond Poulidor and José Pérez-Francés, and he outsprinted them to win the stage in Bagnères-de-Bigorre. I couldn't believe how fast they climbed; I felt like those Tourmen of 1948, over-geared and having to push my bike for long stretches, sweating madly in the heatwave temperatures – which produced torrential thunder showers the next day.

When the Tour had a rest day at Aurillac, I was in the saddle riding across the incessant undulations of the Massif Central to be in place for the marathon 236.5-kilometre fourteenth stage to St Etienne, from where I headed for Grenoble. I made it to the city at the foot of the Alps just in time, and standing a mile from the stage-finish, I was thrilled to snap a photo of Bahamontes as he emerged from a solo break through the pre-alpine peaks of the Chartreuse, after attacking on the Col de Porte. I then watched him make a left turn over the ancient stone bridge that spans the fast-flowing, grey waters of the River Isère, before he headed to the finish at Grenoble's outdoor velodrome.

x   x   x   x   x

With just a bike for transport (I didn't use any trains on that trip), it was sometimes a struggle to make my self-imposed rendezvous as I jumped ahead of the Tour every evening and then made early morning starts. I always tried to ride on roads parallel to the Tour route, and intercept it where I planned to watch that day. This was impossible in the mountains, of course, and on those days I would start extra early, as in the Pyrenees. Sometimes, I would fall foul of an over-zealous *gendarme*, who would stop me riding on the course and force me to walk. That happened the day after the Grenoble stage, although I did find a 'bypass' to ride on – a steep, narrow back road that took me out on to the Tour route part way up the Col de la Croix-de-Fer. So my one view of the race to Val d'Isère was only 50 kilometres into the 202-kilometre stage.

Even so, I was able to see another side of the Tour, with Anquetil himself riding at the head of the peloton – not relying on any *domestiques* to set the tempo – on what was the steepest part of the Croix-de-Fer. (Twenty-three years later, I would be driving a Press car coming down this same stretch of road, with the speedometer touching 110 kilometres per hour, as we tried to keep up with the breakaway riders, Greg LeMond and Bernard Hinault, on the way to their famous 1–2 finish at L'Alpe d'Huez.)

After watching Anquetil and company cruise by, with about six hours left in their stage, I followed (a lot slower!) in their wake before turning left over the Col du Glandon and descending to my overnight stop at La Chambre, a village at the foot of the Col de la Madeleine. I met up there with a couple of English club cyclists who had also been watching the Tour, and who planned next day to ride the valley roads to Grenoble, and take a train back home. In the morning, I was happy for their company as we did a three-up team time trial down the Maurienne valley, on the same roads, I later reflected, where in 1930 André Leducq and his French team-mates were engaged in a memorable pursuit to save Leducq's yellow jersey after he crashed twice descending the Galibier.

Like Leducq, I was thankful for the fast start to my day, which would make it easier for me to reach Chamonix before the finish of this momentous Stage 17. After my two companions headed west, I headed east and north, past Albertville and up the long, gradual climb of the Arly Gorge to the ski resort of Megève, and then on towards Chamonix. I'd hoped to get some nice views of the highest peak in the Alps, Mont Blanc, but low clouds masked the glacier-covered mountain, and a steady drizzle had set in. I knew that this rain would also make life difficult at the end of the stage for the Tour riders, who first headed over the Little St Bernard Pass into Italy and then over the Great St Bernard into Switzerland, before tackling the day's, indeed the whole Tour's, *pièce de résistance*, the Col de la Forclaz.

x   x   x   x   x

There was no live television coverage of the Tour in those days, so following the Tour from a distance meant tuning into one of the three main French radio stations, which gave updates on the hour throughout the day. So I'd grown adept at stopping at the appointed time, turning on my little transistor radio and finding out where the race was and what was happening. Then, using this information and the Tour timetable printed in the paper every day, I knew how much time I had to get to a certain place. On this stage, I was planning to be at the finish in Chamonix about 90 minutes before the riders came in.

What I'd gathered so far was that both Poulidor (who was lying only 2mins 52secs back on overall time) and race leader Bahamontes had attacked several times on the day's second climb, the Great St Bernard. Bahamontes took 90 seconds out of Anquetil by the summit, but the Spaniard later claimed that if Poulidor hadn't worked with his French rival, Anquetil might have cracked. As it was, Bahamontes was caught on the long descent, and then Poulidor counter-attacked, despite some strong head winds caused by localised thunder showers. The attacks had raised the day's average speed higher than estimated, so I would have to crank up the pace of my own personal time trial to make it to the finish in time.

Time trialing is what enabled Anquetil to win his first three Tours (1957, 1961 and 1962). In 1962, for instance, in time trials of 43 and 68 kilometres, he gained a total of 6 minutes 26 seconds on Belgian Joseph Planckaert. That margin enabled Anquetil to overcome runner-up Planckaert by 4mins 59secs in Paris. With those statistics in mind, the Tour organisers decided to make it harder for Anquetil in 1963, when the two individual time trials were cut to 24.5 kilometres and 54.5 kilometres (a reduction of 30 per-cent compared with 1962). That was the good news for the climbers like Bahamontes and Poulidor; the bad news was that there were no mountain-top finishes that year. Anquetil had used this to his advantage in the Pyrenees, by catching the climbers on the Tourmalet descent and then out-sprinting them to take the one-minute time bonus. Bahamontes' main retort was his solo Grenoble victory, where he gained two minutes (plus the one-minute bonus). This had taken the riders over the Col de Porte – which is nowhere near as difficult as the Forclaz. If Bahamontes could again take a two-minute win, plus the bonus, at Chamonix he would have enough time to hold off Anquetil in the last time trial, and so win his second Tour.

On arriving in Chamonix, still wearing my thick, yellow cycling cape, I managed to find a place behind the low railings just beyond the finish line. As I said earlier, the Tour was much simpler in those days, and the finish area was not what it has since become: a jungle of TV trucks, satellite dishes and cables, VIP stands, and ten-foot-high barriers. From where I was standing, I was able to see the finish-line and, although there was no live TV, I could follow what was happening out on the course by listening to the radio reports from the Forclaz, along with the announcements made by the speaker at the finish.

I knew that the radio commentators, wearing their long canvas coats and black berets, were riding on motorcycles just behind the leaders' group; so listening to their words was almost as good as being there. They were saying that the sun had returned to the race as Poulidor reached the foot of the Forclaz, where he was launching another attack. The French hero would eventually blow up on the rugged climb, which has pitches as steep as 18 per-cent (1-in-6), and he would lose some four minutes by the 1,526-metre (5,006-foot) summit.

Remembering this climb from 1948, St Raphaël-Gitane director, Geminiani, was about to hand to Anquetil the special climbing bike that might help his rider stave off any attacks by Bahamontes. Back then, free-wheel blocks had only five cogs (usually 14 to 21 teeth), while the normal chain wheel combination was 52 and 46 teeth. Geminiani had asked his mechanic to mount a 26-tooth sprocket on Anquetil's special machine, even though it was then against Tour rules to exchange bikes – except in the case of a puncture or mechanical failure.

This is where Geminiani's infamous cunning came into play – although the truth of the upcoming incident didn't come out until much later. Approaching the start of the climb, before the course turned off a wide tarmac road on to the old Forclaz's stony goat track, Anquetil put up his hand, signaling some sort of mechanical problem, and it seems that he removed his front wheel even though the tyre wasn't flat. Geminiani then shouted, for the benefit of the commissaire in his team car, that Anquetil had something wrong with his derailleur. Indeed, after the mechanic had handed Anquetil the special climbing bike with its extra-low gearing, the commissaire inspected the original machine and verified that the derailleur cable was indeed broken. (Geminiani later told a journalist that his mechanic had some cable cutters concealed in the sleeve of his jacket and severed the cable before returning to the car.)

Mounted on his new bike, Anquetil was soon back with Bahamontes, ready for their monumental duel. When Bahamontes put in a sharp acceleration, Anquetil was the only rider in the ten-strong front group able to claw his way back to the Eagle of Toledo. Even with his 26-tooth sprocket, Anquetil still had to get out of the saddle on the steep hairpins; but the lighter bike meant that he was able to climb faster and ride in front of his rival for long stretches. This was a big psychological advantage for the Frenchman. Bahamontes tried another sharp attack, then another, but Anquetil didn't panic and each time he was able to gradually pull back to his rival. Bahamontes accelerated one last time near the top of the Forclaz, but he was only a few seconds clear at the King of the Mountains banner.

The special bike had served its purpose. Anquetil now needed his heavier bike to tackle the steep descent, an ensuing climb over the Col des Montets, and then the last downhill into Chamonix, still 27 kilometres away. So just beyond the Forclaz summit, he was simply given back his first bike (with a new derailleur cable fitted). This second switch wasn't illegal because it was simply returning his original mount.

Despite his great success, Anquetil had never engendered much enthusiasm from French cycling fans, who much preferred the more exciting approach to the sport displayed by newcomer Poulidor. Back at the finish-line, there were groans from his supporters when Poulidor cracked, while the reports of Anquetil managing to stay with Bahamontes didn't elicit much reaction from the crowd waiting in the rain.

'Baha' was my favourite, and I was hoping that he'd still be able to get away from Anquetil and win the stage. But when the two men appeared through a heavy downpour at the end of the curving run-in to the finish, Anquetil was ahead, pounding his highest gear. He easily took the sprint, but didn't bother to raise his arm in triumph, even though the winner's bonus put him into the yellow jersey and virtually assured him of his fourth Tour victory. But that was Anquetil's unemotional character.

He may not have been the most popular of riders, but seeing him up close in what was perhaps his most comprehensive performance in the Tour was still a great thrill. My strongest memory was watching him walk back towards the podium, on his way to donning the *maillot jaune*. He took a comb from his back pocket and then pulled it through his wet, blond hair with a smooth flourish. Anquetil's always immaculate appearance reinforced his image as an invincible athlete. And there wasn't any harm in having the wily Geminiani on your side…

STAGE 20, 1964: BRIVE–PUY DE DÔME, 237kms.

Chris Sidwells

Anquetil versus Poulidor: it was one of the big box-office bouts in Tour de France history, and it was the Tour contest of the sixties. Raymond Poulidor in the blue corner, son of the soil, warm, generous with his efforts, valiant in defeat. Jacques Anquetil in the red, a demi-god, cold and aloof, calculating, distant, superior. At least that is how the Press liked to tell it.

Of course, nothing in life is so simple. Both men were the sons of farmers, though there was a world of difference between life on the land in Normandy, where Anquetil's father was a smallholder and Limousin, where Poulidor's father was a farm labourer in an almost feudal land system. Nor was Anquetil as cold as he was portrayed. True he did not suffer fools gladly, but once he trusted someone, they were as dear to him as his own family. Poulidor, on the other hand, let very few people into his private life.

They also had a lot of respect for each other, which over the years almost blossomed into friendship. In fact, Poulidor says now that there is rarely a day goes by that he does not think about, and miss, his old sparring partner, who died of stomach cancer in 1987 at the age of 53.

Why then did the Press cook up an animosity that wasn't really there, seasoning it with differences that did not really exist? Well, partly because such stories sell papers. Get the supporters fired up and involved, and you hold everyone's attention. Partly, though, it was because Anquetil really did believe that Poulidor was the one rider who had the physical wherewithal to beat him in the Tour. It made sense therefore for him to base his race on beating Poulidor, and to do that he waged a constant mental, as well as physical, campaign against him. To anyone watching it looked like war.

In the end, though, Anquetil was so much his master that, according to one of Poulidor's team-mates, the British rider Barry Hoban, Poulidor became overawed by him. No wonder: Mâitre Jacques, as the other riders called him, combined class on a bike that even his rivals admired, with deep intelligence, and an amazing character whereby he simply would not let himself be beaten when he needed to win. But Poulidor did get close – once. 'Twenty-Two Days of Suspense,' the French Press called the 1964 Tour de France, but in truth it came down to just one day. One day on an extinct volcano in the middle of France.

The Puy de Dôme climb, where their duel took place, is part of a chain of similar volcanic features which ring the city of Clermont-Ferrand, but it stands far above them. Gaunt, dark and dreadful, it looks like the Devil's Tower in Wyoming, the one where they shot *Close Encounters of the Third Kind*. Appropriate that, because it was the third Tour encounter between Anquetil and Poulidor, and their battle would provide the race with its closest result up till then.

The two contenders started the 1964 Tour in very different physical and mental states, and with very different ambitions, or at least very different pressures. Anquetil was going for immortality. He had just repeated his 1960 victory in the Giro d'Italia after a desperate battle with the top Italians, and their fans, who pushed their own riders on the climb, and hurled abuse at Anquetil. This meant that in the Tour he was going for two records: he planned to equal Fausto Coppi in winning the Giro and Tour in the same year; and to become the first man to win the Tour de France five times.

Poulidor was simply going for victory. He had won the Tour of Spain with much less effort than had been required of Anquetil in the Giro, and was rested, ready and fit for the Tour de France. He was only two years younger than Anquetil, but had seen far fewer battles. He had only ridden the Tour for the first time when he was 25, and now at 28, he was at the height of his physical powers and ready to go for it with nothing to loose, but everything to gain.

Anquetil had other worries too. In 1962 the Tour had gone back to the trade team formula and, apart from a brief flirtation with the national format in 1967 and '68, would stay with them to the present day. In 1964 the St Raphaël team was one of the best around, full of tactically astute riders like Jean Stablinski, and all dedicated in the big tours to Anquetil.

Well, nearly all. The young German, Rudi Altig had caused a rift between the two of them when he won the 1962 Vuelta a España. Anquetil had been unwell in the race and eventually retired, but he felt that Altig had betrayed him. He did not altogether trust him still, and he was another cause for concern.

Then there was the other opposition: as defending champion, Anquetil had them to worry about, too. If he took his eye off any one of them they could easily cause an upset. Federico Bahamontes, for example, the Spanish genius of the mountains. 'The Eagle of Toledo', winner in 1959 and (along with Belgium's Lucien Van Impe) the holder of the most King of the Mountains titles in Tour history, was a very serious threat.

So was Vittorio Adorni from Italy, a man wanting revenge for his recent defeat at the hands of Anquetil in the Giro. So was Jan Janssen from Holland, who would win the Tour in 1968, and, in certain circumstances, so could be Britain's Tom Simpson, who had won Milan–San Remo that year..

Anquetil had a lot on his mind, and it showed when he lined up for the start in Rennes. He looked thin and pale, worried and distracted. His comments to the Press were full of indecision: 'maybes and perhaps'. The first job his *directeur sportif* was going to have to do in this Tour was get Anquetil thinking straight.

Raphaël Geminiani was the perfect man for that job. A good talker (he still is) he knew Jacques as well as anyone; knew what made him tick, and what buttons he had to press to make him perform. He also respected him immensely, which is something which speaks volumes for Anquetil as a person since, in 1958, when Geminiani was still a rider, they were the worst of enemies. That year Anquetil would not have Geminiani in the French national team, and would not lift a finger to help him when Geminiani, riding for the Centre-Midi regional team, had a chance of actually winning the race.

Whatever Geminiani said on this occasion it worked. By the first few stages Anquetil was in the right zone, talking of victory, and doing everything he could, in his clinical way, to ensure it.

The course helped him too – the French organisers had seen to that. Barry Hoban remembers: 'Anquetil was Lévitan's darling: there were mountains in that Tour, but usually so far from the finish that the climbers could not press home their advantage. There were only two stages that really suited them – Luchon to Pau, and the Puy de Dôme. If Anquetil could out-psyche the climbers on those, he was sure to win.'

Félix Lévitan was a co-organiser of the Tour, a small, delicate-looking and quietly spoken man, who was responsible for the race's commercial side. The other organiser was Jacques Goddet, much more voluble, and responsible for overseeing the Tour's day-to-day workings. Between them they ran the Tour de France, and their word was law. Poulidor might have been very popular in his own country, but Anquetil was known throughout the world; he was even the BBC's International Sportsman of the Year in 1964. It did the media profile of Lévitan and Goddet's race no harm for a sportsman of International stature like Anquetil to win it, so you can see why they would cut its topographical profile to suit him.

Early on though, it looked as though Anquetil's team had scored an own goal. Rudi Altig worked so hard on the stage into Germany, where he took the yellow jersey, that he took with him a little French climber, Georges Groussard, and when the mountains came Altig's work virtually put Groussard in the lead.

Giving a climber a lead looked like a problem, but the fact that it was this particular climber, turned out well for Anquetil. Groussard belonged to a strong team, Pelforth-Lejeune, a team that contained contenders like Jan Janssen and Henri Anglade. They now took over the responsibility of chasing many of Anquetil's most dangerous rivals to protect Groussard's lead, saving St Raphaël from doing a job that would otherwise have been theirs.

After the Alps, Bahamontes was the best of the favourites in second place overall, Poulidor was just behind him in third and Anquetil was fifth. But Anquetil had almost ridden in an armchair. For example, Bahamontes took the big Alpine stage, from Thonon-les-Bains to Briançon, working all day only to see a three-minute lead at the top of the Galibier reduced to 90 seconds on the long descent. In contrast, next day Anquetil took a one-minute bonus for winning a sprint on the Monaco track, after a stage which saw the riders climb the highest road in Europe, the Col de Restefond. But the Restefond was 140 kms. from the finish, and only two minor climbs in between the summit and Monaco. More than enough time for a re-regroupment at the front.

Now the race went into Anquetil's home territory – the time trial. He was invincible against the watch; Raphaël Géminiani once described him as, 'a still, a jet engine and a computer', such was his ability to ride alone and spread his effort through every single kilometre of whatever course was thrown at him. He won the first time trial, at Hyeres, and began to look invincible.

Then an unexpected threat to his chances of winning occurred, and it did so on a day when he didn't even ride his bike. Anquetil was always a law unto himself. Professional bike riders live by following what they call *le métier,* the craft, the way of doing things: what to eat and when to eat it; what to drink and what to leave alone; when to train, how far, how fast; it is all part of *le métier*, part of the lore.

Not for Anquetil – he lived by his own laws. On rest days in the Tour the riders always go for a little promenade on their bikes to stop their legs seizing up. 'Let them train on their holidays if they want,' said Anquetil on the 1964 rest day in Andorra. He would not go out and instead went to a *mechoui*, a kind of barbecue put on by one of the radio stations.

A lot has been said about what he ate and drank there, or didn't. Geminiani says that he hardly had anything. Barry Hoban says, 'Jacques and Janine (Anquetil's wife) were drinking champagne, of course they were; they were the Posh and Becks of the day. The glamour couple. It was expected of them.'

They were, indeed, a glamorous couple, and their rest-day celebrations served to emphasise the gulf that existed in the sixties between the stars and the rest. Barry Hoban again: 'Many of the top rider's wives would be on the Tour; there was a huge gulf between them and the rest of us. They were like royalty, and could behave like it at times. Most of the rest were expected just to serve.'

Next day, though, Anquetil was in a sorry state. The course climbed within the first couple of kilometres, out of Andorra and up the Envalira Pass, and he just could not get going. His legs would not respond; so as soon as his rivals realised that, they piled on the pressure. Anquetil was dropped.

His faithful *domestique*, a useful long-legged, climber called Louis Rostollan, stopped with him, but despite encouraging, bullying, and even pushing him, Rostollan could do nothing to rouse him. Anquetil was on the point of retiring from the Tour when Geminiani, following behind in the team car, found him. As ever, he knew just what to say: 'Jacques, if you are going to die, get to the front and die there. A man like Jacques Anquetil does not die in front of the broom wagon.'

Even in his misery, Anquetil could not help but laugh at what Geminiani had said to him, and the fact that he delivered his little speech with a deadpan serious expression on his face. The comedy of the moment appealed to him, his anxieties went and he soon made up all the time he had lost.

Towards the end of the stage Poulidor did something that his team-mate Hoban is still at a loss to understand. 'He was in a group containing all the favourites, riding on the flat roads towards Toulouse, when he felt a spoke break in his rear wheel and unbelievably he stopped to change bikes. It wasn't that much of a problem – he wasn't going to sprint at the finish. All he had to do was loosen the release on his brakes. Instead, he stopped, and on those flat roads with no team-mates in the front group who could drop back to help him, he couldn't get back on. He ended up losing more time than he lost the Tour by. But I'm not saying that he would have won if he hadn't stopped, Anquetil would still have found a way to beat him. It is just an example of how less tactically astute Poulidor was.'

Poulidor gained some time back by winning next day. Then Bahamontes turned on a virtuoso performance on the day of the four cols, Luchon to Pau, but the last climb was still 60 kilometres from the finish; so although he won, he didn't gain the time he should have.

'What Bahamontes did that day was something the climbers don't do today,' remembers Hoban again. 'The road went upwards in the first kilometre, and before we'd tightened our toe-straps Bahamontes attacked down one side of the road and Julio Jiménez, another great Spanish climber, went down the other. It was amazing, Jiménez eventually fell back, but Bahamontes stayed out there all day.'

It was amazing, but Anquetil survived it. The Pelforths helped, still working to keep Groussard in yellow, and Anquetil let them. Bahamontes had now taken his best shot and missed; all Anquetil had to worry about was Poulidor, and he took care of some of that worry the next day when he won another time trial, beating him by 37 seconds. Now Jacques was in yellow. But was he in it by enough?

The stage was set for a thrilling finale on the Puy de Dôme. Two stages – one at Bordeaux where Hoban was robbed of a stage win by the French sprinter André Darrigade who received a huge hand-sling from his compatriot Jean Graczyk, and one at Brive – did nothing to affect the overall classification. Would Poulidor go for the knock-out punch he needed? Maybe an attack of the sort Bahamontes was famous for could have won the Tour, but Poulidor also knew that whereas Anquetil might allow the Spaniard some slack, he would allow him, Poulidor, nothing.

The profile of the stage from Brive to the top of the Puy de Dôme looked like an upturned saw. The race wandered out of Coreze and into Cantal, by way of twisting, winding country roads, forever climbing and descending between steep, wooded valleys. It was the kind of day which gradually saps a bike rider's strength: heavy weather and heavy roads on top of nearly three weeks of racing. It was a perfect day to gain time, or to lose it.

At the top of the Col de la Ventouse, they could see the Puy, towering menacingly before them. Anticipation was running through the peloton, as everyone knew the race was entering its final act. Would Poulidor attack Anquetil? There was no doubt that the final five kilometres of 18-per-cent gradient suited him, but was it enough to get back the 56 seconds he was behind Anquetil, and to get the cushion he'd need for the final time trial in Paris?

The peloton held its collective breath as it trudged towards the expected battle. Anquetil had watched Poulidor all day, and as yet he'd done nothing. He was gambling on the Puy, and as the bunch approached it around the outskirts of Clermont-Ferrand, Poulidor made the first move, and he did so with the help of one of his team-mates.

'On the run to the bottom of the Puy, Poulidor told me to start making it hard for Anquetil,' Barry Hoban remembers. 'So I hit the front with him on my wheel, put my head down and gave it everything I'd got. I was hammering along the road and we got a gap. In fact I went so hard that I was the first rider to reach the foot of the Puy, but I think I was last but one at the top.'

Behind him, Anquetil kept his head. He used a team-mate, too, and got Rudi Altig to make the pace for him. It was an intriguing match: as amateurs, both Hoban and Altig had been pursuiters on the track. Altig had even been a World Champion at the specialty, and he managed to peg back the Anglo-French tandem's gains.

As soon as the race hit the climb the hard day they'd already had getting there took effect. After just one kilometre only Anquetil, Poulidor, Bahamontes, Jiménez and Adorni were left at the front. No team-mates, just the best riders, on their own, with only their courage and what was left of their strength to play with.

Bahamontes was the first to attack, but Anquetil knew now that there was not enough road left for him to present a threat to his overall lead, so he let him go on to take the stage victory. Jiménez was next, but there was nothing he could do overall either. All this activity did was get rid of Adorni.

Now they were alone, the two contenders, George and the Dragon, head to head. It was time for each to show what he'd got. Poulidor had it all to do; he kept piling on the pressure, but Anquetil refused to ride behind him. No, that would give his rival confidence; Anquetil rode directly alongside Poulidor, imposing his presence on him. Poulidor could see him out of the corner of his eye. Every time he pressed harder on the pedals, Anquetil was there, alongside, looking straight ahead, impassive, burrowing at Poulidor's confidence.

How deep was he digging? Poulidor didn't know, at least not until years later when Anquetil told him. One thing Poulidor did know was that a steady acceleration was not going to get rid of Anquetil. He had to attack.

He did. With three kilometres to go he made a blistering attack, but Anquetil answered it. He tried again, but Anquetil replied once more. Each time he refused to sit behind Poulidor, but rode back into his place beside him. Now, though, the strain was showing on both their faces. Poulidor has said that he rarely suffered again in his career like he did that day. Anquetil looked like death.

Then he cracked, one metre, two, three ... with 800 metres to go Poulidor was five metres ahead. Anquetil's face was awful: drawn, deep-sunk eyes. He couldn't climb out of the saddle any more, and his progress was reduced to a desperate, lunging crawl.

Poulidor's face was a mask of frustration; he had broken his rival, but it was too late. There simply was not enough road left for Poulidor to gain the time he needed, and he knew it.

Anquetil lost 42 seconds in those 800 metres. He had given everything and suffered incredibly to reach the line, but he had won the race. At the end of the stage Anquetil was still fourteen seconds in front of Poulidor, with two flat stages and a 27.5-kilometre time trial from Versailles to Paris to go. That was Anquetil's territory and there was no way Poulidor could beat him over it. And so it proved.

Anquetil won the time trial, putting more time into Poulidor, to win the 1964 Tour de France by just 55 seconds, the narrowest victory margin up until then. But the race also ended the Anquetil era in Tour history. He could not face riding it the following year, and in 1966 he retired from the race with bad health – once he'd made sure that Poulidor could not win, either. Poulidor may not have managed to slay his dragon, in fact so bloodied was he by his battle that he never did manage to win the Tour, but he did manage to wound his rival, and in doing so brought down the curtain on the rule of the first five-times winner – the first great super-champion of the Tour de France.

STAGE 14, 1971: REVEL–LUCHON, 214kms.

Rik Vanwalleghem

However rich Eddy Merckx's *palmarés* looked between 1966 and 1976, the first real sign of weakness began showing in 1971. For five years the opposition had looked in vain for the weak spot in his armour. It had been a fruitless search. Merckx was simply better at everything and his rivals grew deeply demoralised. But then things changed.

It wasn't obvious from his abundance of victories, but if you watched really closely from the end of 1971 you could see Merckx, the once winged god, was now flying closer to earth. The proof came on 9th July 1971, when Luis Ocaña destroyed him on the Tour stage to Orcières-Merlette. The Tour organiser, Jacques Goddet, wrote when it had finished: 'From today things are no longer as they were.'

That 1971 season started as usual for Merckx: he won Milan–San Remo, for the fourth time. Everyone knew he was the favourite, and that he would break away on the Poggio. Yet they could do nothing about it. The 'Cannibal' became the 'Cannonball', rolling along the Via Roma unstoppably, majestically. So 1971 was going to be a year like all the others: a predictable Merckx year.

At the time some people said that Merckx's dominance was casting a cloud over cycling. Although this wasn't really true, Classics specialists could do nothing but look on with sorry eyes as Merckx pushed Rik van Looy off his throne and invaded their territory. He won, seemingly at will, whether it was after a lone break or in the sort of sprint that had brought him victory at Ghent-Wevelgem over Jan Janssen and Ward Sels in 1967. As if that weren't bad enough for Janssen, he then had Merckx kick metaphorical sand in his face later in the year in the World Championship in Heerlen, where Janssen again finished second.

Stage-race riders had just as much to complain about. They, too, had to be happy with crumbs from the well spread Merckx table. Mountain stages, time trials, it was the same overall result: the Cannibal took the lot, driven by an insatiable desire to win that nobody had ever seen. By the end of 1970 he had had two wins in the Giro d'Italia, two in the Tour de France and eleven victories in the Classics.

Even race organisers were in trouble. On the one hand they couldn't keep Merckx out, because a race without him lost half its audience. Criterium organisers fell to their knees to get him to ride. On the other hand, they knew he'd probably win. And where was the attraction of a race where the only mystery was second place? Merckx in his best years won half the races he started.

Journalists also grew bored. They simply ran out of words to describe this phenomenon. And television had an even greater nightmare: the prospect of direct pictures across Europe with nothing to show but a single camera following Merckx for an hour and a half.

Merckx's knife drew even more blood. Potential sponsors walked away rather than start a team they knew Merckx would flatten in race after race.

The excitement behind the scenes was all the greater, then, that dark Sunday in April when Liège–Bastogne–Liège reached its exciting end. Georges Pintens made up a four-minute deficit in 60 kilometres. Merckx still won the sprint, but Pintens became a symbol of the damage that could be wreaked on Merckx, whose *soigneur*, Guillaume Michiels, found him sitting on a stool in the shower, exhausted.

From then on Merckx rode under a microscope as he was examined for any signs of weakness. Every little setback, or any minor divergence, could be a sign that the end was near.

There was new alarm a few weeks later in the Dauphiné-Libéré. This time Merckx had to deal with a weakness on the climb of the Granier. He blamed it on a faulty chain. But the word from the bunch was that he'd wobbled. Riders spoke of nothing else but this sudden vulnerability, of the few metres where Merckx had reached his limit. Above all, it inspired Luis Ocaña, the Castilian toreador whose life's ambition was to beat Merckx and win the Tour.

Merckx knew something was wrong, that something inside him had changed. He blamed it on the bad crash he'd had in a track meeting at Blois in September 1969, when his pacemaker, Fernand Wambst, died. 'I was never my normal self from then on,' he says. 'It affected my pelvis and pinched a nerve. Climbing was never a pleasure after that. Sometimes I sat crying with pain on my bike.'

As if that wasn't enough, Merckx had to cope with a troublesome knee in the Dauphiné Libéré, just before the Tour. 'I got a terrible pain on the last day, exactly where I'd been operated on behind my kneecap,' he says.

The Merckx aura had also changed. 'Will Merckx kill the Tour again?' *Paris-Match* asked on its cover. There was an anti-Merckx feeling at the start in Mulhouse.

The competition, led by Ocaña, was determined to dethrone him. And the Spanish soldier could reckon on the unspoken sympathy of three-quarters of the peloton. They'd relished the way Merckx had been pushed so hard to catch him on Mont Ventoux that he'd had to be revived with oxygen.

Merckx dismisses that incident. 'There just wasn't enough air near the finish,' he says. 'A bit further up I saw Vandenbossche faint. They took him to an ambulance. I thought: "That's the way out of the problem." So I gave the impression I was also on my knees. That way I could have a rest in the ambulance, which got me down the Ventoux and off to my hotel in no time.'

Word spread in 1970 that Merckx had only won the Tour so easily because the opposition was weak. This was hardly true, but, nonetheless, it was a charge that upset his rivals and, in 1971, Ocaña, Thévenet and Zoetemelk all swore to make it clear there was no armistice.

The coffee-brown troops of the Molteni dominated the prologue in Mulhouse, but the difference was insignificant. The first real test was the Puy-de-Dôme. Merckx's vulnerability showed immediately the race reached this old volcano outside Clermont-Ferrand. Ocaña won and took 15 seconds out of him. The time may not have been much but the encouragement for the Spaniard was enormous.

Warning number two: the stage from Saint Étienne to Grenoble. Merckx punctured coming down the Cucheron. There were 30 kilometres to the Col de Porte. Merckx tried to close up to the Ocaña group but got stranded at 100 metres. Thévenet won, with Guimard, Zoetemelk, Van Impe and Ocaña behind him. Merckx lost 1min. 38secs. and the yellow jersey. 'That was a serious blow,' Merckx says. 'The Porte was a col I liked. I had digestive problems and so I didn't recover properly.'

The French Press was jubilant. 'Merckx bested in the Tour for the first time,' it crowed. The feeling swelled to outright euphoria on 9th July. The stage from Grenoble to Orcières-Merlette would be the definitive proof of the change from god to mortal.

That morning Merckx had his suspicions. He suspected the field had watched the way he'd ridden and would start an early attack. He and his team-mates went for a 30 kilometre warm-up before the stage, to be ready for anything. But he didn't retaliate when Ocaña attacked on the Côte de Laffrey, the first real obstacle of the day. Zoetemelk, Van Impe and Agostinho slid away with him, but Merckx decided to stick to his own tempo and see how great the damage was at the summit. 'I had no wish to blow myself up,' he says. 'I wasn't an explosive climber: I had to build up steam and I wanted to make it a long chase.'

There'd also been an unbelievable communications breakdown with the team's management. 'On the Laffrey there was a group 45 seconds behind me with three team-mates in it. But Driessens, the team manager [with whom relations grew worse day by day], didn't tell me. Otherwise I'd have waited for their help and things would have turned out differently.'

The problems that confronted Merckx gave the opposition wings, Ocaña especially. The impulsive Castilian rode with oily smoothness and shed his breakaway companions off his wheel. Behind, nobody would help Merckx. The field sat grinning on his wheel. What joy to see the man who had so often belittled them now being left to wallow in his own misery.

Merckx and Merckx alone rode on the front, and he saw the gap open hand over hand. 'Some of next day's papers said I'd thought of chucking it in,' he says. 'That's nonsense. My head was drooping from exhaustion and I began to forget about winning a third Tour, yes. But pack it in? No, never.'

In Orcières-Merlette the gap had opened to nearly nine minutes, or eight minutes, forty-two seconds to be exact. Things looked bad. Merckx, generous in defeat, praised his great rival. 'Ocaña showed us today that he is cycling's El Cordobes,' he said, referring to the legendary bullfighter of the era.

Merckx had no illusions. But during the rest day at Orcières he talked to the team's doctor, Calli, and went for a training ride with a handful of team-mates to improve his morale. 'We devised a counter-offensive for the following day,' he says.

Ocaña felt cocky on the morning of the 11th. Cocky enough to spend a long time talking to reporters. No one, including the Spaniard, expected the defeated Merckx to retaliate quickly, especially since the first kilometres from Orcières went straight downhill. But the flag had barely dropped when Merckx went off with a handful of team-mates and a few others – opportunists hoping to profit from the counter-attack.

'Oh no,' groaned the bunch.

A bitter Merckx rode behind his team-mates Stevens, Huysmans, and the crazy Wagtmans, who rode himself into the ground. It was a nightmare charge at an average 45 k.p.h. towards Marseille, the lead over the bunch constantly changing. Ocaña gathered a few of his allies around him to limit the damage. By the Vieux Port at Marseille, Merckx – who was beaten for the stage by Armani – had cut his deficit.

'The team made another tactical error,' he says. 'Bruyère got dropped from Ocaña's group and the team management let two riders wait for him. Instead, they should have stayed with Ocaña to disrupt the chase. If that hadn't happened we'd have beaten the bunch by fifteen minutes.'

And he was upset, too, that the talented Spanish Kas team, which fell through the ice during that crazy stage, was again saved by Félix Lévitan, the head of the Tour. 'Rules are rules,' Merckx says. 'All the Kas riders finished outside the time limit. But people didn't want Ocaña to lose fellow countrymen.'

Merckx then made up for his catastrophic ride through the Alps. 'It was clear that Ocaña was the stronger in the mountains,' he admits. 'But he'd already had a bad day in the Tour and it made me speculate. I decided to attack until I collapsed.'

The rivalry with Ocaña had come to a peak in the time trial at Albi, which Ocaña had won. 'Driessens went round protesting that Ocaña had been paced by a TV car,' Merckx remembers. 'I believed him and began complaining to the media. Unjustly, it turned out later. Ocaña and I were like cat and dog for months afterwards.'

The spat inspired Ocaña to make a bold prediction at the start of the Revel–Luchon stage. 'Today I deliver the fatal blow,' said the flamboyant Castilian, who still had a comfortable 7mins 32secs lead. In fact it was Merckx who hauled Ocaña through the fire, and tried heaven and earth to outwit his opponent.

Ocaña glued himself firmly to Merckx's wheel. The flanks of the Col de Mente provided the backdrop for a battle of the cycling gods. The sky grew black and hellish weather lashed the summit, the ditches overflowing in the rain. With contempt for death, Merckx started the dangerous descent.

'I knew Ocaña used an ultra-light bike for the climb and that he only had 24 spokes in each wheel,' he says. 'That makes the bike less stable and you pay for it on the descent.'

Merckx forced Ocaña to take deadly risks, only to make the first error himself. His bike went from under him coming out of a bend and the bars hit him in the groin. He bit back the pain and got back on his bike. A fraction later Ocaña slid on the same bend. He too survived and scrambled upright, only to be hit full-on by a flat-out Zoetemelk. And that was the end of the race for Ocaña: a dismayed De Muer, his Bic team manager, held the yellow jersey wearer to him, like Mary with Christ.

Merckx refused the yellow jersey on the podium in Luchon. He licked his wounds. 'I was in bad pain, which the following day gave me a hard time in the stage over the Peyresourde,' he remembers. 'But I managed to get through the stage.'

Now, so many years later, Merckx admits for the first time that he wouldn't have won that Tour without Ocaña's crash. 'It's pure mathematical logic,' he says.

Ocaña's elimination gave him wings again. On the road to Bordeaux he settled accounts with Cyrille Guimard, who, en route to Marseille, had shown himself to be an ally of Ocaña. Merckx cleverly organised an echelon to ride the Frenchman out of the points jersey. And he won another stage, plus the finishing stage to Paris, where the Cannibal won his third Tour in a row.

It had been an obvious transition Tour, the one in which Merckx had shown for the first time that he could be beaten. Ocaña was not the only one to have stolen his halo. He was regularly battered by another Spaniard, Mañuel Fuente. And there was no shortage of others who had hurt him. Agostinho rode away from him; Van Impe and Zoetemelk too. And Bernard Thévenet, who won a stage in Meribel-les-Allues and came fourth overall to raise French hopes.

Merckx could impose his will for another three years, but his domination changed fundamentally. Previously he attacked where he wished, on any terrain. He went away under his own power. After 1971 he had to be more measured, set the foundations, look for the weak spot in an opponent.

From the way he rode the 1972 Tour de France you'd think he was back to the Merckx of old. He rode without problems to his fourth win. But that was without Ocaña. The much anticipated duel between them came to nothing. The Spaniard had spent the winter revelling in his star status and had neglected his preparation. His fitness was inconsistent and he retired on Stage 15. 'I would have ridden away from him,' Merckx says. 'There was no talk of a duel.'

The ambitious Frenchman Cyrille Guimard did challenge him but paid a severe price, leaving the race after Stage 18 with an injured knee. More in the background, however, Thévenet improved his reputation. He won the stages over the Ventoux and the Ballon d'Alsace, and France took him quietly to its heart as a potential Tour winner. If only that devilish Merckx hadn't been there!

In 1973 French bike fans saw their hopes come true. Merckx was sick of the constant feeling against him and stayed at home. 'I was stupid,' he says now. 'I could have been the first to win five Tours in a row. I had already bettered Ocaña and Thévenet in the Vuelta. But it was clear that what people wanted was an 'open' Tour. The organisers had laid on a specially tough edition with an unusual number of cols.'

Pierre Chany of the French paper *L'Équipe* described it as *'un Tour farci de cols, l'un des plus montagneux de l'histoire'* – a Tour stuffed with cols, one of the most mountainous in history.

Ocaña won in Merckx's absence and speculation began again. 'Merckx wasn't ready for an Ocaña like this,' was the view. The Tour boss, Jacques Goddet, led the chorus in singing the praises of the unmatchable Spaniard, who, in his eyes, was so much more colourful than the 'boring' Merckx.

Thévenet was second.

Nineteen seventy four started as a disappointment. Merckx's domination had again lost some of its shine: no major win in the spring; a tiring win in the Giro; a badly healed injury. But Ocaña was in an even worse state after a pitiful spring with bronchitis. Zoetemelk hit a parked car in the Midi-Libre and was out of contention. Thévenet had sunstroke in the stage over the Télégraphe in the Tour. So Poulidor, at the age of 38, became Merckx' s principal opponent. He came second overall. Merckx won seven stages in that Tour, plus the prologue, and you'd think he was once more unbeatable. But rot had set in under the surface.

All the same, he once more put his rivals on the wrong foot at the start of 1975. He spent a happy spring winning Milan–San Remo, the Tour of Flanders and Liège–Bastogne–Liège. He set himself up for a historic sixth Tour. And he made such an impressive start to the Tour in northern France – he and Moser attacking repeatedly – that nobody doubted he could do it. The stage to Roubaix was so hard that Fuente was sent off home and a number of favourites, including Luis Ocaña, were already facing a two-minute deficit.

Merckx stretched out his lead in the two time trials that came before the mountains. So what could possibly go wrong? The answer: Bernard Thévenet. He was 2mins 20secs behind at the start of the first mountain stage and, in theory, no danger. But folk were going to be surprised.

The whole situation overturned when Merckx hit the first major obstacle. His talent as a climber had started to rust away. He let Zoetemelk and Thévenet get away on the road to St Lary-Soulan. The loss was only a matter of seconds, but there were three mountain-top finishes to come. While Ocaña was humiliated and eventually gave up, Thévenet struck on the Puy-de-Dôme: he made up 34 seconds on Merckx, who wasn't helped by a fanatical French supporter who punched him in the stomach on the way up.

It was clear the Tour would be played out on the way to Pra-Loup, where Merckx, the Yellow Jersey, led with a substantial 58 seconds on Thévenet. The advantage would be even greater at the end of the stage… but it would be the Frenchman in yellow.

Merckx was still sitting pretty at the foot of the final climb before Pra-Loup. He took the descent furiously and, with just six kilometres of climbing to the line, he had a minute and ten seconds on Thévenet. Tour win number six was in the bag. He pushed on at full power. Then, 4,000 metres from the line, the lights went out. He began plodding, as though he was sticking in the tar that was melting beneath the burning sun. And then up from the background came Thévenet, triumphant now, strengthened by Merckx's unexpected weakening.

The die was cast. Merckx tried hopelessly to outwit Thévenet, but he had to recognise his defeat.

In March 1976 Merckx again gave the false impression that the sands of time had left him untouched, winning Milan–San Remo for the seventh time. In fact, this was his last major victory before the inescapable process that led to his retirement at the start of 1978.

The child of the gods had finally been shown as human. It had been ten years; but even the great Eddy Merckx couldn't halt the march of time.

'The Elegant Powerhouse'

*From an original painting of Eddy Merckx, reproduced
by kind permission of Joe Scherrer*

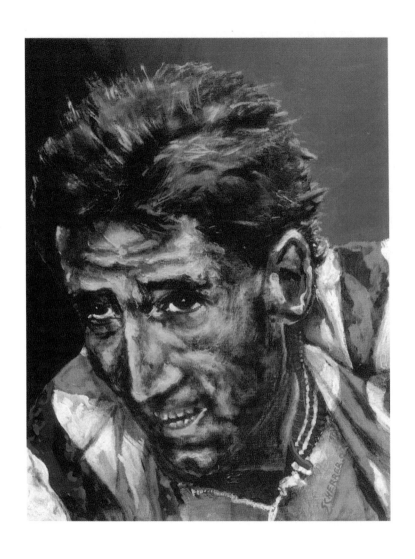

'The Classics Legend'

*From an original painting of Sean Kelly, reproduced
by kind permission of Joe Scherrer*

STAGE 12, 1982: FLEURANCE–PAU, 249kms.

Keith Bingham

It was a Golden Stage indeed when Ireland's super roadman-sprinter, Sean Kelly, confirmed that he had added another skill to his range of talents, and become a fine climber.

The year was 1982. That spring Kelly – or 'Killy' as Radio Tour insisted on calling the Irish star – had shown he could time trial, and climb well in the shorter stage-races, when he won Paris–Nice with a final stage victory in the Col d'Ez mountain time trial.

In July on Stage 12 of the Tour, Kelly added another string to his bow. He transformed himself into a solid all-rounder with a spellbinding display of climbing which raised even Hinault's dark eyebrows! After failing to win a flat road stage, as had been expected, Kelly upset the form book to win the first Pyrenean stage at Pau after a fearless descent out of the clouds.

This unexpected victory by a sprinter gave Kelly a firm grip on the points jersey and he would become the first non-Continental to win the green jersey when the Tour reached Paris. Apart from this one stage win, Kelly scored five second places and twelve times finished in the top eight.

Ironically, Murphy's Law saw to it that Kelly's win at Pau would also be his fifth and last stage win, despite continuing to ride the Tour until 1992, and going on to win a record four green jerseys in his outstanding career.

The day was significant also because the Breton, Bernard Hinault, second on the stage, strengthened his hold on the yellow jersey he had snatched in the time trial the day before from Phil Anderson. The Aussie had worn the leader's jersey since his victory on Stage two – an historic feat in itself.

But to set the stage, so to speak, the story must focus first on how both Kelly and Anderson took the race to Hinault in the first week, forcing the Frenchman to sprint it out in virtually every Rush sprint before he finally restored order at what the French refer to as the next 'rendezvous'. These are the time trials and certain selected difficult mountain stages when damage is inflicted, and a pecking order more firmly established in the overall placings.

This initial skirmishing was breathless stuff. It was the first time English-speaking riders had dominated. It was also my first 'ride' with the Tour and the sheer scale of the thing blew my mind: 3,500 people – officials, publicity, Press, all on the heels of just seventeen teams of ten riders, 170 riders in all!

The 3,500-kilometre, 21-stage journey began in Basle in Switzerland. From there, like an invading army, it pushed its way into France, dived into Belgium, before returning to the homeland for good. We trekked across the blustery north to Britanny, then south to hotter climes and into the Pyrenees and down to the tropical Med, before heading east across the Alps, and finally north to Paris. Only by travelling with the vast motorised division which surrounds the crack battalion of riders, as the late Geoffrey Nicholson so aptly described the Tour, do you get an inkling of what it must take to ride the thing!

There is no shortage of stories for the eager scribe to tell, and such enthusiasm keeps you on the go for the three weeks. But I discovered the Tour is no picnic. You spend all day in the car, most of the evening in the Press centre, or driving to find a rider's hotel and, later, still longer drives to find your own, and then, oh yes, a meal. And then there are the transfers – one of 400 miles across northern France in the 1982 Tour. All in all, this can play havoc with your system, so you can only imagine what the riders go through.

I recall Anderson suffering horribly in the mountains, paying for his ten days in yellow. Lungs fit to burst, his whole body wracked with pain, Anderson was comforted by a team-mate repeatedly telling him, 'Phil, Phil, you're not going to die!'

No cold factual analysis can ever portray a rider's journey to the depths of the soul.

There was the burning heat down in the south and the racket of the cicadas, a large broad insect. 'I hate them,' confessed Anderson. On one stage it was so hot the organisation suspended the supply of cold drinks to keep what was left for the riders.

But I digress. Let's get back to basics, the Rush sprints. After all, they were the hors d'œuvre for the main course, which Kelly served up on Stage 12.

So hotly contested were the Rush sprints, that at one of them Hinault, Kelly andAnderson left the bunch trailing as they hurtled the final kilometre to the sprint. Not surprisingly, a squad of motorbike photographers roared after them creating a bridge for the peloton. Tour boss Lévitan went absolutely spare over the radio.

Kelly in One Hell of a Rush

The 1982 Tour was a race of two quite distinct halves. The first on the flat, was dominated by high-speed scraps to gain precious seconds at the Rush sprints. These carried time bonuses which could catapult you into the race lead and a taste of glory: Twelve seconds for first, eight for second, four for third.

The generous time bonuses in the finishing sprints: 30 seconds, 20 and ten could not be ignored, either, by anyone wanting a tilt at the yellow jersey. This was what interested Kelly and Anderson, and consequently Hinault, who like the prudent investor looking to the long term, needed to keep them both within arm's reach.

The second part of the Tour included three time trials where Hinault made his moves and, of course, the high mountains where he consolidated his lead. It would be the fourth of his five Tour victories.

Let's look at the first act. The curtain went up with Kelly second on the opening road stage in Basle, snatching the bunch sprint 38 seconds behind stage-winner Ludo Peeters of Raleigh, the new Yellow Jersey. But not for long. Anderson bagged it the next day, when he won the longest stage of that year's race, 246 kilometres to Nancy via the climb of the Ballon d'Alsace.

And Kelly? He again won the bunch sprint, for seventh. On top of that he won two Rush sprints and was second in two others, trailing lone breakaway Jacques Michaud who had mopped them up.

On to Stage 3, from Nancy to Longwy. This was a short hop of 131 kilometres, where the terrible three, Anderson in yellow, Kelly in green and Hinault seventh overall but rising to second this day, tore each other apart for bonuses. Anderson took the first Rush, and so Hinault put a stop to him by putting the whole of his Renault team on the front. They forced the entire peloton into one long, snaking line and, from within this protective cordon, Hinault slid out forward to take the next two Rush sprints.

Although Kelly missed out in two sprints, he was up there for the finish, where he was placed third, once again giving the Irish journalists a collective heart attack.

Next day Kelly really put the cat among the pigeons when he won three of the Rush sprints, at 44, 122 and 191 kilometres. But that's not all. There he was again, at the head of a final mass bunch gallop, but, no, he missed out once more. He was second to the stage winner, another Raleigh star, Gerrie Knetemann. But Kelly had now set the race buzzing, and French heads shaking, for he'd pushed Hinault down to third. There followed some respite, as the Stage 5 team time trial was cancelled when a demonstration by steel workers in the town of Denain blocked the route.

There were no Rush sprints on the Lille–Lille stage next day, over the cobbled roads of northern France, where Dutchman Jan Raas triumphed. The race then transferred by air and road to Britanny for a rest day.

It was the hastily arranged replacement team time trial on Stage 9a that upset Kelly. His team, Sem–Loire, were no great shakers at this specialised, ultra-fast relay and it was won by the masters, Raleigh. Kelly's men, could only finish tenth fastest. After lying second overall, Kelly dropped to eighth, kissing goodbye to any designs on the yellow.

Kelly was down but not out. That same afternoon he moved up one place overall, after taking fifth at Nantes. Then he confounded us once again by just missing another stage victory, taking second at Bordeaux: he won the bunch sprint easily, but Pierre-Raymond Villemiane had slipped away just before the finish. None the less, the second-place time bonus carried him another two rungs up the overall ladder.

But that was it, surely! No flat stages until the final week: Kelly will have to wait for that elusive stage victory. It was so nice to be proved wrong in two days time!

Did Kelly know something we did not? Was it tired legs which saw him slump to finish 31st in the 68-km. time trial at Valence d'Agen on the eve of his Pau triumph? Or was it part of a survival plan: get over the mountain and catch the leaders on the downhill run to the finish, and beat them at Pau!

A sprinter staying in contention over the *hors-catégorie* Col du Soulor and the first-category Col de l'Aubisque? Pull the other one!

Kelly strikes in the kingdom of climbers

Stage 12: 243 kilometres to Pau, the second longest stage of the 1982 Tour. The first of the big mountains loomed ahead. From the start in Fleurance, a town on the plains north of the French–Spanish border, the high Pyrenees could normally be seen as a row of distant humps on the horizon. Today they were hidden in a grey blanket of cloud.

In a few hours the riders would be enveloped in this fog which hid from view the seriously steep mountain slopes which would split the Tour asunder. The previous day's time trial at Valence d'Agen had shaken the field into a new order with Hinault at the head. Now the riders faced their second rendezvous.

A look at the profile showed the road gently tilting upwards for 140 kilometres, before reaching for the sky to ascend what, in effect, was one big climb. The objective: the 1,709-metre summit of the Col de l'Aubique, reached via the shoulder of another climb, the 1,479-metre Col du Soulor sitting just below. You are talking 40 kilometres of climbing with a brief 2.5-kilometre descent between the summit of the Soulor and the start of the Aubisque.

The Col du Soulor was given the highest rating – *hors catégorie* – beyond classification! – because the race came at it cold, after twelve days on the flat. They were warmed up when they reached the Col d'Aubisque, which consequently was given the lower, 1st-category rating.

We were entering the kingdom of the climbers, when the sprinters – with the exception of one particular Irishman who was about to change his spots, and the Aussie, Phil Anderson, who also wasn't known as a good climber – would content themselves with huddling together at the back of the race, on the 'bus', the name given to the last group of stragglers on the mountain road.

This gradual ascent from a mere 170 metres above sea-level at ten kilometres, rising steadily to 476 metres at 130 kilometres – atop the Côte de Labatrale – would pass unnoticed in the car. But to the bike-rider, pedalling at between 30 and 40 k.p.h., this would tug at the leg muscles, and seriously chip away at the energy block.

For the riders the most important thing about the stage was that the finish came some 60 kilometres after the second big climb, which would allow many of them to recoup their losses.

In fact, after the 20-kilometre high-speed descent off the Aubisque, they had another 40 kilometres of gently falling roads to the finish, interrupted only by short, sharp Côte de Rontignon, a third-cat. climb inside the last ten kilometres.

Even so, the seriously high Col de l'Aubisque was considered a barrier for the sprinters who would normally not expect to make up time lost on the long, steep slopes.

Let's pick up the action of that stage after 47 kilometres, when André Chalmel took off alone from the peloton. He gained over fifteen minutes as he approached the first of two big passes, disappearing into the cloud on the 13-kilometre ascent of the Soulor. They had been racing for four hours and forty minutes and had just over two hours riding ahead.

The bunch split under pressure of the chase and Chalmel was caught. We didn't expect to hear Kelly's name mentioned in the selection. In fact, he was at first reported to be sliding back.

This was my 'first' mountain and you can imagine my disappointment at being denied the splendid views. My companions and I never saw a thing through the car windows as we picked our way up the slopes and then on to the descent! But nothing could cloud my imagination. I couldn't see the drops but I sensed them through the windows. I recall my astonishment, followed by excitement at the reports on Radio Tour of how 'Killy' had attacked, and was working his way through the mist from group to group. But the thrill at his daring turned to trepidation at the repeated urgent orders over the race radio: *Attention, presse avant, accélérerer s'il-vous-plâit!* Jeeezus, the blighters were catching us! Then the *motards*, the *gendarmes*, their arms waving, came among us, urging our convoy on.

At that moment I realised the Tour is also, at times, a car race. I recall my story filed to *Cycling Weekly* after that momentous day's racing. It pretty well summed everything up in a few words.

Left behind by the advance party on the mist-enshrouded Col du Soulor, Sean Kelly made a superhuman effort to catch them, took the following Col de l'Aubisque in the best company and, 63 kilometres later, outsprinted 17 men for his much sought after stage victory in the Tour.
The Pyrenees welcomed them on the 12th day, swallowed them in thick mist that made life a lottery for unskilled descenders, and broke up the huge pack so that 18 men plummeted out of the cloud on the north face with a healthy lead …

What a monumental sort-out!

Let's take a look at it in greater detail, to see how Kelly turned the tables and set about taking his place in Tour history.

In those days riders didn't have radio ear pieces and microphones as they do now. They relied on the blackboard man to keep them informed, and team managers who drove up alongside to tell them about their rivals.

But in the dodgy conditions recalled here, neither the blackboard man and certainly not one team manager, dared chance his luck to drive among the riders and so it is fair to assume the leaders had no idea Kelly had slipped the leash – until they came out of the cloud and Hinault looked about him, to find both his adversaries, Anderson as well as Kelly, still on his heels.

In some 30 kilometres, the race had completely changed. Lone leader Chalmel had been mopped up before the summit of the Soulor as the big guns moved forward. So who were these guys who did for Chalmel, who shaped the stage?

That exclusive group included Robert Alban, the gangling climber; American Jonathan Boyer; two Dutchmen, Peter Winnen and the 1980 Tour de France winner Joop Zoetemelk; Hinault; Anderson; and Vallet. But no Kelly – yet!

But Kelly was on a roll. He was limiting his losses by riding hard with Italian climber Mario Beccia.

Kelly was riding so well he caught and despatched the French darling of the moment, Jean-René Bernaudeau. He also reeled in Hennie Kuiper – twice second in the Tour (1977 and '80). And then he passed the Italian favourite, Giovanni Battaglin.

Meanwhile, up front, ahead of Kelly's crusade, the leaders were going so hard they temporarily shed Alban – who was third overall the year before and, so, a man to respect – and, also, the mountain's leader himself, Vallet, although both got back on.

By now the Press had received more information on the composition of the group.

Driving them were Spain's Lejarreta brothers, Marino and Ismaël, helped by Switzerland's Beat Breu. In fact, Breu and Marino were too fast for the rest and it was these two who called on Chamel first, two grey shapes materialising out of the mist to end his brave 123-kilometre escape. At this point they had only ten yards visibility. Soon the rest of the Hinault group passed Chamel as well.

They crested the summit and, trusting to intuition, for they could hardly see, swooped through the hairpins on the 2.5-kilometre descent to the foot of the Col de l'Aubisque.

At the summit, some eight to ten kilometres later, Breu outsprinted Marino, 1min 45secs ahead of the élite group, which at that point didn't expect any more callers.

How wrong can you be? One kilometre from the top of the Aubisque,

Kelly and Beccia joined the leading group. Note that. Kelly caught them on the upgrade! The sprinter actually overhauled the climbers on the climb. Every scribe on the race sat bolt upright.

And when that leading group finally plunged out of the cloud on the long descent they discovered that a certain Irishman was among them. At once they all knew the top spot on the podium at Pau was gone!

But was it? Nothing is certain in this life, especially on the Tour. And Kelly didn't need to remind himself that he had finished second too many times already, when he might have been expected to win.

However, the finish at Pau was in his favour. It is a sprinter's dream. The race files in on wide roads and turns right to enter the huge square which forms a one-kilometre finishing circuit packed solid with tens of thousands of spectators eagerly awaiting to see how the final act in this drama would be played out.

Vallet led around the one-kilometre circuit, then attacked hard to his right on the back straight and a column of riders peeled off in his wake. Not Kelly. Kelly cut loose and took another line, intercepting Vallet on the second-last bend and taking the corner flat-out. It was an intimidating charge, as Kelly carved a perfect line to give him the front while Hinault completely messed up. The Frenchman found himself blocked in on the left and was forced to brake for the final left-hander which Kelly was taking at top speed. Out of that final bend with 200 metres to go, several figures slammed their gears into top and came hurtling for the line.

It was one of those moments you later recall like a slow-motion action replay, as in a dream. Kelly, Anderson, Van der Velde! Who would get it! A sea of bodies and bikes, whistles, the baying crowd, open-mouthed Irish journos lost for words just this once.

After all those missed chances in a frenetic first ten days, Kelly shot home a clear length ahead of Anderson, with Van der Velde third.

Super-climber Kelly. He'd beaten the mountains and won the stage!

The Irish journalists shrieked for joy, linked arms and did a jig in the finishing straight before running like the wind to join the Press scrum which had ambushed the golden hero.

Kelly Looks Back

When Sean Kelly is asked to recall that day, 23 years ago, he agrees that, yes, it was a definitive stage in his Tour career. But he wouldn't ever say he proved himself to be a true climber.

In Noël Truyers' fine book, *Kings of Cycling*, Kelly says that his climbing ability was never enough, that his bone structure was too heavy. Even in top condition, with a racing weight of between 72 or 73 kilos, that was too much. 'Against the out-and-out climbers I have always lost out,' he said.

Looking back today at that stage into the Pyrenees, Kelly agrees the weather conditions played into his hands: 'For a rider of my climbing ability, it was always going to be difficult to know how I would go. I'd been riding well all the previous week. I suppose I was starting to dream ,' he laughed.

'On the route to Pau I found I was climbing well, early on in the day. But in the morning, if you had asked me how I felt, I'd have told you I was worried. But it was cool and foggy on the climbs, as I remember. That made it better for me. I always go well in cooler weather.'

But he confessed that he surprised even himself, getting over the mountains and catching the leaders. Only then did he realise he stood a chance of winning the stage.

STAGE 16 1984: GRENOBLE–ALPE D'HUEZ, 151kms.

Matt Rendell

Swept upwards by a nation's longing, he darts out of the valley like a spirit of the air. A few inquisitive souls already know his name. Some among them have witnessed his sprightly ascents at greater altitudes than these. Yet when the half-human, half-god Prometheus set out for Mount Olympus, what mortal believed he would return with his phial of fire? And who can believe it now, that this slender god on limbs as fine as extruded glass is leaving cycling's Titans squabbling in his slipstream as he rises majestically up Alpe d'Huez?

It defied all logic. Since school, Luis Alberto Herrera had been told that his physique was too fragile for an athlete. It was an impression that fooled his adversaries throughout his career; nothing could have been further from the truth. Yet none of the protagonists on Stage 16 of the 1984 Tour de France, from Grenoble to Alpe d'Huez, had fewer credentials than the little Colombian. Reigning Tour champion Laurent Fignon was a brooding, complex man whose prodigious physique and graceful style had brought him Tour de France victory at his first attempt, as a brazen 22 year old, in 1983. His most dangerous rival was Bernard Hinault, a punchy, compact bundle of restlessness whose cold-blooded sense of purpose had already brought him victory in four Tours de France. Both men knew that the 1984 Tour could be won, and history made, on Alpe d'Huez. No Frenchman had won here before; both wanted to be the first.

Hinault and Fignon were among the leaders all day, as the route looped north-west out of Grenoble, returned around the city, climbed the 1,434-metre Col du Coq and the 910-metre Côte de Laffrey, and crept stealthily along the valley to the foot of Alpe d'Huez. Scotland's Robert Millar was with them. Seven days earlier, he had won the gruelling mountain stage from Pau to Guzet Neige, emerging as one of the strongest climbers of his generation. Now he led the field over the third-category Col de la Placette.

The second mountain prize of the day fell to Herrera's veteran team-mate, Patrocinio Jiménez. The best young rider in the 1974 Tour of Colombia, overall victor in 1976 and mountains' king in 1976, 1979, 1980, and 1981, Patro had been his nation's finest climber in the period before Colombia's Tour de France adventure had started in 1983. That year, he had finished second in the mountains category, aged 31. Like his compatriots Ramón Hoyos in the 1950s and Javier (el Ñato) Suárez in the 1960s, if Patro had been allowed to compete at the highest level from his early twenties, a Colombian might have entered the annals of cycling's greatest climbers long before Luis 'Lucho' Herrera.

On the first-category Col du Coq, Patro slipped back and the Spaniards Ángel Arroyo and Pedro Delgado headed the leading group. Second in the previous year's Tour, Arroyo had already won on one of France's legendary climbs, the Puy de Dôme; now he wanted to add another. Delgado had finished an excellent fifteenth in the 1983 Tour, his first. Also there was the Swiss climber Beat Breu, who had won on Alpe d'Huez two years before and was eager to repeat the feat.

Over the Côte de Laffrey it was Lucho Herrera who led with Fignon, to be caught, with twenty kilometres to go, by Hinault, Arroyo, Millar and Breu. Hinault immediately attacked; at the foot of Alpe d'Huez, his advantage was 30 seconds. For the first three kilometres of the climb, Fignon seemed the strongest of the chasers. Then Lucho made his move.

For many watching or listening, or even reading the papers the following day, the sparrow-like form rising inexorably up one of the Tour de France's most prestigious slopes was excessively exotic: a coffee-coloured impostor from a banana republic complicating the racial homogeneity of white European bike-racing. Not the international teams who had travelled to Colombia in 1982, 1983 and 1984 to ride the ten-stage Clásico RCN as pre-Tour altitude training; they knew what Lucho Herrera was capable of, and had nothing but respect. Fignon had been there weeks before the 1984 Tour. So too had Greg Lemond in his World Champion's jersey. Hinault wouldn't compete in Colombia until 1986, but his *directeur sportif* at the great Renault–Gitane and Renault–Elf teams, Cyrille Guimard, had been there to witness Herrera win overall victory and the mountains category in three successive years. When, at the end of 1983, Hinault agreed a lucrative contract to move to Bernard Tapie's wealthy La Vie Claire team, Guimard had tried to sign Herrera to replace him. The Colombian subsidiary of German battery manufacturer Varta, who sponsored the Colombian team at the Tour de France, had had to match Renault–Elf's substantial offer to keep their star. His performance at the 1984 Tour de France alone justified the expense.

The stresses of climbing at this velocity are beginning to take their toll. Breu's body can no longer wring enough oxygen from the air to fuel this pace. Now, in turn, Millar, Arroyo and Fignon also allow the Colombian to escape. Presently, Herrera reaches Hinault and passes him at such exhilarating speed that the Frenchman does not even attempt to respond. He is alone now, his tiny frame transfigured in defiance of gravity, the relentless pitch of his effort sending out a harmonic across the landscape, through the altitude and across the planetary distance to his homeland.

Sport is where modernity banishes the realm of miracles. Sporting success is the stuff of popular sainthood, the spontaneous canonisation that medieval popes mustered huge bureaucracies to suppress. When, in July 1955, Gabriel García Márquez published his biography of Lucho Herrera's forebear, the brilliant climber Ramón Hoyos, he noted that in Colombia's most humble households, beside the holy image of agonising Christs and compassionate Madonnas, a photograph of Hoyos had been pinned, cut from the newspapers. However, behind sport's *locus amœnus* lies a lesser dimension where the human drama of sport's global institutions unfolds. Since that is where the decisions took place that brought Lucho Herrera to this transcendent effort through the mountain air, let us leave him dancing out of the saddle and tune into a grandiose soap opera of more worldly ambition.

The story of the Tour de France from 1947 to 1987 is the story of a power struggle and personality clash between two great organisers and *hommes de presse*. Jacques Goddet and Félix Lévitan codirected the Tour and shared the offices of *L'Équipe* for 40 years. No two men could have been more different. Goddet was a bourgeois born in privilege. His father, Victor, had been the administrator of the sports newspaper *L'Auto*, and had played an important part in the creation of the Tour de France by encouraging Henri Desgrange to back the first Tour in 1903. Desgrange had regarded Jacques as a surrogate son, and had explicitly cultivated the boy as his successor. Sent to study in England at the age of sixteen, Goddet had acquired a lifelong passion for rugby and an eccentric sense of dress, most notoriously in the colonial-style shirt, shorts and wide-brimmed hat he sported at every Tour de France from 1929 to 1989.

Jacques owned and directed *L'Auto*, first with his brother, Maurice, and then alone until 17th August 1944, when General De Gaulle's ordinances against the collaborationist Press that had continued to publish during German occupation came into effect, and *L'Auto*, after two World Wars and forty-four years in publication, had ceased to exist. During the hearings, *L'Auto* and its director Jacques Goddet were complimented by the judges. *L'Auto*'s chief print-layer Roger Roux and motorsport editor Maurice Henry had been senior Resistance leaders, editorial secretary Jean Lafitte had hidden Jews in his Montmartre apartment, while three of its most prominent journalists, Louis Lapeyre, Marcel Oger and Odette Farge, had had close ties with the Resistance. But there was no waiving the decrees.

It was at this moment that Émilien Amaury, a pillar of the Resistance, former director of the news agency Havas and then owner of the newspaper *Parisien Libéré*, muscled in in Goddet's defence. Amaury convinced Goddet to sell him 50 per cent of the future Tour de France, then appealed for clemency in *L'Auto*'s favour. When this failed, Amaury advised Goddet to prepare a new paper on the same basis and with the same staff as *L'Auto*, even seeking permission for the new journal, *Vitesse*, to be printed on yellow paper like *L'Auto*. The request was refused and the yellow jersey of the Tour de France leader remains as the only reminder of *L'Auto*'s yellow pages. *L'Équipe*, a new sports paper on white newsprint with Goddet at the helm, was the compromise solution. Amaury sent an agent to assist Goddet, but also to keep him in check: his name was Félix Lévitan.

Lévitan had risen from lowly social status through hard work and a driving ambition. Goddet regarded him as a parvenu. Where Goddet would delegate responsibilities, Lévitan issued curt orders. '*Il faut se soumettre ou se démettre,*' was his central precept: follow your orders or find another job. Lévitan was a devoted husband all his life; Goddet had four wives and observed: 'I always wanted to marry the woman I loved at the moment I loved her.' Lévitan was rigorously prompt; Goddet was frequently late. The rows between them were legendary. One that took place during the 1982 Tour de France, as Bernard Hinault cruised to his fourth Tour win, was to lead indirectly here, to Lucho Herrera's sublime ascent on Alpe d'Huez, and much further. If global cycling today belongs to Americans, Australians, Balts, Kazakhs, Latin Americans, Russians, Scandinavians and Ukrainians, and is beginning to attract South East Asians and, more slowly, Africans, it is due in great part to the results of Jacques Goddet and Félix Lévitan's slanging match.

Each had clear ideas of the direction the Tour should take to ensure its future. Both sought to internationalise the Tour de France. Lévitan proposed to do so by declaring the Tour de France 'Open' and inviting foreign national amateur teams. Goddet's solution was a Tour de France departing from a great capital – Washington or Moscow – and spending just two-thirds of its itinerary in France.

The urge to internationalise had deep roots in global sport and in cycling lore. Soviet success in the Olympics was a key feature of the Cold War. However, the amateur–professional divide meant that Western professionals and the cyclists of the Soviet bloc had never been allowed to compete on level terms. The cyclic appearance of riders so peerlessly dominant that they drained the sport of all uncertainty – Alfredo Binda before the Second World War, Fausto Coppi after it, then Jacques Anquetil, Eddy Merckx, and Bernard Hinault – set the cycling milieu dreaming of heroes from behind the Berlin Wall who might shake Western European cycling to its foundations.

The first Great Eastern Hope was Poland's Richard Szurkowski. Szurkowski won the Peace Race – the Eastern bloc's Tour de France – three times and was crowned World Amateur Champion in 1973. The 1974 Paris–Nice was declared 'Open' to permit Szurkowski's participation with an amateur Polish team. He had an immediate impact, finishing Stage 2 second, on Merckx's wheel, and Stage 5 third. On Stage 6 Szurkowski missed the winning break and lost eight minutes to the stage-winner, Merckx. A fine performance, but not one to change history. The second Great Eastern Hope was Sergey Sukhoruchenkov. Sukhu had dominated the 1978 and 1979 Tours de l'Avenir (the amateur cousin of the Tour de France), then pulled away from the peloton with twenty miles to go to win the road-race at the Moscow Olympics in 1980 by the biggest margin since 1928. Neither athlete had ever been able to ride the Tour de France.

The developing world, meanwhile, had begun to mark the Olympics, most notably with the superb distance runners of Kenya and Ethiopia. If cycling had made little progress in Africa, at least one developing country already had a magnificent cycling tradition. Colombia's cyclists had been hungering for international recognition since the founding of their own national tour in 1951. Just two years later some did compete in Europe, travelling by sea to the Route de France, the old amateur version of the Tour. Most had been disqualified by the end of day one for finishing outside the time limit. By day four it was over. None had ever ridden over such flat terrain; none could keep up with Europeans twice their size. If they had made it to the mountains, global sporting history might have been different.

In 1957 Fausto Coppi had visited Colombia with Hugo Koblet. Coppi and Colombia's greatest climber, Ramón Hoyos, grew close, and in August 1958, the two champions met in Milan. Hoyos, who had won his fifth Tour of Colombia in May, had been contracted by the Swedish bicycle manufacturer Monark, which had a factory in Medellín, to ride a number of amateur events in Europe culminating in a six-day track race in Stockholm starting on 29th August. The World Championship course in Reims, insisted the Italian, might have been designed with Hoyos in mind. But the race would take place on 31st August, during the Stockholm event. His ambitions whetted, Hoyos contacted the Colombian Cycling Association for permission to ride in the worlds, but the answer was no: the Association could not risk upsetting a major presence in Colombian industry. By the time a second letter arrived on 27th August, reversing the Association's earlier decision and authorising Hoyos to ride in France, he had fixed his travel plans. Hoyos dutifully flew to Stockholm the following day, only to learn that the six-day competition had been postponed until the second week of September. It was too late for Hoyos: there was no way of reaching Reims in time.

That was the end of Colombia's European ambitions until the age of Martín Emilio Rodríguez Gutiérrez, known as Cochise. World Amateur record-holder for the hour in 1970, and World Amateur 4,000m Pursuit Champion in 1971, most Colombians regard Cochise as the greatest rider in their national history. Excluded from the 1972 Olympic Games under the strict rules governing amateurism – Colombia hadn't the resources or the structures to provide its athletes with covert funding through the universities or the military on the American or Soviet models – he turned professional immediately, with the team funded by the Italian bicycle manufacturer, Bianchi. His team leader, the 1965 Tour de France champion Felice Gimondi, has warm memories of Cochise: 'He was a complete rider. Cochise could climb with great dexterity, but he could also pull the group along at 50 k.p.h. on the flat. His experience on the track gave his pedal action formidable power. If he'd come to Europe aged 22 or 23 he could realistically have hoped to become a team leader and achieve much more than two stage wins in the Giro d'Italia.'

Some of European cycling's mandarins agreed. Rino Negri of the Italian daily *La Gazzetta dello Sport* wrote: 'I cannot explain how Cochise lost so much time. If he had come to Europe five years ago, he could have been a sort of Eddy Merckx.' In France, Le Soir baptised him 'the South American Pele of the bicycle, as fine an ambassador as *o rey do futebol*'.

Yet it was not the extrovert Cochise but another Colombian, one who failed in Europe and returned home to transform Colombia's cycling culture, who indirectly made Lucho Herrera's Alpe d'Huez victory possible. In 1974 Raphaël Antonio Niño Munevar had ridden for Jolly Ceramica beside Giovanni Battaglin, one of Italy's most exciting prospects. Now a frame manufacturer, Battaglin's memories of Niño are ambivalent: 'When Cochise came to Europe, he surprised us. He was not only a complete rider technically: he was intelligent, excellent company and ballsy. I had a word with him about Colombian riders, and he recommended Niño. With Cochise's help we made contact, and arranged to bring him to Europe. But Niño never adapted to life away from home, and it came out in his riding. Don't misunderstand me: in the mountains during the Giro d'Italia, he was strong and helped me a great deal. But I always felt he had an extra gear, which he rarely used.'

Niño's unhappy experience in Europe ended after a season, but it was not wasted. In Europe he had studied every aspect of team organisation with cold detachment. He had returned home with clear ideas about team finance, organisation and tactics with which he revolutionised Colombian cycling. He found sponsorship from a major national bank, the Banco Cafetero. Then, as undisputed team leader, he hired his own *domestiques* to ride themselves to breaking point for his benefit, according to the European tradition. If he had a puncture, they were paid to stop and give him one of their wheels. If he had a mechanical problem, they were paid to give him their bike. In return, the collective team winnings were pooled and divided out equally.

The ruthless application of European tactics, combined with Niño's uncommon physical capacities, gave him success beyond compare. He won four RCN Classics and six Tours of Colombia: only absence or injury prevented him from winning eight or nine. Many connoisseurs in Colombia regard Niño as Cochise's lieutenant in the hierarchy of Colombian cycling. For a decade, every other rider in Colombia scratched for crumbs beneath Niño's table. Yet the margins of his victories were narrow: Colombian cycling had strength in depth.

In 1980 a Colombian delegation entered the Tour de l'Avenir, the amateur equivalent of the Tour de France. With just four weeks to prepare his riders for their redoubtable expedition, time was against Raul Mesa, the team director. Time, and Sukhoruchenkov, now focused on his third consecutive victory. France, meanwhile, awaited Latin America's giants with baited breath. When the giants failed to show, and the diminutive figures of the Colombian climbers disembarked instead, the awe dissolved and pity took over. Sukhoruchenkov and his ruthless technical director Viktor Kapitanov, the 1960 Olympic road-racing champion, would eat their frail physiques for breakfast.

On day two the team time trial reassured the pessimists: Colombia lost over five minutes to the victors from Czechoslovakia. But as the race continued, the South Americans held back the expected storm of Russian ascendancy and, on day four, Alfonso Flórez, a balding, moustachioed figure with crossed eyes and an iron resolve joined a ten-man breakaway that gained over five minutes on Sukhu. The Russian didn't care: he was marking Patrocinio Jiménez. They had ridden against each other at the Tour of Cuba, and Patro was the only Colombian he credited with realistic title hopes. But, in April, Alfonso Flórez had lost his Tour of Colombia title by just eleven seconds: he had brought a terrible hunger to France and now began to ride away with the race. As evening drew in on day five, 13th September 1980, after judiciously joining the winning breaks day after day, he had become the first Latin American ever to lead a European stage-race.

On the flat Flórez gritted his teeth; in the mountains he darted into the sky. His overall lead had expanded to six minutes by Stage 8, when Sukhu rocketed away from the field with the Frenchman Frédéric Vichot, and led by four minutes at the foot of the final climb, La Joux Verte. Ascending with ruthless delicacy, Flórez kept his nerve and ate into the Russian's advantage. He crossed the col less than two minutes behind. On the final descent into Morzine, the two men squeezed such speed from the mountain air that their adhesion on the spiralling road edged towards zero. The heavier Sukhu, lurching downwards in a glissade on the limits of control, could only claw back a few seconds. Day after day, Sukhu stared down defeat with the pride of a champion, but on 21st September 1980, Alfonso Flórez rode into Paris as the first Tour de l'Avenir champion from the developing world.

With precedents like these, Goddet and Lévitan recognised that the future lay in internationalisation. Each, however, wanted to see their own plan enacted. Lévitan published his vision in a newspaper article. Goddet held a Press conference. Each accused the other of betrayal, but it was Lévitan – with the support of Émilien Amaury – who carried the day. Amateur teams from beyond cycling's Western European pale were invited: the USA, Russia and East Germany. Colombia, too, was on the guest list.

When the invitation arrived at the Colombian Cycling Federation in Bogotá, it was received by the President, a visionary, an inspirational motivator and a man of limitless energies named Miguel Ángel Bermúdez. The corpulent, charismatic Bermúdez bullied, cajoled and charmed his way towards obtaining the political support to take a Colombian team to the Tour de France. But he also needed 35 million pesos, and this was no time to be looking for hand-outs – in 1982 six of Colombia's greatest industries had reported losses totalling 5.64 billion pesos. Bermúdez asked seven major Colombian businesses for five million pesos each. Of the seven, only one, the battery manufacturer Varta, gave a positive reply. The project looked to be foundering, when Varta's managing director,

Saulo Barrera, took a massive gamble. He agreed to underwrite the entire budget. So began an expedition Colombia has known ever since as 'The Great Adventure'.

The Colombians were an unqualified success. Patrocinio Jiménez finished third in the mountain time trial on the Puy de Dôme; his teammate Edgar Corredor finished third in the stages finishing at Alpe d'Huez and Morzine. But they would have to wait another year before their first stage win. Lucho Herrera had been too young to compete in the previous Tour de France: the Colombians competed as amateurs, and Tour regulations stipulated that they should be aged at least 23. When it came, it would be the first stage win by an amateur and the first by an athlete from the developing world in Tour history.

Now, on the slopes of Alpe d'Huez, Lucho, the cyclists of Colombia, and the claims of riders from far beyond Western Europe and the Anglo-Saxon countries, are finally coming of age. He tunnels through the colour and celebration towards the finish line and, as he raises his hands in victory, the bike beneath him lurches slightly to one side. It seems ungainly, too big for this diminutive physique, as if the skinny kid with the too-long limbs were somehow out of place at the greatest annual sports event on the planet. He isn't: he's here, crossing the line alone on Alpe d'Huez because, irrespective of colour, creed, education or nationality, this is what he was born for.

STAGE 17, 1986: BRIANÇON–ALPE D'HUEZ, 162kms.

Alex Bannister

I remember the closing moments of the 1986 Alpe d'Huez stage so well that I can play back the tape in my head at will. Under a bright blue sky, a tanned Bernard Hinault is coolly leading the yellow jersey of Greg LeMond into the village of Huez at the top of the final climb of the day. To the left of picture, a lady in red hurtles alongside the pair for as long as she can manage, whereupon a bare-chested man in blue Addidas shorts takes up the chase. Paul Sherwen remarks that it's great to see the two team-mates reunited so spectacularly after everything that has passed between them, and Phil Liggett chips in with an apt something about the strongest pair in the race ripping the field apart in the style of the great Tour champions.

And then it happens – after a few moments tapping along the flat stretch through the village, just beneath the ski lift, Greg nonchalantly pulls alongside Hinault and puts a friendly arm around the Frenchman's back. Broad smiles spread across both of their faces and they embark on a relaxed conversation that lasts all of twenty seconds. Phil chips in that the scene is more reminiscent of two old pals out for a Sunday morning club run than a key stage of the Tour de France.

Moments later, the two riders turn the famous final corner for the long drag to the finish and Phil brings in an hysterical Kathy LeMond. She predicts that Greg has told Bernard that he should win the stage and then declares that 'She knew it!' when the pair sail towards the finishing line hands aloft and linked in joint celebration. Phil and Paul aren't often silenced, but by this stage there is a sense of awe in the studio. It's the first time Phil has seen anything like it in all his years on the Tour, and Kathy says that it's great to see that they are still such friends. A few moments later Greg and Hinault enjoy a huge buddy's hug – Hinault collects the stage win, and Greg puts on a bright new yellow jersey. Perfect harmony.

It's not just because I have watched that tape maybe 50 times that I can remember it in such detail. From my sofa in Surrey, this was my spectacular introduction to the world of the Tour de France and, not surprisingly, I was absolutely captivated by the mind-blowing emotion and scale of the event. As a fifteen year old, I struggled to talk after climbing the long drag through old Sunningdale, so I had to agree with Phil that it was incredible that two grown men could cycle up a 7,000-foot mountain and have the energy to hold a cheery conversation at the top. I also agreed that it was incredible how the rest of the field had been blown apart, and I certainly agreed when Paul and Kathy remarked that it was great to see that the pair were still best friends.

In fact, it was only when I wound the tape back years later that I realised I may have been a bit naïve that summer afternoon. But, equally, the more I learned about the events that led up to that stage, the greater that one epic moment of reconciliation seemed – even if things were a bit more complicated than Paul, Phil, Kathy and I supposed that day. You can wind back to the start of the 1986 Tour to get a greater insight, but you really need to go right back to the late 1970s and early 1980s to get any idea of just what it meant to see these two characters linking hands and chatting on that sun-baked Alpe that summer afternoon.

Take Hinault. A quick romp through his history will tell you most of what you need to know about the man. Born in Brittany in France, Hinault started out life as a simple, stubborn, outspoken and bellicose Frenchman who had got into fights for fun at school, and who could still lash out at spectators or protesters who got in his way. He had no time for the half-baked opinions of journalists, and he had no time for the cobbles of the famous Paris–Roubaix Classic either. He did win it in 1981 – just to prove he could – and then he never rode it again. As a youngster he hated school and would wile away lessons staring out of the window longing to be free to go fishing or ride his bike. At seventeen, he lived in a barn for three days, stubbornly refusing to come home after an argument with his father.

But like all the great champions, his talent on the bike was apparent from his first turn of the pedals. And he was cocky with it. 'I'll bring you the winner's bouquet,' he said to his mother on the morning of his first ever bike race in 1971, at the age of sixteen and a half. His mother told him not to be such a clever dick, but sure enough he did bring back the winner's bouquet that afternoon. And he won the next three races as well, for good measure. But then, any sixteen year old who could race lorries up the hill from Yffiniac at 50 k.p.h. had to be a bit special.

Years later, the newly nicknamed 'Badger' was up to the same trick, but by now it was in races rather bigger than that first test at Planguenoual. Hinault came to his first Tour de France in 1978 at the grand old age of 23, declaring to anyone who would listen that he was going to win it, and he duly did so, in addition to leading a riders' revolt at Valence d'Agen about the excessive number of transfers which were limiting the amount of sleep a rider could get. Again, confidence wasn't in short supply – 'Mr Mayor, when I'm talking to you, just shut up and listen,' he claims to have said.

Two years on, in 1980, despite controversially having to retire from his third Tour de France while leading the race, Hinault was as confident as ever, this time before his one and only victory in the World Championships at Sallanches. 'I had no doubt that I was going to become World Champion and I told my team so. I asked them to set such a fast pace from the start that the weaker riders would go out the back. I wasn't in the least worried and, as I hoped, the race went perfectly.'

Not that the Bernard Hinault who turned up to the 1986 Tour had enjoyed an entirely trouble free career. In 1983, a problem with his knee became so serious that he was forced to miss the Tour and have an operation to sort things out. It was the same year that his long standing partnership with Cyrille Guimard also broke down. People were starting to say that the Badger was finished, but, as it happened, he started a new team with the controversial businessman, Bernard Tapie, embarked on a new training regime with Swiss coach, Paul Koechli, and gradually set about fighting his way back to the top.

And the return was gradual. In the 1984 Tour he was a definite second best to a dominant Laurent Fignon, who had also won the year before. And it was only in Fignon's absence that he took the 1985 Tour ahead of rising American star and team-mate, Greg LeMond, who had made a remarkable third-place début the previous year, and now made do with the runner-up spot. He faithfully rode in Hinault's support despite proving the strongest in the final time trial of the race. And, to be fair, this support was gratefully received. That evening in Paris the Badger thanked LeMond for helping him to his fifth Tour victory and promised he would return the favour by devoting his final season to helping Greg win his first. And no one doubted that he meant what he said. Hinault may have been an aggressive rider, but he was a nice enough guy off the bike – someone you could trust.

So this was one half of the duo I watched tapping through Huez that summer afternoon. But his self-assured confidence was a world away from the blond American sheltering in his slipstream in case a patriotic spectator lashed out and upset his race.

Not that there was that much between the two men in terms of natural talent. Like Hinault, victory came easily to the young LeMond, who was a junior World Road-Race Champion in 1979 – in fact, like Hinault he had enough talent to bag the first four races he ever took part in. Within a year he was racing his fellow Americans in the intermediate class and, at sixteen, in his first year with the juniors, he won so many times that he began to get bored with these easy victories.

But that problem didn't last. As a young professional still destined for the top, LeMond seemed to lack the necessary panache to climb the final step from runner-up to victor. So much so in fact that by 1985 he was starting to get a name for himself as a 'nearly man', someone with the talent but not the mental approach to be the best.

Despite his famous World Championship victory in 1983, his palmarès was dotted with near misses and his team boss, Bernard Tapie, was beginning to get disgruntled with his million dollar wonder-kid. 'Second, third, second, third. Second place is the same as twenty-fifth place,' he moaned to the French Press.

'Hinault has a very strong character,' LeMond would say to any journalists who probed. 'He says he's going to win and sometimes he does win, but I never say it ahead of time. I don't say "I'll win the Tour." I say that I hope to win the Tour.' And of being a team leader: 'Sometimes in a race when the team's not doing well, when our riders aren't at the front, I have a hard time shouting, "Get up here!" Hinault would just yell at them.'

Coach Paul Koechli had similar things to say: 'It's up to Greg to impose himself. Sometimes he still seems timid.' Hinault noticed the same fault: 'Greg's a top-class rider, but he seems too unstable, incapable of accepting the responsibility which the race leader needs. He worries too much.'

Let's just say that Greg was having a hard time coming out of Hinault's shadow. And who can blame him? The Badger's shadow was big enough to eclipse the whole of France, and most of Spain and Italy as well. By the beginning of the 1986 season, he'd won five Tours, three Giros, two Vueltas, the World Championship, nine Classics, the Dauphiné three times and the Grand Prix des Nations five times. Despite Greg's Worlds win and his undoubted talent, everything was conspiring to tell him he was second best.

So, against this background, it must have been a huge relief to know that he had his French friend and mentor well and truly on his side for the 1986 Tour. Hinault was a stubborn man, a racer, but he could be counted on to keep a promise, couldn't he? After all, the young American had backed off when he could have put time into him on the 1985 stage to Luz Ardiden, so Hinault owed him. In any case, Hinault would be 32 next year, and his strength would be on the wane.

Of course, sitting on my Surrey sofa for my first ever Tour, I didn't know any of this – I only knew what I saw, and what Phil and Paul told me. And what I saw was the Badger attacking like a man possessed from the moment the race rolled out of Boulogne.

And the old man seemed to be having a high old time of it, too, darting off the front whenever the mood took him. You couldn't say the same for LeMond – his worried little face and concerned post-stage comments made it quite clear that this wasn't the script that he had been given. Hinault had cast himself as the faithul lieutenant, but he was throwing himself into the role of arch-villain with theatrical abandon. He wasn't supposed to be this aggressive, and he certainly wasn't supposed to be this strong – strong enough in fact to win the first major test of the Tour, the 61.5 km. time trial around Nantes.

Much more worrying for the American, though, were events three days later on the first big mountain stage from Bayonne to Pau. Mountains were supposed to be Hinault's weak point (like Induráin's!), especially in this twilight of his career, but he contemptuously threw out this piece of wisdom with a devastating attack in the company of Spaniard Pedro Delgado on the viciously steep Col de Marie Blanque. By the end of the day, he had taken the yellow jersey hostage with a lead of more than five minutes over a shell-shocked LeMond. Was I missing something? Were these supposed to be the considered actions of a team player riding for his leader?

Incredibly, Hinault was at it again the next day to Superbagnères with an early attack on the descent of the Tourmalet. By the bottom he had another 1min 43secs on LeMond – that's a lead on general classification of more than seven minutes. If things stayed like this, it was obvious, even to me, that there could be no way back for LeMond. Hinault would have to throw his bike in a ditch and walk if he was to let the American back into the race, and that seemed to be the last thing on his mind.

Of course, history relates what happened next. In the great turning-point of the Tour, what should have been the *coup de grâce* for the Frenchman, turned into an ugly suicide attempt as his strength wilted in the Pyrenean heat. By the time the group containing LeMond had caught Hinault on the valley road before the final climb, Hinault was already shattered, and only a superhuman effort up the final climb allowed him to limit his losses and conserve 40 seconds of his race lead from the resurgent American at the top. Albeit against his will, the Badger had finally been caged. Surely now it was time for him to end his ad lib and set about honouring his forgotten debt?

Not so. By the time the race hit the Alps, even with the tide now flowing solidly in the direction of the American, Hinault still seemed hell-bent on turning his final grand Tour into an epic. He was going – he would keep his promise to retire at 32 – but he had no intention of going quietly. And when he attacked in the company of third-placed Zimmerman, LeMond now had no doubt that he couldn't trust the Badger, even if he did have the strength that day to ride so strongly up the Col du Glandon that he was to become the first American to wear the yellow jersey that evening.

And that's where the race stood as I turned on my TV set on that hot day in July. LeMond was facing what could have been a serious threat from second-placed Zimmerman, but what certainly was a far greater danger from his own team-mate and 'helper' back in third. Alpe d'Huez is always a big day, but in 1986 the anticipation was immense. Even Phil's usual humdrum run-through of the day's route had morphed into a *tour de force* as he weighed up the possible outcomes while purring over a profile that took in the Galibier, the Croix de Fer and the legendary hairpinned ascent to Alpe d'Huez. Anything could happen.

And just about anything did. Right from the start, Hinault was throwing down the gauntlet yet again, and pitching the race into turmoil by attacking on the very first climb of the day before tearing down the descent as usual. But back down the road something very unusual was happening. Buoyed up by the yellow jersey, LeMond wasn't panicking. Instead, he paced up to Hinault in the company of Bauer and Ruiz-Cabestany and it was second-placed Zimmerman who was left struggling further down the road.

Look at the tape when Greg finally catches Hinault on the valley road. It's another fascinating moment. They're deep in the valley, now, on a long, flat, straight stretch with mountains all around. As LeMond coolly taps past the mischievous Hinault he doesn't cast so much as a single glance at the captured escapee. Hinault's gaze too remains fixed on the road ahead. You might expect a shake of the head from LeMond, an argument maybe, even a full-scale no-holds-barred, bike-in-the-ditch fight. Either way, it's an unusual moment. But perhaps not as unusual as what happens next.

Of course, Hinault claims he could have dropped LeMond on the second climb of the day, but in any event, by the time they reached the top of the Croix de Fer we were already enjoying the most memorable image of the race, perhaps of the decade: by this stage the race had exploded to leave LeMond and Hinault alone, yesterday's grand champion and his chosen successor swooping down the descent at speeds topping 60 m.p.h. and demolishing the rest of the field in their wake. At last we were seeing the two strongest men of the race giving the display of unity we had expected from the beginning.

With the Swiss Zimmerman now over five minutes back, the race was all but over, save for the serene sight of five-time Tour winner Hinault lovingly shepherding his team-mate round every one of the twenty hairpins of Alpe D'Huez. In fact, in this surreal instant there doesn't really seem to be a race at all, or a rivalry for that matter.

Greg revealed later that he was scared that a patriotic spectator may lash out at him on the climb, but he was safe under the wing of his protector and, finally, helper. 'By finishing hand in hand, I think we gave a wonderful image of what sports are all about,' said Hinault after all the embrace and emotion of the finish. I couldn't have agreed more.

And that should have been that. Hinault had finally kept his promise and Kathy, Paul, Phil and I could turn off our television sets knowing that all had worked out for the best in the end – hugs all round. What better way to celebrate the dignified passing of power from one generation to the next on cycling's greatest stage? Greg's nightmare was over, and Kathy was delighted that everyone was friends again. With a bit of luck, and the passage of time, Hinault's exuberant attacks on the early stages could be relegated to footnote status. I was busily papering over them already. Hinault had come through and, as the sun dipped low behind the Alps that evening, everything was just fine.

But when the sun rose the following morning everything was not fine. Far from it. Hinault was now nearly three minutes back on LeMond, but instead of turning off the heat on his American protégé, he turned it up to maximum by declaring that he still planned to try and take his sixth historic Tour win in the final time trial: 'Let me say it one more time: the Tour isn't over,' was his message, before offering the scant consolation that he wouldn't attack Greg any more if he didn't regain the lead during the final time trial.

For the fragile American, this was the last straw. Just 24 hours after the great reconciliation, Hinault was once more pinching at the nerves of the American who was spitting: 'He made promises to me he never intended to keep. He made them just to relieve the pressure on himself.' Even Hinault admitted later, 'I've really thrown everything at Greg in the last 48 hours. I've pushed him as hard as I can and spared him nothing – not words, not deeds – and have put him under the maximum pressure. If he doesn't buckle, that means he's a champion and deserves to win the race.'

And what of the famous promise? On that front Hinault was making the same lame excuses that he sticks to today: 'I did everything for his own good … I attacked all the time to get rid of our rivals … I never attacked him personally, even though I could have had his scalp at Alpe d'Huez.'

Even to this day Hinault and LeMond remain irreconcilable – Greg, with good reason, maintains that Hinault never meant to keep his promise; Hinault, meanwhile, clings to the notion that he was merely shaking up the race and trying to toughen up his young protégé. The only thing everyone can agree on was that by his actions Hinault had created the masterpiece of the 1986 Tour, one of the greatest and most talked-about Tours ever. Without his panache, and with no other strong contenders, the race could so easily have amounted to nothing at all.

It's interesting to speculate why, despite that one epic day, Hinault's promise was never kept, and I suspect that even more than Hinault's love of attacking – his natural racer's inability to play the supporting role on a bike – what really threw the spanner in the works was the Badger's Indian summer of form. After all, when the promise was made in 1985, shortly after losing the second time trial, Hinault was pleased enough to have escaped with a fifth tour, which many experts believed LeMond could have won. Not even Hinault, himself, could have predicted just how strong he would be coming into his sixth.

I think Hinault came to the race with an open mind. He was looking to make mischief, to enjoy himself, to be aggressive and to see how things turned out. He would win his sixth Tour if things worked out that way – and after the first day in the Pyrenees things were working out that way – but he would have been happy to support Greg had his tactics failed. Greg summed it up when interviewed in Velo magazine that August: 'No one could have predicted how strong Hinault would be this year – neither him, nor me. That's what messed everything up. Hinault this year was ten times stronger than he was a year ago, when he won his fifth tour.'

And when, on his very first roll of the dice, his lead built to five minutes in the Pyrenees, who could blame him for looking for a sixth victory? I am certainly grateful that he did – if he hadn't done so, his panache may never have fired my imagination for the sport, and, who knows, LeMond may have remained for ever the timid American.

Hinault may not have kept his promise to help LeMond win the 1986 Tour – he couldn't have done much more to prevent him – but at least his argument that he was toughening up the fragile LeMond holds water. After all, without that baptism of fire, LeMond might have spent his whole career as a 'nearly man'. And would he have had the mental toughness to rise from the ashes of his accident in 1987 to pull off the greatest coup of all time by winning the 1989 Tour by those famous eight seconds?

ICE COLD WAR ON LE TOUR, 1986
Saint or Sinner? – Hinault versus LeMond

Keith Bingham

When France's Bernard Hinault equalled the record of five victories in the Tour de France in 1985, he promised to help his young American team-mate, Greg LeMond, who'd finished runner-up, win his first Tour in 1986. He did so, after a fashion, but seemingly only when it suited him! And not before trying his darndest to take a record sixth victory for himself! That's how I interpreted Hinault's tactics in the Alps, which were a smokescreen under which, as well as taking out LeMond's rivals and his own, he really hoped his American team-mate would roll over, too. But this wasn't immediately apparent to many in the press who were taken in by the show of unity between the pair at l'Alpe d'Huez.

Nicknamed the 'Badger' for his stubbornness and courageous attacks, Hinault knew he was riding his final Tour and wanted to go out in style. And boy, did he do so. The French hero's breathtaking and glorious attack with 130 kilometres to go on stage 11 from Bayonne to Pau in the Pyrenees wowed the French public – and everyone else. It was a thrilling, awesome display of power, which tore the field to shreds. Double Tour winner Laurent Fignon was the main casualty. He didn't start the next day.

On that stage Hinault eventually finished second to Pedro Delgado and took the yellow jersey with a lead of 5–25. According to Sam Abt in his book Greg LeMond, The Incredible Comeback, Hinault's motives were clear. He had wanted ten minutes to ruin his La Vie team-mate's quest for a first Tour win. Well, if that was the case, I was unaware of that on the day, or anything the team had decided. It seemed to me that Hinault had been first to take the initiative to give La Vie Claire the overall lead, not LeMond, and good luck to him, I thought.

But when, a few stages later, Hinault attacked in the Alps I smelt a rat. For by then, LeMond had the overall lead. And to my mind, Hinault's actions were definitely out of order. But first, let's go back to the Pyrenees.

When Hinault blew up spectacularly on the day after his great escape, that opened the way for the American to make his move, not only for himself, but in a bid to keep the jersey in the team should Hinault lose it. And LeMond did so with the team's permission. And so it was that he at last stepped out of Hinault's shadow with an equally epic ride to Luchon across four major climbs to finish atop Superbagnères. LeMond won the stage while Hinault struggled in eleventh to retain the yellow jersey, but conceding 4–39 to LeMond, who closed to only 40 seconds behind overall.

The French press went ballistic. How dare LeMond put Hinault's attempts at a record sixth victory in jeopardy. They challenged Hinault at the finish, demanding to know, had he, Hinault, given LeMond permission? To which Hinault caustically replied. 'I am not his father, he can do what he wants.' A battle royal was shaping up for supremacy in La Vie Claire. Who would succeed?

LeMond showed he was ready to take the crown in Paris – and become the first American winner of Le Tour – on the first Alpine stage (stage16) from Gap to Serre-Chavaliar. This was when he took the initiative as Hinault again faltered. This time, LeMond took the overall lead from his team-mate when he finished third to stage winner Eduardo Chozas. Hinault dropped to third overall at 2–43, but he put a brave face on it. After all, La Vie Claire still had the jersey.

What followed – as I saw it – was a very clever plot. For although Hinault made out that his attacks the next day were to wipe out his and LeMond's opponents, his real target was the American. Figure this. What's a man to do when he finds he's in the form of his life? If it was you, wouldn't you want to be the first man to win six?

Hinault was a brilliant tactician, one of the hardest men in the game, a fighter, the patron, a winner of single day classics as well as all the Grand Tours. He thought that LeMond, a new breed of rider who focused mainly on the Tour, lacked the necessary aggression. That was my take on it at the time, and how I saw and wrote it up in my daily despatches from the press convoy.

After his adventures in the Pyrenees, Hinault was exhausted and no one could have expected him to recover and mount a series of attacks over the mighty Col du Galibier a few days later. It was astonishing. The team's official line was that these attacks were intended to get rid of their arch rival, the Swiss star Urs Zimmermann, second overall, and so allow Hinault to move up to second behind LeMond. Entirely plausible, except the move also left LeMond behind – for a while!

And I sensed mischief afoot. I saw the day's action as a mighty showdown between the two in the Alps. Only in later biographies would the truth emerge.

At the time, I had no hesitation in translating Hinault's ingenious attack off the Galibier as being intended to weaken LeMond's resolve, so that in the time trial two days from Paris, Hinault might see off the American for good and ride to a record sixth victory. If LeMond hadn't chased Hinault he would have lost the yellow jersey. So he chased, and in doing so took Zimmerman back to Hinault. Whereupon, the French star put in another attack!

Instinct. Intuition. Call it what you like, but the reporter is a detective who must unravel what's really going on. You can ask all the questions you like, but if there's a dodgy plot no one is going to tell. And this was one right dodgy plot.

My instant reaction when Radio Tour announced Hinault's attack from the yellow jersey group was, 'Hinault tries to take back the yellow jersey from team-mate Greg LeMond.'

That was the story I filed to *Cycling* and my editor Martin Ayres. He had watched the TV news which swallowed the other story, the one which shaped up in the closing stages of that stage, after LeMond had come back to Hinault for the second time. The story which made the headlines was the 'best buddies' embrace – the La Vie Claire pair crossing the line at L'Alpe d'Huez together, shoulder hugging, where the American gifted the stage to his French team-mate. In my view this show of unity was a sham, at best, a cover up for what had happened five hours earlier, on the Galibier. I wasn't alone in coming to this conclusion. A Belgian journalist and I discussed it, laughing at the other scribes for swallowing the lie.

When my story landed on my editor's desk that same evening, he accepted my take on it without question. But not everyone appeared to do so. I recall asking a top British scribe what he thought about Hinault's 'attack' on LeMond. He was horrified, saying no, that wasn't what he did at all. Impossible.

'What makes you so sure?' I said. He replied that he had an interview with Hinault after every stage and he'd never said anything to him. To which I replied, 'Do you think he'd would really tell you what he was up to behind LeMond's back?'

It was a great story, about one of the sport's greatest riders. For Hinault was a tough fighter, a winner, a natural. For sure, after his fifth victory the year before, he had promised LeMond he would help him win his first Tour. But 12 months on, the great man could sense a record-breaking sixth victory was within his grasp if LeMond should not be up for it! For Hinault didn't think the American had command of the situation. Might not be up to seeing off his rivals. So to help him assert himself,

Hinault simply set about doing what he plainly thought LeMond should be doing, and take the race to Zimmermann and the rest, get rid of them. It was a double-edged sword, for in doing this, it was my contention at the time that he hoped also to get rid of LeMond.

My case at the time was that Hinault knew exactly what he was doing. Here's how I saw the action unfold as it happened, as filed to *Cycling*.

Stage 18, Briançon–L'Alpe D'Heuz, 162.5 km.

This was one of the greatest days in Tour history as Bernard Hinault tried to take back the yellow jersey he regarded as his own from team-mate Greg LeMond.

Like two prize fighters the pair went in search of the truth over the terrifyingly high Col du Galibier, where the snows never melt and ice lines the roadside. Then over the Col du Télégraph, the Col de la Croix de Fer, and finally up the famous 22-hairpin climb of L'Alpe d'Huez, to complete the alpine 'circle of death'.

On the descent off the Galibier, Hinault had dived into the attack, and his prey was LeMond. He plunged to a 20-second lead before LeMond reacted. In the press room that night, word had it that LeMond was only prompted to react by Spain's Ruiz Cabestany, who was reported to have said to LeMond, 'You'd better go after him, hadn't you?'

LeMond took off, taking Cabestany with him, and big rival Zimmerman and they joined Hinault. They began the next climb, the short haul up the Télégraph, and two kilometres from the summit, Hinault attacked again.

At St Michel de Maurienne in the valley, some 11 kilometres later, LeMond rejoined Hinault, together with their team-mate Steve Bauer, and Ruiz Cabestany. But no Zimmermann, who would lose 5–15, and his second overall place to Hinault.

So, Hinault had got rid of Zimmermann, as he said they must. But not the other guy!

Soon, Hinault and LeMond had only themselves for company on the descent off the Col de la Croix de Fer where race director Félix Lévitan riding in his car behind the pair, was aghast at the risks Hinault was taking on the 30-kilometre descent. I wrote: 'Hinault, like a wounded animal running amok with the weapon that had struck him – LeMond – embedded in his side.'

Far-fetched? I didn't think so.

And so, LeMond having shown his strength, stuck to Hinault like a limpet mine. The pair continued, alone to the finish, winding up through the 22 hairpins of l'Alpe, where LeMond gifted the stage to his teammate. They were all smiles!

At next morning's press conference, the plot thickened. It took place in the unlikely setting of the Church of Our Mother of The Snows at L'Alpe d'Huez, a modern building in the village. This is the story I filed.

It was an unusual sight. LeMond, Hinault and coach Paul Koechli were dressed identically in white jogging suits. They were sat before the huge church organ in the centre of the church, daylight from the conical tower above pouring angelic light on them! Had they come to confession? We would get no satisfactory answer.

Koechli played down the story about a rift, but admitted that before the Tour he had been concerned that his two stars would not declare war on each other. After fencing questions from the floor, with much putting of heads together to frame their answers, the trio admitted this much, that until the time trial at St Etienne, with four stages to go, they had agreed: 'may the best man win'.

After that, if he is still on top, LeMond can keep the jersey and Hinault would not attack him! *Would not attack him! Do you read that?*

x x x x x

The meeting ended. Outside the church they split up, the LeMond camp and the Hinault camp, each surrounded and tackled individually by reporters.

LeMond said: 'This is a very stressful Tour for me. It is an unusual situation. We are two leaders in one team.'

'The big question, Greg,' I said, 'is, did Hinault attack you yesterday?'

LeMond drew in a deep breath. 'No. We had planned it. Sure, it was dangerous. I'm sure he might have thought it would be nice for him to get away all by himself to the finish.'

He left us to read between the lines. He told us how he read the unfolding drama, after Hinault had attacked off the Galibier and on the Télégraph. 'I realised that if I just sat there with Zimmermann, there was always the risk he would drop me if I didn't feel so good later. And I felt it better to have Stephen Bauer [team-mate] there and for all of us [Hinault, LeMond, Bauer] to get away. It was to the advantage of the whole team.'

And so that's what happened, the three of them on the front, clear of Zimmermann. Whatever Hinault may have wished for, LeMond had proved equal to the task, worthy of the yellow jersey.

Now Hinault fell into his other role, guardian of his young protégé in the yellow jersey. On the Col la Croix Fer LeMond was told he must not ride so hard, save himself.

'We played it for security, worked together until the bottom of L'Alpe. I stayed next to him,' said LeMond. But then he gave the clearest indication thus far that he and Hinault were at loggerheads.

'The whole way up the climb, until the last kilometre, regardless of what the public says, I didn't feel like attacking Bernard.' (Attacking Bernard? He has considered paying back Bernard for earlier attacks? – I recall thinking afterwards.)

'But that would have been useless, stupid,' LeMond continued, once again, trotting out the party line. 'It would have shown we were not working as a team. It would have shown we were individuals and I think the way we finished yesterday was perfect. We couldn't have done it better.'

So, all's well?

Not in Australian Phil Anderson's book. Tension was high in the LeMond camp when racing resumed after the rest day, with stage 18 from Villard de Lans to St Etienne, for this was the eve of the time trial, when we would see who was king of Le Tour.

My lead for that day's story began with a report of Anderson of Panasonic engaged in a furious row with Hinault, whom he accused of towing the pack up to the yellow jersey group which had taken a 20-second lead during the stage! Was he pulling back LeMond, not wishing to see him extend his lead of 2–43 the day before the race against the watch?

Deep down, LeMond must have known that Hinault's cards were not on the table! But the American never publicly questioned Hinault's loyalty during the race, and denied there was any rivalry between them. He spoke instead of his concerns at rumours that the public believed that 80 per cent of the peloton were racing against him.

He certainly believed that a 'select few' wanted to see Hinault win. And why not? And he felt the need to remind us of what happened in 1985. 'If I hadn't been there last year he wouldn't have had his fifth victory.'

During the '85 Tour, the boot had been on the other foot. Then LeMond had been in a position to challenge for the yellow jersey when his team-mate Hinault faltered and looked to be in danger of losing the overall lead. But LeMond, who wanted to be given his head, dutifully followed team orders to hold back. Hinault won, LeMond was second.

A year later, many in the press felt LeMond was getting paranoid. Certainly he was tense, feeling the pressure on the eve of becoming the first American to win Le Tour.

The evening before the time trial, he said: 'If I don't win because of an accident and Bernard wins because I've been knocked out by some rider in the peloton, I just say it will be his worst victory ever and that's a bad way to go down in history for Bernard.'

The final showdown – stage 19, a 58-kilometre time trial at St Etienne. Hinault won, beat LeMond! But only by 25 seconds, in a time of 1–15–36. It meant LeMond still commanded a healthy overall lead of 2–18 on the French hero.

The battle of minds was over. And Hinault, with a broad smile, at last conceded victory to his American teammate two days out from Paris.

So it was that LeMond sparked a new era for *Le Tour*.

And I filed the following after that fabulous victory, from the Champs-Elysées press centre that afternoon.

> The Star Spangled Banner rang out on the Champs-Elysées, heralding the first victory by a non European.
>
> Greg LeMond, 26, triumphed just as experts said he would when he dominated the Tour de l'Avenir, regarded as the junior 'Tour' in 1982.
>
> All his fears melted away as was cheered by tens of thousands on the crowd-lined Champs-Elysées.
>
> The war of nerves, of accusations of betrayal within the team worked against LeMond who unfairly lost some credibility as a true leader when the chauvinistic French press accused him of hiding behind Hinault on the big Alpine stage to l'Alpe d'Huez. They conveniently overlooked the fact that Hinault, in my view, had attacked LeMond that day.

LeMond covered the 4,100 kilometres in 110 hours, 35 minutes and 19 seconds. That was three minutes 10 seconds quicker than Hinault and over 10 minutes faster than the Swiss hope, Urs Zimmermann, third. The La Vie Claire team swept the board. Hinault won the mountain jersey for the first time after the specialist climber, Scotland's Robert Millar, fell ill and retired.

LeMond's long apprenticeship under Hinault was over. It included third in the 1984 Tour, second in 1985, a month after finishing second in the Giro d'Italia. In 1986, he was fourth in the Giro, a month before embarking on this historic, turbulent Tour, when the old master was finally forced, most reluctantly, to give best to the younger pretender to the throne.

Later that night, at our overnight accommodation en route for the Channel ports and home, the hotel's manageress enquired who had won, le Breton? Or le American?

'The American,' we said.

'Bon,' she smiled.

Curious Revelations

When Bernard Hinault published his autobiography, entitled *Memories of the Peloton* in 1989, the foreword, written by John Wilcockson, clearly alluded to Hinault's attempts to win a record 6th Tour, even though his chief rival was his team-mate, Greg LeMond.

It says that in his autobiography, Hinault explains why he 'made attacks against LeMond' during the 1986 Tour.

Hinault recalls how he rode that Tour. He was there for the glory, to enjoy his last Tour, he says. He reaffirms that he had given his word to Greg LeMond that he would help him win, and that's what he did.

He did this by trying the wear out his rivals, to help LeMond. He attacked them, not LeMond personally, he said. 'It wasn't my fault that he didn't understand this.'

Keith Bingham *Cycling*

STAGE 21, 1989: VERSAILLES–PARIS, 24.5kms

Chris Sidwells

In 1789 a Parisian mob stormed the Bastille prison in the centre of the city. They then marched to the King's Palace in Versailles, deposed their monarch, and thus gave birth to France as a republic. It was a triumph for freedom, a great day for the French and a great day for Paris.

Two hundred years later the organisers of the Tour de France thought they would celebrate the French Revolution by running the last stage of their race as a time trial that would follow the route the revolutionaries took, only in reverse. With any luck the stage could turn into a triumphal march for another Parisian, the top French rider of the day, Laurent Fignon.

It didn't, and what is more Fignon was beaten at the last minute, on the Champs Élysées, in front of a holidaying crowd of his own people, and by a man from a country whose influence the French have a deep-seated fear of. America was the country, Greg LeMond was the man, and he beat Fignon by the closest margin the race has ever seen – just eight seconds.

To say it was an exciting Tour does not do it justice – neither the race nor that final time trial stage. No one had a clear hold on events: the balance of power swung one way, then the other, then back again. It was a story of endeavour, of tenacity, of bad luck, of intrigue and of favours. In short it was the story of the Tour de France distilled into a single year. It was also a story which began in the trauma room of an American hospital over two years before the 1989 Tour de France had even started.

On 20th April 1987 LeMond, who only the previous year had become the first American to win the Tour de France, was on a hunting trip in California with some of his family and friends when his brother-in-law accidentally shot him. Surgeons from the University of California saved his life in a two-hour operation, but could not remove some of the lead shotgun pellets that riddled his body because they were too close to his heart. They are still there today.

'I will return. I do not know when, but I will return – that is certain' were the first words LeMond said to the reporters gathered around his hospital bed. In fact, he probably never did return to the rider he was in 1986, but neither would he have guessed that his comeback to the top level of cycling would take so long, and be so tortured, or that so many people would write him off.

LeMond says that the next two years were the most difficult of his life, as time and again he would look like he was finding something of his old strength, only for it to suddenly disappear. Things got so bad that in the 1989 Giro d'Italia he had to suffer more than he ever thought possible just to keep going in the mountain stages. Not once, though, did he think of taking the easy option of retiring, even though a reported one-million dollar insurance pay-out would have made that option attractive. Great bike-riders just don't think like that.

Laurent Fignon had been through difficult times, too, before 1989. The winner of the 1983 and 1984 Tours, he had failed to mount a serious challenge between 1985 and 1988, due to injury and patchy form, but in 1989 he had come back with a bang, winning Milan–San Remo and the Giro d'Italia in the run-up to the Tour. It looked like it could be the mercurial Frenchman's year again, at last.

His biggest rival on the face of it would be the Spanish winner of the 1988 Tour, Pedro Delgado, only he almost wrote himself out of the plot in the first three days. After completing his warm-up for the prologue time trial around the streets of Luxembourg city, Delgado thought he had time for a few minutes of quiet riding before he was due to start. He didn't.

Realising his mistake, his manager, José Miguel Echávarri, rushed him to the line 2mins 54secs after he should have been there. Two days later Delgado was dropped by his Reynolds team during the team time trial. They waited, but still he lost another five minutes.

Nearly eight minutes lost in two days, Delgado's fight back to third overall at just over three and a half minutes by the finish in Paris would be the sub-plot of the Tour, but it was nothing like the block-busting thriller the main event turned out to be.

Fignon had the best start of all the favourites by finishing second to Holland's Eric Breukink in the prologue. His Super-U team then handed out a rare beating to Breukink's Dutch Panasonic team, the unofficial World Champions at the discipline, in the team time trial, putting Fignon well up in the overall standings.

LeMond didn't start badly, either. Fourth in the prologue time trial surprised everyone, but confirmed what LeMond knew. Towards the end of the Tour of Italy he had discovered the medical reason for his fluctuating form and put it right. During the final week of that race he managed second place in a 53-kilometre time trial, and felt sure that his come-back was now on.

He was right. The fifth stage of the Tour was a 73-kilometre time trial in Brittany, between the towns of Dinard and Rennes. Pedro Delgado's bad luck turned to good when, as an early starter due to his low overall position, he had good conditions and beat better time triallists to take second on the stage.

Later on in the day, the capricious Breton weather turned sour, and those higher on the overall classification were slowed by rain; all except Greg LeMond. He sliced through it to record the fastest time, and he did so by using an American invention that most of the Europeans had laughed at when they first saw it.

A ski equipment designer called Boone Lennon, who was also a keen cyclist, had worked out that if cyclists could get their arms in line with their bodies like skiers do, rather than to their sides, they would reduce their frontal area, therefore cutting wind resistance. So he invented a set of clip-on handlebar extensions, which allowed riders to rest their arms in front of them and still control their bikes. The new sport of triathlon had adopted them enthusiastically – hence their name – tri-bars. Cycling, however, was a little slower: the Americans of the 7-Eleven team had used them first; the rest wouldn't be so reticent after this Tour.

LeMond was ecstatic after the time trial. He was back, and what's more he was back in yellow. He took over the race leadership and it tasted very sweet. 'Whatever happens, this is the greatest day of my life, even better than winning in 1986. People gave up on me, but now I have proved them wrong,' he said after donning the jersey. He had dreamt about wearing it again, but must sometimes have wondered if he ever would.

The adoption of new equipment ideas was just one of the changes cycling was going through in the late eighties. Hein Verbrugggen, who took over the presidency of the UCI in the eighties, had coined the word 'Mondialisation'. He wanted the sport to grow into a worldwide one, and attract nations other than those it traditionally had appealed to.

His policy had been a success. LeMond had already been World Champion and a Tour winner. The Irish rider Sean Kelly dominated single-day Classic races, and in this Tour would take a record fourth Green Jersey as the points winner. His countryman, Stephen Roche, had even equalled an Eddy Merckx record in 1987 by winning the Giro, Tour and World Title in the same year. The peloton, which formerly spoke only

French, Dutch, Italian and Spanish, now contained Australian, American, Scandinavian, British, and Canadian voices.

Raul Alcalá became the first Mexican in Tour history to win a stage when he crossed the line at Spa Francorchamps in Belgium on Stage 3. The international flavour of the 1989 race continued with victories for Portugal through Acacio Da Silva, Ireland with Martin Earley, and Scotland's Robert Millar.

But the main battle was between Fignon and LeMond. While Millar was scoring his fantastic stage victory in the Pyrenees; soaring up to the ski station at Superbagnères, with Pedro Delgado just able to hold on and ride behind him, Fignon attacked late to gain a few seconds on LeMond, and to take the yellow jersey.

A few days later Fignon showed the wild, stubborn spirit which governed his racing, as it did his life, when he attacked with country-man Charly Mottet on Bastille Day on the rolling, boiling-hot run from Montpellier to Marseille. It was an attempt to stand the race on its head, and the two French heroes relayed each other for over 50 kilometres before LeMond's desperate chase brought them under control, and provided a springboard for Vincent Barteau to achieve what every French pro cyclist dreams of doing – winning the stage on 14th July.

Stage 15 was a mountain time trial from Gap to Orcières-Merlette in the Alps, and again this knife-edge race saw the pendulum swing the other way, as LeMond bested Fignon by a few seconds to take the jersey back again. Steven Rooks won the stage, ahead of the Spanish workhorse, Marino Lejarreta, who had already ridden the Tours of Spain and Italy that year.

LeMond gained a few more seconds next day, between Gap and Briançon. He did it by being more alert than the Frenchman, and with a little help from a fellow North American. Steve Bauer, from Canada, had been fourth in the previous year's Tour, but had lost a lot of time and any chance of a high overall placing in the Pyrenees. On the descent of the Izoard, shortly before the finish, LeMond and Mottet passed him and thought, 'why not lend Greg a hand?' So, after they'd passed he left a gap. It quickly grew and Fignon couldn't close it.

Seconds gained through sleight of hand. Fignon answered with a show of strength. Next day on Alpe d'Huez he followed Pedro Delgado when he attacked behind the long-haired climbing wizard and stage winner, from the Dutch village of Oss, Gert-Jan Theunisse. LeMond couldn't follow; near the top he cracked and had a desperate struggle to limit his losses, but Fignon took back the jersey by 26 seconds.

At the finish LeMond was desperately tired, but his pale blue eyes burned with defiance. 'There are a lot of traditionalists who say that after Alpe d'Huez, it's over. That's a lot of bull. I haven't given up,' he said.

However, Fignon piled on the pressure with some devastating riding. On the stage to Villard-de-Lans he changed to his big chainring and launched an attack near the top of the first-category St Nizier climb that not even the uphill specialists could follow. He rode alone to the finish, stretching his overall lead to 50 seconds; meanwhile, behind him, an exhausted LeMond played poker with Delgado. The Spaniard was chasing with the Dutch duo of Steven Rooks and Theunisse, but LeMond was not doing as much work. Delgado slowed to let the American through, but he refused. They stared into each other's eyes, and slowed right down, but Delgado broke first and resumed the chase. If he hadn't, Fignon would have won the Tour.

The pony-tailed Frenchman was magnificent in the lead, riding into the wind, sometimes at 50 k.p.h. not caring about anything but gaining as much time as he could. With what was happening behind it looked every bit as though it was the race-winning move. In fact, everyone thought it was, except one man – Greg LeMond. 'It isn't finished,' he said after the stage. 'If he [Fignon] wins the Tour it won't be by 50 seconds. He is going to have some sleepless nights between now and Sunday, I can tell you.'

He was having them already. Fignon had begun to suffer from a saddle sore which required nightly lancing. His nerves were also beginning to shred. He looked fairly cool after containing LeMond the next day to Villard-de-Lans, and taking second place at the finish behind him, but it was just a mask.

Fignon is very French: he wears his heart on his sleeve and says what he thinks. The Press, sensing the brilliant story of a Parisian winning in the bicentennial year of the Revolution, were now hounding his every move. But Fignon knew that their story was not already written, his saddle problems meant that he was riding in constant discomfort. In the final time trial it would show.

The state of his nerves showed when he lost it with a television camera crew, who were following his every move. 'They have been following me for three weeks, even when I go for a piss,' he said in his defence. It wasn't pretty from the other side of the camera as he spat at and harangued the TV people on a station platform before boarding the TGV to Paris, and the final stage.

The scene was set for a thrilling finale. Paris had been celebrating the Revolution all summer, and it was looking like this could be another day in the glorious history of *La Patrie*. Tricolours were everywhere, fluttering in the sunshine which bathed the Champs Élysées, as thousands of French lined the route from Versailles to Paris. Those that weren't there tuned in their TVs and radios, and held their breath. The sense of French expectation hung in the still air until you could almost taste it.

Only Fignon knows how much the pressure of the day was getting to him, though he showed no outward signs as he calmly went through his warm up. Some idea of how much tension both must have been feeling can be gauged by an outburst of temper LeMond had at his team mechanic when he found that his tri-bars had worked loose on his bike. The problem was fixed by packing out the clamps with slivers of metal cut from a Coke can, according to Jose De Cauwer, LeMond's team manager.

LeMond started second to last, two minutes in front of Fignon. On the line he looked composed and with his handlebar fixed, ready to get on with the job. Any emotion was now hidden deep beneath his dark glasses. As he launched himself down the ramp from the time trial start-house, Fignon rode past the other way having completed his warm-up. They didn't look at each other.

Fignon climbed the steps to the start-house with a sense of purpose. He had problems, but no one could tell, and he certainly did not look like a man climbing up to the guillotine. No problems had occurred with his bike, his Super-U team were too big a set-up for anything like that to happen. But although everything was working as it should, Fignon's bike wasn't equipped with tri-bars, neither was he wearing an aerodynamic helmet like LeMond. Some experts reckon that those things can save between two and five seconds per kilometre; this time trial was 25.5 kilometres – you do the sums.

By the time Fignon started LeMond was getting on for two kilometres down the wide, straight and slightly downhill Avenue de Paris. He was riding very smoothly, crouched in his aerodynamic position, arms out in front of him, and powerfully turning his top gear (55 x 12). The rumbling of his rear disc wheel warned the packed crowd of his approach, and though they were mostly French, they sportingly cheered the American, little knowing he was about to spoil their day.

The crowd was really waiting for Fignon, and not a sound could be heard from his bike as he was carried along the same route by a wave of hysteria. He was going fast, but it didn't look like the controlled effort LeMond was making. If you study pictures of the Frenchman in that time trial, he is sitting awkwardly on his bike. The saddle sore was making him do that.

The course threaded its way through Viroflay, Chaville, Sevres, then Issy-les-Moulineaux where the Tour de France has its headquarters. Then over the Seine by the Pont d'Issy and along the right bank of the river by the Quai Saint-Expury, named after one of France's aviation pioneers. By then LeMond was flying: already 21 seconds up on Fignon at the 11.5-kilometre check, he was gaining time in every kilometre.

The next part of the course, which ran alongside the Seine, was absolutely flat for six kilometres, with just a steady bend around the river to the rider's right. LeMond was rock solid, still gaining. Fignon now was getting news of his losses from the System-U manager, Cyrile Guimard. He was in and out of the saddle, trying to get more from his body in order to stem the ebbing tide of his lead. He was also trying desperately to ease the pain he was suffering from his injury.

If the American needed a lift he got it now as the course passed the Avenue du President Kennedy, the Rue de B. Franklin and went along the Avenue de New York. It was as if Paris itself was turning against Fignon; by the end of that section he had lost 34 seconds in 19 kilometres. There was 6.5 kilometres to ride and only 16 seconds left of his overall lead.

On to the Place de La Concorde for the first time, and on to the circuit that is used for the final road-race stage today, LeMond raced down the Quai des Tuilleries, back up the Rue de Rivolli, crossed the Place de La Concorde and up the Champs Élysées, breathing down the neck of third overall Pedro Delgado.

If LeMond needed a carrot, the Spaniard provided it now as he rounded the Rond Point des Champs Élysées and thundered back down to the finish, almost catching Delgado, who had started two minutes in front of him. It was the fastest time – 33 seconds better than time trial specialist, Thierry Marie; 26 minutes 57 seconds for 25.5 kilometres!

LeMond stopped just after the line and was mobbed by reporters. It was going to be close. The TV producers split their cameras between LeMond's face and Fignon, still desperately pedalling as he made his way along the most famous street in Paris. The joyful cheering had now turned to desperation in his ears.

Tracing LeMond's wheel tracks he rounded the Rond Point, where the Roosevelt Metro station mocked him still further. Then the cameras flicked back to LeMond. Time was running out as the seconds ticked away and LeMond's face was a mask of disbelief.

Back to Fignon, trying to urge every gram of strength from his tired, pain-wracked body. Inside 300 metres to go and he still led the Tour de France. Inside 200, he had lost it.

LeMond's face exploded in a huge grin, still almost unsure it had happened, as he punched the air in triumphal delight. But he had won; the clock showed it. Eight seconds. Eight seconds it took Fignon to cross the line, still fighting, still not believing. Eight seconds and Greg LeMond had won his second Tour de France, the one no one ever thought he could.

STAGE 17, 1990: LOURDES–PAU, 150kms.

Luke Evans

Greg LeMond's third Tour victory was by far his most clinical and, as the race unfolded, inevitable. While that may not have made the 1990 Tour the most dramatic when compared to his two previous Tour wins in 1986 and 1989, LeMond's final week experienced one big blip in what until then had been a smooth trajectory on the graph. The hiccup took place on Stage 17 from Lourdes to Pau, and it had smoke temporarily pouring from the air brakes on the American Z Tour juggernaut. In the soaring temperatures that roasted the great convoy as it began trekking north from the Pyrenees on the last leg to Paris it was a timely reminder that the Tour's third week is no time for an afternoon siesta.

Ironic, really, that the rider who came to the seventy-seventh Tour kitted out with Scott's weird drop-in bars, his LeMond TVT carbon-fibre frame, Oakley Mumbos, Giro Air Attack helmet and full-zip rainbow jersey should be temporarily KO'd by a puncture, that irksome little devil that sits on the shoulder of every cyclist from the humble commuter to the highest-paid racer the sport had yet seen.

No amount of money can prevent the finest bicycle in the world from bumping to a halt with a flat, but Z boss Roger Zannier's millions were not wasted on that Wednesday as his blue-liveried team was paid handsomely to react to just this kind of crisis. Leaders in the team classification, they were one of the best Tour outfits in recent memory with men for the mountains like Robert Millar, Ronan Pensec and Atle Kvalsvoll, and bullet-proof all-rounders like Gilbert Duclos-Lassalle and Jerome Simon.

A disaster was avoided and LeMond would go on to win the 1990 Tour in the least flamboyant way possible – with not a stage win to his name and only two days in yellow: the prologue (as defending Champion from the previous year); and the final day, Stage 21 Bretigny-sur-Orge to Paris (182.5 km). That is the story from one perspective – in no way does it do justice to the Minneapolis man's achievement in a multi-layered and fascinating Tour that, in hindsight, heralded the start of a turbulent new decade: an era of astonishing performances and historical firsts with a near-apocalyptic conclusion. Welcome to the Nineties.

There was a very good reason why in the final week of the Tour LeMond was still sporting his white jersey with the multicoloured bands celebrating his world title at Chambery the previous year. That reason was a little-known Italian called Claudio Chiappucci. Broad-smiling, cyclo-cross-riding Chiappucci had been a relatively anonymous member of a four-man break which took more than ten minutes (10 mins: 35 secs to bunch winner Olaf Ludwig) out of the peloton on Stage 1 of the race. With a team trial in the afternoon the first road stage of the 1990 Tour was little more than a three-and-a-half-hour leg-loosener around Futuroscope's flat and featureless prairie in western France. A soft break containing Steve Bauer, Ronan Pensec, Frans Maassen and Chiappucci quite simply, and routinely, disappeared up the road. The finale, however, was not in the script: they never came back. LeMond had a team-mate in there thanks to be-quiffed rocker Pensec, but race favourites Pedro Delgado (Banesto), Laurent Fignon (Castorama) and Gianni Bugno (Château d'Ax) were wrong-footed from the off, and that would play into LeMond's hands later.

A storming ride by his 7-Eleven team-mates on the afternoon of the first stage (sixth place) ensured Canada's Steve Bauer remained in yellow for nine days. In 1988 he had finished fourth overall in the Tour, but the pressure and nerves of a full-on first week in northwest France with lots of bad weather and cross-winds took a heavy toll on the man who had narrowly missed out on victory in Paris–Roubaix earlier in the year. On Stage 10 from Geneva to St Servais, the second day in the foothills of the Alps, Bauer's climbing legs deserted him and Pensec stepped up to the plate for his moment of glory.

LeMond could now play a game that was risky for his own Tour ambitions but mightily torrid for his immediate rivals, one of whom had already packed his bags and returned to Paris.

Fignon's departure – he climbed off his pearlescent Raleigh halfway through the longest stage (301 km. Avranches–Rouen) run off in pouring rain, robbed the 1990 Tour of one of the few champions who could eyeball LeMond. The pony-tailed Parisian had conceded more time after being held up and involved in crashes on the early stages. He was also still suffering from a leg injury sustained in the Giro which saw him pull out of the race he had won overall one year before. As he glumly turned round in the road, his plastic rain mack dripping with rain-water, all hope evaporated that the Castorama man would put the record straight after his humiliating eight-second defeat to LeMond on the final stage of the 1989 Tour de France.

Without Fignon, the French shifted expectations to Pensec in a Tour where the host nation could also cheer for mountains' leader Thierry Claveyrolat and his unpredictable team-mate Charly Mottet (RMO), and a young pro from the south, Gilles Delion (Helvetia), who went on to win the young riders' classification. After an *étape royale* (Stage 11) to Alpe d'Huez, when Pensec conceded only 48 seconds to stage-winner Gianni Bugno (the first Italian to win on the Alpe since Fausto Coppi in 1952) French fans dared to hope that they might have happened upon a surprise Tour winner of their own. It was a stage where LeMond fought hard for the stage win but after his second crash of the race (on Stage 5 he fell off without incident on the wet road to Rouen) which saw him colliding with an old lady in the crowd and dislocating a finger on his left hand, he very nearly crashed again trying to brake on the final corner of the ski-resort finish. The back wheel locked and his bike slewed sideways as LeMond narrowly avoided piling into the barriers. He then had to start a long sprint in a high gear which effectively led out Bugno, that year's Giro winner, who grabbed the chance to take the coveted stage.

Behind LeMond, who was by now racing in a parallel universe to the Stage 1 breakaway crew, Pensec was towed up the Alpe by on-form team-mate Millar and at the top he was 38 seconds ahead of Chiappucci. That night the Italian was pretty much written off as Pensec gained new respect as the outsider who might go all the way. Team Z were firmly in the driving seat but LeMond was a back-seat passenger and possibly beginning to wonder if he would ever take the wheel.

Twenty-four hours later Chiappucci was in yellow after Pensec had unexpectedly cracked in the 33.5-km. time trial from Fontaine to Villard-de-Lans (Stage 12). *La Grande Boucle* had turned again. Pretty soon LeMond would have to accept that from the Stage 1 hiatus a very real and threatening challenge to his third Tour victory had finally emerged with just over a week to go. While the bookies' favourites were having bad days (Erik Breukink), ill health (Delgado) and tactical balls-ups (Bugno and Delgado) the man LeMond insisted on calling 'Cappuccino' would pop up as his most dangerous adversary.

Just like the tiff between Lance Armstrong and Marco Pantani that was to enliven the Tour ten years later, Chiappucci was visibly irritated by LeMond's mangling of his name, deliberate or otherwise, and he was to fight like the pesky devil that was later to become his trademark, and prominent tattoo. LeMond was a veteran of the mind game – his spats with Bernard Hinault and Fignon were vintage stuff. Belittling the Italian champion was not beyond LeMond and, as the countdown to Paris started and the mercury began to rise and bubble the roads of the south, he may well have decided that now was the time for total war.

With the American more than seven minutes down there was still a serious job of work to be done by the Z team and they wasted no time laying into Chiappucci on the stage that followed the time trial. Stage 13 from Villard-de-Lans to St Etienne (149 kms.) was a classic, rolling stage with a fourth- and second-category climb which was run off at an average of 28 m.p.h. and finished half-an-hour ahead of schedule. Fast-moving groups caused havoc from the start and when LeMond and Breukink found themselves in front they threw everything into the break to pull back minutes on Chiappucci and put valuable seconds into a dithering Bugno. A good day's work by the Z men had hauled LeMond to within 2mins 34secs of Chiappucci, with Breukink still threateningly in between at 2mins 2secs.

There was little change as the race headed for the Stage 16 showdown to Luz Ardiden. Mottet won Stage 15 (170 kms. Millau to Revel) which cheered up the French, but Millar dealt a blow to LeMond when he retired with a stomach upset on the same stage. The Scot had ridden like his old self in this Tour and was the only climber who could have protected his American team leader on the *hors-catégorie* mountains of the looming Pyrenees. Chiappucci, meanwhile, lost thirteen seconds to LeMond on the Stage-14 finish at Millau, then clawed back three the following day. But when LeMond emerged from his personal motor-home to face the microphones each day he was now confident, very upbeat, and cited Delgado and Breukink as the only riders who might keep him off the top step in Paris.

LeMond won the Tour on the sixteenth stage from Blagnac to Luz Ardiden (215 kms.). It was the last big mountain stage of the race and, profitting from the strength of Induráin who was in the same break , he cut loose from Chiappucci with eight kilometres to go, leaving the Italian 2mins 19secs adrift to close within five seconds of the Yellow Jersey. There may have been five stages to go but only one was strategically important: the Stage-20 time trial (45.5 kms.) round Lac de Vassiviere where Chiappucci was sure to concede minutes rather than seconds to LeMond. On the stage to Luz Ardiden Chiappucci had ridden like a true Tour hero, attacking on the first climb, the Col d'Aspin, at one point putting two minutes between himself and LeMond before the inevitable chase began. Even when he was caught, after the descent of the Tourmalet, the pugnacious Italian bluffed it out on the front of the leading phalanx of riders on Luz Ardiden. Bravado was not enough by then, and eight kilometres was all LeMond needed to muscle his way ahead, not just of Chiappucci, but also of Delgado and the other big loser on the day, Breukink, who conceded over three minutes in the blazing finale.

Which brings us to Stage 17 of the 77th Tour de France. The race was wrapped up and heading for home with just a twentieth-stage rendezvous against the watch in which the transfer of the yellow jersey from Chiappucci to LeMond was a mere formality. Well, that was what we assumed as the Press cars filed away from the tacky pilgrimage of Lourdes, and sped across the early climbs of the Aubisque and Col de Marie Blanque (78 kms.), before pressing on to the finish after a long, rolling run-in to Pau (150 kms.). Heartily sick of the free Mars bar choc-ices chucked into the window from the race caravan by now, we nevertheless dutifully tucked in to the cool ice-cream as another hot and sultry Pyrenean day cranked into life.

Radio Tour filled the Peugeot with news of an early break of nineteen riders splitting off from the peloton after two kilometres. No danger-men on general classification, just a couple of interesting names for the notebook: 24-year-old Russian Tour débutant, Dimitri Konyshev (Alfa-Lum) and another fan of the long game, that man Bauer again. On the steady climb of the Aubisque and up the 'easy' side of the fearsome Marie Blanque, described by the Spanish writer, Javier García Sánchez, as 'a climb resembling the scored back of a wild boar',* the break gained ten minutes on the watchful bunch.

An attack by Delgado started the serious racing near the top of the Marie Blanque. All the favourites moved clear in a twelve-man group that began the precipitous descent with 72 kilometres to race in a clockwise loop to Pau with just three small climbs in the last 30 kilometres. It was after the summit that LeMond picked up the puncture that, one way or another, guaranteed a great first paragraph for every Press member that night. Normally a rider with a puncture is given a new wheel within seconds of the team car arriving and screeching to a halt as the mechanic is catapulted from his back-seat reverie into a frantic wheel-swop.

This time around, however, nothing could get the Z team's Fiat past the exhausted 'autobus' riders as they zigzagged up the narrow Marie Blanque, and LeMond waited a full agonising minute before finally receiving a wheel. More time was lost when the wheel pulled over and he was forced to make a complete bike change 100 metres later. The next time-check put the isolated American 1min 27secs behind Chiappucci,

---

* Javier García Sánchez, *Indurain: a tempered passion*

who, lest it be forgotten, was still wearing the maillot jaune and so,was not obliged to wait for anyone. According to a motorbike cameraman distanced by LeMond on the descent of the Col it was the fastest, most reckless piece of downhill riding he had ever seen. Team-mates Jerome Simon and Eric Boyer, who had started the descent with LeMond, rejoined the American at the bottom where Gilbert Duclos-Lassalle and Atle Kvalsvoll were waiting, having been instructed by the advance Z team car to pull out of the break.

For 21 kilometres the Z train, with LeMond doing big turns on the front, rode as hard as they had done in the previous sixteen days, rode as if the result of the Tour depended on it. Chiappucci and Delgado drove the bunch along, but on this short stretch of road LeMond and his team proved beyond doubt that as an individual, and as a team they were the strongest in the race. The gap was bridged, in the end, with a crushing display of power-riding that not only marked the end of the road-race battle for the yellow jersey, but also painted LeMond's attackers in an unsporting light. The Z team leader was vocal in his distaste for the tactics of Chiappucci whom he accused of attacking when he knew LeMond was in trouble. More mind-games or was *le patron* genuinely angered?

With 20 kilometres to go the *status quo* was restored to the bunch, but up front young Belgian Johan Bruyneel (Lotto), who would become Lance Armstrong's *éminence grise* as manager of his Tour teams nine years later, attacked on the third-category Côte de Notre Dame de Pietat and left the leading thirteen-man break. Only Konyshev went across and Bruyneel could not hold off the powerful Russian who recorded an historic first Tour stage win for his country.

In the final time trial LeMond, as predicted, crushed Chiappucci and at last got his hands on the lead with one day to go. His advantage going into Paris was a comfortable 2mins 16secs on the Italian and 2mins 29secs on third-overall Breukink. One year after his duel with Fignon LeMond again found himself against an opponent without tri-bars in the final time trial. If Chiappucci had ridden more conservatively on the Luz Ardiden stage and used a low profile with tri-bars in the final trial would the final result have been closer? By the following year the Italian had risen to world number one on the UCI rankings and future successes proved that he was no one-Tour wonder.

Another rider who would surprise the sceptics was a tall, reticent *super-domestique* to Pedro Delgado. Miguel Induráin rode for his Banesto team leader in the 1990 Tour; he won the stage to Luz Ardiden and finished 10th overall at 12mins 47secs. Most, in fact nearly all that time, was lost when he sat up at the bottom of Alpe d'Huez having thrown everything into dragging the lead group to the foot of the climb where Delgado subsequently cracked. He also lost 30 seconds nursing Delgado to the finish at St Etienne. Take those days out and Induráin could quite comfortably have won the 1990 Tour.

In 1991 he took the first of five consecutive victories in one of the most impressive series of performances ever seen. In 1990 he had plenty of opportunity to study the style and tactics of LeMond. On Luz Ardiden the sublimely smooth-pedalling Navarran cruised up behind LeMond as he fought his machine, lunging pigeon-toed and bow-legged in a frenzy of effort as he hammered home his advantage over Chiappucci. Induráin's acceleration 350 metres from the line, which left LeMond floundering, heralded the end of the champions of the Eighties.

Looking back, the 1990 Tour was a fascinating race and a true foretaste of the new era to come. Apart from Konyshev's success for Russia, we also celebrated the first East-German stage win and green jersey thanks to Olaf Ludwig (Panasonic). Future Classics super-champion, Johan Musseeuw (Lotto), popped up as a formidable sprinter with two stage wins, and Phil Anderson (TVM) trialed Shimano's still-new STI Dura Ace levers. On a more portentous note October 1990's edition of *Winning* magazine contained a worrying article by sports-scientist Ed Burke. The headline read: 'EPO: heart stopping performance'.

STAGE 13, 1992: SAINT GERVAIS–SESTRIERES, 254kms.

John Pierce & Adrian Bell

'There are certain days in the cycling season that professional cyclists live in fear of; today we find such a day.' – Phil Liggett

The day in question was Saturday, 18th July, and the route that struck fear into those seasoned professionals would take them 254.5 kilometres from Saint Gervais, in the shadow of Mont Blanc, up through the heart of the High Alps: a second-category and two first-category ascents, the hors-catégorie 2,770-metre Col de l'Iseran before the final, first-category climb to the summit-finish at Sestrières in Italy. The fact that the stage started at 8.45 a.m., some three hours before a normal Tour road-stage, gives some idea as to the severity of the day's racing that the peloton could look forward to.

And what a formidable peloton it was – one of the most richly endowed that had assembled at the start of a Tour de France in years. At its head was Miguel Induráin, winner the previous year and victor in the Giro d'Italia two months earlier; leading the challenge was World Champion Gianni Bugno, runner-up in 1991 and Giro-winner in 1990, who had conspicuously avoided this year's Italian race specifically to prepare for the Tour. Also there was triple Tour-winner Greg LeMond; double Tour-winner Laurent Fignon (who had also won the Giro in 1989); Stephen Roche, winner of the Tour–Giro–World Championship triple in his glory year of 1987; Pedro Delgado, winner of the Tour in 1988; plus two other Giro-winners – Andy Hampsten (1988) and Franco Chioccioli (1991). As if that didn't represent sufficient talent and ambition to stir up the peloton on a stage with so savage a profile, there was always the spirited Claudio Chiappucci.

Variously nicknamed 'the Devil', 'the Bionic Man', 'Locomotive', Chiappucci was simply irrepressible. An excitable and pugnacious rider, he was constantly on the attack over any kind of terrain – a throw-back to an earlier era when the peloton was less easily controlled by strong team tactics and individual attacks more often bore fruit. Chiappucci had burst into real prominence during the 1990 Tour: the major beneficiary of a first-stage breakaway that was allowed to get out of hand, he only finally relinquished the yellow jersey to LeMond at the end of the Stage-21 time trial to finish second overall. The fact that too often he failed to profit from his adventurous, all-or-nothing riding did not prevent others, more averse to wild risk-taking, from putting his aggression to use for their own advantage, most famously Induráin at Val Louron during the previous Tour. On that day Chiappucci claimed the polka-dot jersey, and Induráin the yellow; and they wore them all the way to Paris. Since then Induráin had beaten Chiappucci in the recent Giro and, furthermore, inflicted the indignity of catching and overtaking him in the streets of Milan during the final time trial. So, as the riders prepared to leave St Gervais on the morning of 18th July to begin their high-altitude switchback ride towards Sestrières, the Italian, it might be supposed, had a point to prove.

More than that, in fact, he had a promise to keep. When the route of the 1992 Tour had been announced the previous autumn, revealing that the thirteenth stage would take the race into Italy to finish at Sestrières, Claudio had told his father he would win that stage. He would win it for him, and for the memory of Fausto Coppi, for it was on that very stage to Sestrières that the *campionissimo* had sealed his Tour victory in 1952, riding solo over the last 21 kilometres of the final ascent to finish seven minutes ahead of the second-placed rider. It is a legendary stage win and it had a particular resonance for the Chiappuccis, father and son. Claudio's father, a racing-cyclist in his day, had been a prisoner of war in 1943, in the same North African POW camp in which Coppi, himself, was being held. They had occupied the same bunk-house, slept on the same floor, and shared their memories and their hopes. Chiappucci Senior never tired of telling that story to his young son, and the boy never tired of hearing it. So the dream was born, and the promise made. Was it foolish Italian sentimentality, or an appointment with destiny? Chiappucci didn't have the same engine as Coppi, but he had the same spirit.

On the start-line at St Gervais, the Frenchman Pascal Lino was the leader on general classification, as he had been ever since the end of Stage 3 in Bordeaux. It had been an outstanding achievement, defying every morning's predictions. Here was proof, if ever proof were needed, that wearing the yellow jersey gives you wings. Lino had managed to survive RMO's comparatively weak showing in the team time trial at Libourne and even, on Stage 9, Induráin's individual onslaught in the Luxembourg time trial. This had been a dazzling ride against the clock that would go down as one of his greatest: the Navarran took a full three minutes out of his own Banesto hare, Armand de las Cuevas, and 3mins 45secs out of third-placed Bugno. It was a ride which prompted Charly

Gaul, once the 'Angel of the Mountains', to comment: 'Today I saw an angel fly past.' But Lino had held on: sixth that day at 4mins 6secs, just two seconds slower than Lemond and four seconds quicker than Roche meant he had done enough to retain his jersey by nearly a minute and a half.

Gianni Bugno, having prepared so assiduously for this Tour, was bitterly disappointed. He had anticipated losing time to his Spanish rival in the time trial, but not on this scale. For some, the Tour was now as good as over, but that was to ignore the fact that on a single Alpine climb it is perfectly possible to lose time hand over fist, and on the road to Sestrières there were five such hazards, one after the other.

Five minutes covered the first seven riders as they left St Gervais. Induráin was 1min 27secs down on Lino; Roche was a further half-minute behind; then a gap to Delgado at 4mins 6secs, LeMond at 4mins 27secs; and Bugno, sixth overall, another twelve seconds back. And in seventh place, Chiappucci, already wearing the King of the Mountain's jersey, was poised at 4mins 54secs.

Twenty kilometres into the stage, on the second-category Col de Saises, Chiappucci attacked, suddenly and alone. Even by his standards this seemed a crazy, near-suicidal venture. Richard Virenque (in the same team as race-leader Lino) and Thierry Claveyrolat gave chase and soon joined him; together these three crossed the 1,633-metre summit. The break had been made, but it was in no sense decisive: other riders, their ambition seemingly undaunted by the steadily rising morning temperature and the steeply rising roads, were still able to bridge the gap. So, by the time these three reached the summit of the next climb, the first-category Cormet de Roselend, after 70 kilometres, the leading group, which included Ireland's Sean Kelly, had swollen to ten. Britain's Sean Yates, wearing his National Champion's jersey, was riding well in eleventh place, just one minute in arrears. At the 1,968-metre summit, Chiappucci again took the mountain points from Claveyrolat and Ruiz-Cabestany. Insurance, perhaps? If all else failed that day he would, at least, make his hold on the polka-dot jersey more secure.

On the descent to Bourg St Maurice a crash, which saw Iñaki Gaston taken to hospital with serious facial injuries, disrupted the cohesion of the leading pack. Chiappucci continued to drive the group which now was thinning out on the long climb up through Val d'Isère, so that when, after 120 kilometres, he arrived at the foot of the third mountain of the day, Col d'Iseran, he only had Virenque for company. Ahead lay a further 135 kilometres to the finish at Sestrières and, more immediately, seventeen kilometres of unrelenting climbing to the 2,770-metre top of the mighty, *hors-catégorie* Iseran which had not been included in the Tour itinerary since 1963. On the lower slopes of the col, the irrepressible Chiappucci dropped his French confederate (who in the second half of the '90s would take the KOM title five times). From now to the end of the stage he would have only himself and his dream for company

At the summit, after 137 kilometres, Chiappucci crossed first, 2mins 22secs ahead of the second group which was led by Roberto Conti. Virenque, who had been caught by this advance guard of the peloton was third, followed by Franco Chioccioli, the winner of the pervious years Giro d'Italia, and the magnificent Pascal Lino in his yellow jersey, and still the leader on the road.

The peloton, at 3mins 44secs, was led over the top by Britain's Robert Millar, riding beside Induráin, a length ahead of Bugno. The Italian World Champion had wanted to seize this day to exact some revenge for the damage Induráin had done to him at Luxembourg. He wanted also to be *the* Italian to triumph at Sestrières, all the more so because he had come under fierce criticism at home for his refusal to ride that year's Giro, while Chiappucci had grabbed all the headlines. Now his crazy rival had scuppered all that with his wild, impetuous attack on the very first col – doing a Coppi – and Bugno had spent the day riding alongside the infuriatingly calm, impenetrable Spaniard who seemed unperturbed at the lead Chiappucci was building, mountain after mountain. But if Bugno was suffering psychologically, others were physically. Delgado and Fignon, both Tour-winners, had lost time on the Iseran, and Lemond was trailing at eighteen minutes; he was destined to lose a good deal more than that.

After the descent of the Iseran, Chiappucci's advantage had gone up to over four and a half minutes – he was close to becoming the leader on the road – and, with 80 kilometres of the stage remaining, still the 'big guns' had not yet started firing. Ahead lay the nasty first-category Col du Mont Cenis with its average gradient of 7 percent, and, climbing relentlessly, the muscular little Italian never once faltered. Behind him, the Bugno could stand the tension no longer and began to accelerate: with Induráin on his wheel he reeled in, and disposed of, the yellow jersey group. So, the two favourites for the '92 Tour reached the summit a length apart, still, despite their counter-attack, three and a half minutes after the solitary figure in the polka-dot jersey. If Induráin's ride at Luxembourg had been an omen for the next three Tours, so too, was this calm, controlled, powerful performance in the highest mountains.

Thirty seconds later came the American, Andy Hampsten, the winner of the 1988 Giro d'Italia, and Franco Vona who had won two stages in the recent Giro d'Italia. At 4mins 57secs came Robert Millar, leading Gert-Jan Theunisse, Fignon, Roche and Delgado. Half a minute further back Richard Virenque was now shepherding his team-mate Pascal Lino, but all their combined effort was not going to be enough to keep him in the yellow jersey.

Miguel Induráin was now, effectively, the race leader, but the magnificent Chiappucci, who had gone clear after just 20 kilometres on the first climb of the day was the master of a break that could, conceivably, survive to the end of the stage. Except that, in the Susa valley, Hampsten and Vona joined the two chasers, Induráin and Bugno. As he crossed the border into Italy, with less than 50 kilometres remaining, Chiappucci's lead began to tumble. In Oulx, at the base of the final eleven-kilometre climb, it was down to 1min 45secs on the chasing quartet. His days looked numbered. Bathed in sweat, he became possessed by the mission in hand and now drew on all his reserves.

Behind, in the chasing group of 'favourites', Franco Vona was the most active. Sensitive to the savage criticism in the Italian Press about the timidity of the home riders, and their reluctance to attack Induráin in the Giro, he now pressed repeatedly. Each time, Induráin rode with him, and each time, as the group was prized apart, Hampsten would simply tow Bugno back up. Then, the World Champion simply cracked. Resplendent though he might have been in his rainbow jersey, he simply could not lift his pace sufficiently one more time. Hampsten's similar fate followed immediately afterwards, because Induráin saw his chance to take serious time from the man whom he regarded as his closest challenger.

At last the big man had made his move and he was free, because Vona, a great climber on his day, was also unable to respond to this fantastic attack. He began to close in on Chiappucci like a missile. We were set for an incredible finale but, whatever the outcome, we had witnessed a ride by Chiappucci that people would talk about for years to come, just as they continue to speak about the ride Coppi had made to Sestrières in 1952. Some say better than Coppi, for Chiappucci, out ahead by himself for 130 kilometres had truly ridden in *le grand style*. With just five kilometres to go, they passed through the outskirts of Sestrières, Chiappucci's lead falling rapidly, vulnerable now to the surge from the defending champion.

Then they were enveloped in the crowd, a sea of hysterical *tifosi*, waving, shouting, spilling down from the hillside to the left and completely blocking the road. The leading motorcycles of the *Carabineri* and Tour Commissaires came to a halt. Chiappucci, himself, had to fend off the wobbling motorbikes, and plead with the crowd to let him weave a path though. There have been huge crowds, and sometimes difficulties, on the Alpe d'Huez stage, but this was double anything the Tour had ever seen, for here was an Italian, wearing the King of the Mountains jersey, winning a stage of the French Tour, in Italy. That screaming, back-slapping crowd was a gauntlet all the early riders would have to run. Fignon remembers:

> I asked Jean-François Pescheux, who was on a motor-bike, to open a passage for me, because they were making me frightened. It was the first time I'd seen anything like that. Perhaps it was Chiappucci's exploit that had made them like that.

Anywhere but in Italy Chiappucci might not have made it: he was rocking on the bike; he was too exhausted to ride out of the saddle – 'riding with his knees', as they say. Bobbing relentlessly, he heaved himself into the final 500 metres of the stage and, all of a sudden, the road – lined now with crowd barriers – became very wide, and very empty, which made him all the more vulnerable: he began to falter. He tried again to get out of the saddle but could not support himself. At 150 metres he tried to lift his arms in a victory salute, but his body would not support the effort. Then at 25 metres, in front of his very own fan club, he lifted his head, blew kisses to the huge crowd as his arms came up, and slapped his hands together over his head. As he crossed the line in 7hrs 44mins 51secs, an average of 33 k.p.h., he burst into tears.

Behind him, Induráin was in trouble. It rarely happened in the whole of his illustrious career, but suddenly, inexplicably, he cracked. Perhaps it was the frightening pressure of the crowd, although Induráin always refused to offer that as an explanation; perhaps he had neglected to give himself sufficient food or drink; perhaps the final acceleration to reach Chiappucci's back wheel and close in for the kill had demanded too much, even of him. But whatever the reason, Induráin cracked: one moment it seemed certain he was going to capture the fading Chiappucci; the next, his power had simply evaporated; he was riding on empty. And inside the final kilometre, through the mêlée, Franco Vona passed him to take second place, 1min 34secs after the jubilant Chiappucci. Induráin finished third at 1min 45secs, but he did take the *maillot jaune*, and he did hold it all he way to Paris for the second of his five consecutive victories.

No wonder it was a day the riders had lived in fear of: fourteen abandoned and one finished outside the time control, and others, like LeMond and Luc Leblanc, who both lost 50 minutes, were among the eleven who retired or failed to make the time limit the next day on the road to Alpe d'Huez. It was a day the riders would not forget, either. Jean-François Bernard, who in those years was Induráin's protector on the lower slopes of the cols, recalled that it was the only time Induráin felt too exhausted even to climb the stairs to his room after dinner. For Stephen Roche, who had been prominent among the chasing group as far as summit of the Col du Mont Cenis, the final ascent to Sestrières was a col too far:

> After the stage I didn't want to speak to the Press; normally I'm very talkative, but when your head is empty, and you can barely stand up … I was destroyed.

François Lemarchand remembers it as the hardest stage in all the ten Tours he rode:

> And I'll never forget the look on Duclos-Lassalle's face; he got terribly angry and he was saying to me, 'I haven't seen the 20-kilometre kite; where is it?' And I didn't dare tell him there were still another 70 to go.

Duclos-Lassalle abandoned the following day, on Stage 14.

And Claudio Chiappucci? His aggression did not let up: first lambasting the Gatorade riders, Bugno and Fignon, for their lack of attacking initiative *en route* to Sestrières; then returning to the fray, himself, the following day. But now Induráin was in the yellow jersey, and had publicly acknowledged the battling Italian as his one serious remaining rival. Chiappucci never gave up, attacking whenever the road reared upwards, but he could not escape Induráin's vice-like grip: shoulder to shoulder they rode over the Galibier and on to Alpe d'Huez. Over the next three days, Hampsten, Chioccioli and Roche would each be permitted enough leeway to record a stage win, but not Chiappucci: his opportunity had already come on the road to Sestrières.

And how splendidly he had taken it – a 235-kilometre break on the toughest stage in memory, the last 120 of which he had ridden on his own. 'It was the greatest ride I have ever seen in all my days as a professional, on one of the greatest stages they have ever had in the Tour as well,' so Roche later described Chiappucci's exploit. It was truly a ride to set alongside Coppi's stage win from Bourg d'Oisans to Sestrières, over many of the same roads 40 years earlier. First over all five cols, he had guaranteed his polka-dot jersey and second place on the podium in Paris. He had realised his dream, and honoured his promise to himself and to his father.

STAGE 7, 1996: CHAMBERY–LES ARCS, 200kms.

John Deering

'Come on, it'll be great. A few days in the Alps, in the sun, in July... and a bit of bike-race watching.'

Louise, Pete, Veronica and I were trying to decide on the venue for a joint summer break. We'd already had one good camping trip that year, down on the Gower for a spot of Welsh surfing and mountain-biking, making good use of the funky new tent Louise and I had got as a wedding present the previous September.

Pete was up for France, as he'd been a canoeing instructor down in the Ardèche a few seasons earlier, and had been keen to get back to the stunning scenery ever since. Veronica was happy to get away anywhere; she loved travelling and new places. Louise wanted some mountain-biking and sunshine as our honeymoon in the Lake District had been a rain-lashed affair to sorely test any romantic notion that camping was fun. But I had an ulterior motive...

I was a cycling fan, you see. The sort of fool that risks his job by bunking off work to watch mountain stages of the Giro d'Italia on Eurosport with his equally daft mates and a couple of Stellas, or 'Paul Wellers' in the coded language sometimes needed to fool bosses and spouses. Unfortunately for me, the first bike race I had ever watched with more than a degree of vague curiosity had been the 1989 Tour de France, which turned out to be one of the greatest races in history. Unfortunately? Yes, because I'd been craving that giddy high of emotion and drama so beautifully administered by Greg Lemond, Laurent Fignon and Pedro Delgado to be repeated ever since. Like a hopeless drug addict who still needs to score but can't recapture the rush he used to get in the old days, I would squat in front of the video late at night listening to David Duffield talking about Eccles cakes and Fausto Coppi in the same breath. Squatting in front of the video long after everybody else had gone to bed in the same way as Lou Reed used to tighten an old leather belt round his arm and hold the end with his teeth.

The intervening Tour de France years had seen mighty Miguel Induráin exert the sort of stranglehold that hadn't been seen since Alfred Hitchcock made *Strangers on a Train*.

Big Mig crushed the opposition according to his strengths. And his biggest strength was his strength. To me, he had often been unfairly accused of being boring because he didn't attack enough. It seemed unfair because he found it difficult to attack, possessing no natural 'jump' to distance his opponents. Instead, he ground them into the road with his relentless power and speed. His strategy usually consisted of two Tour-winning ploys: a) kick everybody's arse in the first long time trial; and b) kick everybody's arse again in the first mountain stage. This would invariably be enough to decimate the pre-race list of potential usurpers down to one or two. Whether it be Tony Rominger, Gianni Bugno, Claudio Chiappucci, Alex Zülle, or Marco Pantani, Big Mig could then follow him around France happily for a couple of weeks, knowing that he wouldn't get far away. Such was the ease with which he controlled the race. Jesus, the year before, he hadn't even waited for the first mountain, just the first medium sized hill ... he'd shot up the road to Liège and spread-eagled the field.

So I'd done a bit of homework. The '96 Tour had been laid out in such a way that the peloton would hit the Alps very early, with a massive stage that went over the Col de Madeleine, the Cormet de Roselend before finishing at the ski-station at Les Arcs. The following day there would be a mountain time trial from Bourg St Maurice up past the awe-inspiring Barrage des Tignes to the British skiers' paradise of Val d'Isère. This would surely be the time to see Induráin in his pomp, putting it to them on the way to Les Arcs, and then twisting the knife in the next day's race against the clock.

I got my way.

Some judicious packing got the Mondeo estate on the road. There were four mountain bikes in the boot part, plus two tents, a stove, four sleeping bags and four rucksacks. It was like a tardis, but heavier. I'd never driven in France before, let alone been through the new tunnel, and it was dead, dead exciting. The kilometres galloped past: it's wondrous seeing them click down so much quicker than miles, obvious illusion though it is. Before long we were in Lyon, then winding our way up the Isère Valley below beautiful peaks and deep-green pine forests, and then pitching our tents a couple of clicks downstream of Bourg St Maurice, the little town that sat at the foot of the climb to Les Arcs.

The following day the bikes were carefully reassembled and our happy foursome toddled off along the pretty cycle-track that followed the Isère upstream. We still had a day before the race arrived. The Isère was a white-water canoeist's dream, with most people on our flashy campsite carrying boats rather than bikes, and the stripey poles of their competition gates dangling above the fast-flowing water for much of that stretch. Rounding a crystal-clear mill-pond at the head of our stretch of river, Pete was very excited to see there was a sluice-gate that could control the flow of water over the succeeding rapids.

'Aww man, it must be amazing down here when they have a release,' he gasped. I was beginning to get annoyed that my sport was losing out in the face of all this natural wonder and the mountain sports that go hand in hand with it. I needn't have worried.

We slowly began to coax our bikes up the lower slopes of Les Arcs. It's about sixteen kilometres to the top and not unbelievably tough compared to, say, the Col de Joux Plane, Alpe d'Huez or the Galibier. Or even the Madeleine, which the riders would have to scale first tomorrow morning. But when the closest you've been to an Alpine climb is back-to-back ascents of Box Hill, it feels like something pretty special. There are a few switchbacks near the bottom as the road climbs steadily over a good surface through the pine trees and we each settled into our own quiet rhythm and pace, pausing at the first hairpin to discard the extra layer we'd put on for a distinctly un-Côte d'Azur-like morning. We looked up to the slopes almost directly over our heads and saw a lorry traversing a road a long, long way above us.

'That can't be our road, can it?' asked Louise.

'Nah, don't think so,' I said dismissively.

About two hours later we were puffing along the same bit of tarmac we'd seen the lorry covering, by now at walking pace, weaving along the open tarmac past the Belgian motor-homes that had been parked on the roadside for a week. Fat, middle-aged men wearing sandals but no shirts urged us on cheerily, waving small bottles of Leffe or Jupiler in our general direction, while aromatic smoked meats sizzled on their barbecues and black, yellow, and red flags bearing the disembodied head of Johann Museuuw fluttered from the roofs of their Mobilvettas. Something told me that they hadn't had to employ the same amount of deception to entice their families out to the Alps in July that I had sunk to. These were cycling people.

We were passed constantly by people going faster than us: cycle tourists, keen amateur racers, even the odd young pro. There was a guy I later discovered was a junior with the Mapei development squad who passed us on the way up, then shot back down to the bottom, then passed us *again* before we got to the top. In my mind, by now, Les Arcs was the pinnacle of all cycling. Surely nothing could ever be harder than this. It would be galling to realise in later enlightenment that if the stage-finish had not been seated at the top, it would have served as not much more than an inconvenience for the big boys.

That night the heavens opened. I have never, before or since, witnessed rain like it. We drove to the nearby romantically named town of Aime for a pizza, parking right outside the door, no more than a couple of feet from the warmth inside, yet we were each drenched by the time we were inside.

'Never mind,' said Pete, shortly after discovering that artichokes are apparently *de rigueur* on French pizzas, 'a storm like this, you only get once in a season down here.' Oh. Is that right, Pete?

By the time we had toiled up Les Arcs again the following day, the rain had eased off to the level of merely pissing down. Huge crowds were spread across the hillsides, huddled together under plastic sheeting and bin liners that kindly types had been handing out. There was little respite in the ski resort itself, where few businesses had taken the trouble to get themselves open for what would be the one day in six months that it would be worth their while. We stood for a while shivering in the stairwell of a chalet block, watching the rain fall and people's breath rise in vapour trails into the cool mountain air.

When the rain eased, momentarily, we paced higher up to the finish where a giant videoscreen was relaying events unfolding on the Madeleine. If anything, it looked worse there, with Stéphane Heulot, the latest French overnight sensation, abandoning whilst wearing the yellow jersey. His countrymen up on the mountain with us were distinctly underwhelmed at his lack of what Induráin would probably call *cojones*: they believed that nothing short of a fatal accident should entice a Frenchman into retirement whilst adorned in the fabled golden fleece. A knee or ankle problem was not going to wash with them, no siree, not with any amount of Alpine rain. As Heulot clambered into the Gan team car, tears rolling down his face mingling with the extraordinarily dense mountain rain and the dirt flung up by the back tyres of bicycles moving faster than his, there was a huge 'harrumph' of disapproval. We also learned that our own hope, Chris Boardman, was in trouble.

The rain came down harder again as we headed back down the road to regain our prime position. We were on the inside of a hairpin less than two kilometres from the finish, positioned so we could see them pass us, round the bend, then pass us again just above and behind us. It was perfect, as the barriers that skirt the road nearer the finish began a short distance higher up. You don't want to be standing up there – much less atmosphere. Four years later, I would be leaning on those barriers under the red kite signifying one kilometre remaining to the finish at Hautacam in the Pyrenees, seeing the incredible sight of Lance Armstrong in full flight. The intensity of his gaze, fixed wide-eyed on the road ahead and above would burn itself into my brain. It was the look of a man possessed, an impossible stare to meet.

The caravan spun it's tortuous progress up the Alp, chucking out sweets, badges, samples of instant pasta and money-off vouchers for vacuum cleaners. Veronica in particular was bewildered by the whole concept of the publicity caravan, how something as far removed from cycling as a floor tile could be advertised by writing a brand name across a man's jersey, or how handing a bystander on a mountain a small badge would make him want to change his car insurance provider. She looked on in a mixture of horror and amusement as two grown men fought over what appeared to be something akin to a Murray Mint, thrown casually from the back of a van to the screaming hordes, both of them risking death by rolling and scrabbling across the tarmac to rescue the inconsequential prize from under the wheels of the next tat-purveying vehicle. 'C'est la vie,' she shrugged.

We could see the bottom of the Cormet de Roselend, the last major obstacle before Les Arcs, across the valley beyond Bourg St Maurice. Excitement was building as the three TV helicopters following the race buzzed into view, hovering in the distance above the narrow mountain road. The caravan had all but passed, topped off with a stunning performance from a Nike armoured-car piloted by the spitting image of Yaphet Moto, that tough looking, black American actor, pumping out hip-hop at a rate of decibels likely to bring on epileptic fits among children and the infirm.

Now the road began to bring us Press cars, eager to get their places at the temporary *Salle de la Presse* up in the gymnasium at the finish, cars containing dignitaries, cars containing sponsors. Every now and then, a car with a tannoy would pass slowly, belting out race details. We struggled with the 100-mile-an-hour French sufficiently to learn that Udo Bolts was leading down the Roselend, and the Magoo-like figure of Alex Zülle had fallen off twice.

By the time the race had reached the town below us, unbelievably, the sun had begun to shine. It felt intensely hot, as though the rain had cleaned the air of any filter it had for our protection. Steam rose off the trees like bonfire smoke as the cold rain evaporated at a bizarre rate of knots. By now everybody was on their feet, throwing off the plastic shelters they'd built for themselves, roaring encouragement and clapping their hands for riders still way down the mountain.

I thought the noise was already loud, but then we heard a roar coming up below us like a wave, and we realised the first man must be close to us. As they had done all day, the *gendarmes'* motorbikes sped past in ever increasing numbers, now with a real intensity about their work as they by turns cajoled, instructed and ordered the public to keep the road clear. Still, we leaned out, took an extra step across the road, craned our necks to see who it would be as the noise grew to a deafening crescendo.

'Perhaps Boardman's got back on,' I yelled optimistically in Louise's ear. But there was no doubt that this crowd was going mad for a Frenchman. It was their own that they were yelling for. And then, suddenly, rocketing into sight powering a gear that I would have used to ride *down* the slope, was Luc Leblanc. He had just passed the Swiss star, Laurent Dufaux, now labouring slightly in his wake. We spun on our heels to watch Leblanc corner behind us and shoot up the climb, carried on a huge wave of sound to his most famous victory since becoming champion of the world in Sicily two years earlier.

Now what? Surely Induráin would be the next face we would see; that characteristic grin/grimace hovering just over the handlebars, hands on the drops, spitting men off his wheel like throwing fag ends from the car window on the motorway. It was made for him to take yellow, especially with the jersey having already been so spectacularly ceded hours before the finish by Heulot.

More *gendarmes*, more cameras, more motos, then the roar again. This time it was for the élite group, the group that Leblanc had attacked and broken away from lower down. They absolutely flew past us and into the corner, Rominger with his Mapei team-mate Olano alongside him in the World-Champion's jersey, Batman Bjarne Riis and his boy wonder Jan Ullrich, the Russian Evgeni Berzin – the Giro winer in 1994 – they were all there, all the big names. Or were they?

'I don't remember seeing Induráin,' I shouted to Pete.

'They… they… they just go so fast,' was his flummoxed reply.

'He must have been there; probably just on the far side of someone so I didn't see him,' I reasoned.

Riders were coming up in ones, twos and threes, those dropped from the front on this, the final climb, team climbers who had accompanied their leaders all day, riding in to a high finish. Here, for instance, were two of them now, an Once guy and a Banesto rider. Hang on.

'It's Induráin! *Induráin! Miguel Bloody Induráin!*' I was yelling manically. 'He's been dropped! And Zülle, too!'

The invincible Induráin rode past, head down, broken. Had it ever been seen before? Not in the Tour de France, certainly not. His face was different; broken almost. He spat as he rode by, the grin/grimace gone, a look of emptiness across his distinctive Navarran features that we had never seen on the telly over all those years.

As they rounded the hairpin, Zülle, his jersey and shorts torn from his earlier escapades began to do an incredible thing. He pulled away from Induráin. Like the others must have done out of our sight, he rode away from him. He dropped Induráin.

Miguel Induráin lost the Tour de France right there in front of our eyes in scenes that were unimaginable to any fan that had followed cycling for those past five years of his bruising domination. He rode on all the way to Paris, prompting first anxious talk of comeback attacks and tactics, then, secondly, as he fell further behind Bjarne Riis, compassion and admiration for the way he continued to conduct himself with a bewitching mixture of pride and humility: refusing to give up, even though he knew he was beaten.

A nation mourned. Spain was in pain. In his inspiring book, *Induráin: A Tempered Passion*, Javier García Sánchez says, 'The end of the world came on Les Arcs.'

He goes on to tell of receiving one of the many gifts bestowed on journalists by local municipalities during the course of the Tour – a polo shirt bearing the name of the place: Les Arcs.

> Never in my life will I be able to put on that shirt, I admit that much. On the other hand, I have been unable to give it away, or throw it away. Who knows if one day I will be able to break the spell, forget my weaknesses or fanaticism, exorcise my own ghosts, and put it on if only as some kind of macabre fetish. But not today. Nor have I been able to watch the film of the ascent of Les Arcs, even though someone video-recorded it for me.

x   x   x   x   x

I met Miguel Induráin on the Tour some years later, introduced by a mutual friend. Big Mig was in the Pyrenees as a fan, watching the race with his wife and kids. We chatted for a couple of relaxed and friendly minutes, about his car, about his home, about the race. But all the time, I wanted to say: 'I was there. I was there that day on Les Arcs, Miguel. I was standing right there by the road when you were dropped. I saw you fold up in front of me, but it just made you bigger in my eyes. You became human.'

PROLOGUE, 1999: LE PUY DU FOU, 6.8kms.*

John Wilcockson

A couple of months after I moved to the United States in 1987, Greg LeMond was shot in a hunting accident. The accident, which put shotgun pellets in his back, shoulder and arms, would have been lethal if a California Highway Patrol helicopter hadn't been in the remote area where he'd been hunting wild turkey. He was taken to the trauma unit of a Sacramento hospital where he was operated on to staunch the loss of blood. 'I almost died,' the 1986 Tour de France winner revealed two weeks later, in a one-on-one interview at his spacious home in Rancho Murietta, California. Pale and thin, and wearing pyjamas and dressing-gown, LeMond was a ghost-like figure who had lost all semblance of an athlete's muscle tone and vibrant colour.

Two years later, at the Giro d'Italia, in another interview, LeMond was starting to wonder whether he'd ever recover his former health, strength and resilience. We talked on the staircase of a ski-area hotel in the Dolomites. He said he was on the verge of quitting cycling for ever after finishing with the also rans on the last couple of mountain stages, instead of with the leaders. He was languishing near the foot of the Giro's overall classification, but he said he was determined to fight back.

Six weeks later, on a sunny afternoon on the Champs Élysées, I was jumping up and down with another American racing star, Andy Hampsten, as yellow-jersey-holder Laurent Fignon gasped his way to the end of the Tour's final time trial – eight seconds too slow to prevent LeMond from winning a second Tour de France. What a turn-around! What an athlete!

Ten years later, those memories came streaming back to me. It was the evening of 3rd July, 1999, the opening day of another Tour. This time, another American was performing an athletic miracle, a young man who, too, had almost died. Not from gunshot wounds, but from a virulent cancer. Lance Armstrong.

---

* The editors spent a long time deliberating on whether or not to include this chapter from the 2003 edition. See the Introduction (page x)

There was another similarity between the two Americans. Both won the World Championship early in their careers, LeMond in 1983 at age 22, Armstrong a decade later at age 21. LeMond rode his first Tour wearing the rainbow jersey, coming in third; the following year, he was second to team-mate Bernard Hinault; then he beat Hinault to score his first win in 1986. In contrast, Armstrong didn't seem to be a potential Tour winner, despite winning a stage on his 1993 début. As planned by his then Motorola team, he pulled out of that Tour at half distance; and did the same in 1994.

When I asked him in May 1995 whether he could ever win the Tour, Armstrong equivocated: 'I don't know if I can, but I'd like to contend at some point.' Then, in obvious reference to LeMond's accomplishments, he added, 'I've seen what the Tour has done for American cycling. In fact, the Tour is cycling in America. My goal [this year] is to finish the race, and get a Tour de France under my belt. I look at it as an investment for the future.'

Armstrong, still only 23, did finish that Tour, in 36th, and took a brilliant solo stage win. To take that victory, he called on strength that few riders have shown in the third week of a grand tour; he said it was the strength given to him by his Italian team-mate Fabio Casartelli, who died in an horrific crash a few days earlier, and whose memory the Texan wanted to honour.

A year later, Armstrong was expected to ride a more comprehensive Tour, perhaps take a top-ten placing. He had yet to show climbing ability in the high mountains, but his victories at the top of steep climbs in America's Tour DuPont and Belgium's Flèche Wallonne were indications of future prowess in the Alps and the Pyrenees. He also was working on his time trialing. Over the winter of 1994-95, he did aerodynamic and power testing with U.S. Cycling Federation coach Chris Carmichael (who later became his personal coach), and he then had a Lotus time trial bike made to his dimensions. Using this, he placed third at the Tour DuPont prologue, just beating his arch-rival Viatcheslav Ekimov of Russia. He then used his regular low-profile machine to win the DuPont's mountainous time trial in the Roanoke Valley, breaking Ekimov's course record.

Armstrong repeated his DuPont victory in 1996, but at the Tour – two months later – sick and out of form, he abandoned the race on a day of torrential rain and cold, before the Tour even reached the Alps. He said he couldn't breathe. Reflecting on that day during an interview two months after the Tour, Armstrong said, 'There was nothing I could do. I was physically ill. And I couldn't continue.' The explanation came three days after that interview when he was diagnosed with testicular cancer that had spread to his abdomen, lungs and (discovered later) his brain. The world now knows how Armstrong and his doctors beat the cancer, but it was an experience more gruelling and traumatic than anything he'd experienced in cycling. In one of several interviews after his return to the sport, I asked him if he'd ever thought about riding again when – similar to LeMond a decade earlier – he was lying in a hospital bed, weakened by the very aggressive chemotherapy he'd elected to undergo. 'I didn't think about racing,' he replied, 'but with the chemo, the anti-nausea drugs, it's so hard to think. I had a difficult time reading ... watching tv ... listening, speaking ... No, I never thought about it. I was just a little scared ... a lot scared at times ... and I just wanted to get better.'

Armstrong then remembered, during his periods at home in Texas between the chemotherapy sessions, how hard it was even to ride a bike, let alone think about training. He spoke about one particular ride with his friend and fellow Austin resident, Kevin Livingston: 'I had to get off and lie in a yard I was so ...' He didn't finish the sentence, but intimated that it was more than simple fatigue. 'After 30 minutes [riding], I was just wasted ... completely exhausted ... almost like deadish. I shouldn't have been there. They were scared. Kevin was ready to get a car. But ... I rode home, just needed a little rest.'

Within a year of that incident, and restored to full health, he was racing again. In his first year back, 1998, Armstrong ended his season with fourth place at the Vuelta a España, and fourth at the World Championships in both the road-race and time trial. It was after that series of performances that Armstrong and his new directeur sportif at the US Postal Service team, *Johan Bruyneel*, agreed to tackle the 1999 Tour de France as a potential contender.

Looking ahead to the Tour in late 1998, Armstrong said, 'It's a whole new challenge ... I mean, the Tour de France, whew. I'll give it a shot. I don't want to make any predictions overall, but I'd like to win a stage again and factor in the overall. Top five or ten, I don't know.'

He worked hard that winter, and following coach Carmichael's counsel, focused on developing his power and climbing ability. In May, there were long training rides in the Alps, Pyrenees and the Massif Central, scouting out the Tour's mountain stages. And every month, he did a time trial test up the Col de la Madone, near his then European home, in Nice. Armstrong revealed that in his final test up the twelve-kilometre Madone climb, immediately before the Tour, he broke the unofficial hill record, riding it in 30mins 47secs, compared with the 31mins 30secs of former

Giro and Vuelta winner Tony Rominger. What's more, Armstrong's power output for that half-hour effort was 490 watts – right up there with Miguel Induráin. What no one knew, yet, was whether the American could translate that power into victory at the Tour.

As it happened, the 1999 Tour began with a prologue time trial on a 6.8-kilometre circuit at Le Puy du Fou where Induráin had set a course record to kick off his win at the 1993 Tour. The Spaniard, with two Tour victories under his belt, was the super favourite that year, whereas the 1999 Tour was wide open. The openness was emphasised by the wide diversity of predictions on the eventual outcome. For instance, the respected French sports daily newspaper *L'Équipe* did not include a five-star favourite, as it usually does, but instead offered two four-star candidates: Armstrong and Abraham Olano. Another French daily, *France-Soir*, had two completely different top tips: Michael Boogerd and Pavel Tonkov. And a third French paper, *Aujourd'hui*, named Armstrong and Tonkov as the best bets. And what about the inscrutable English bookmaker Ladbroke? Its odds given the day before the prologue were: 2:1 Bobby Julich; 3:1 Olano; 4:1 Boogerd; 5:1 Tonkov; 6:1 Armstrong.

Julich had finished third overall the previous year behind Marco Pantani and Jan Ullrich – neither of whom was starting this Tour. But it was the other American, Armstrong, whom those with inside knowledge were tipping to win. We already knew his pedigree, and he had shown champion qualities in the meticulous way he readied himself for the prologue on that humid July day in the Vendée region of west France. He had ridden the course several times the previous day, learning the best lines to take through the several tight turns, and the gear ratios he needed on the constant changes in gradient. This was not a straightforward, city-street prologue like the ones taken by specialist Chris Boardman in three of the previous five years. This one was entirely on country roads, most of which had been resurfaced since Induráin won in 1993 – the year which marked Armstrong's début at the Tour de France. The course's main feature was a half-mile-long, 187-foot climb called the Côte de Fossé, which averages 7 per-cent (1 in14), with a short section of 14 per-cent (1 in 7) gradient immediately after turning on to the hill.

What few people knew was that Armstrong started the prologue in pain from a scary crash he'd had 24 hours earlier. It happened as he was riding a fast practice lap of the prologue course, with US Postal Service team-mate George Hincapie just behind him. Armstrong wanted to be at full speed when he reached the course's critical climb, right after a downhill, right turn. Before the turn there was a line of cars on the riders' right, but Armstrong saw that the hill itself was clear and so he was riding hard, when one vehicle – the Telekom No. 3 team car, driven by Belgian Frans Van Looy – pulled out from the line just at the moment Armstrong looked down to check his gearing.

'I was probably doing 55 k an hour,' he recalled. 'George was behind me, and he shouted, "Lance!" As soon as I looked up, it was too late. When I saw him [Van Looy] I had about half a second when he was turning into me. I thought, "This is unbelievable." I just smacked the side of the car, and went flying over the handlebars. I caught his mirror on my right ribs. It looked really bad. But because I had speed, when I hit the ground, I just slid. I really had no road rash, no cuts. I had discolouration; I had a little bruise on my ribs.'

Armstrong handled the emotional fall-out of the crash just as maturely as he was facing the physical and mental challenges that lay ahead. To get the best view of the prologue preparations of Armstrong and Julich, I walked back and forth between their respective warm-up areas at the Postal and Cofidis team vehicles. With Armstrong's start time less than an hour away, he began warming up, riding his race bike on a wind-trainer. At times, three Postal riders would be on the wind-trainers, which were set up beneath a canopy strung between the team's two rented camper-vans.

After his fast-pedalling warm-up, Armstrong went back into one of the vans to dry off. Then, in a long-sleeved skinsuit, he returned to the wind-trainer about fifteen minutes before his 7.07 p.m. start. He looked nervous, slowly turning the pedals, chatting to team boss Mark Gorski, adjusting his rear brake cable, and then listening to Hincapie's comments on his ride. By now, the evening sun had broken through the all-day cloud cover. Armstrong then donned his aero helmet, climbed aboard his time trial machine, and bumped his way across the grass toward the start area.

At the same time, about 30 metres from where Armstrong had been warming up, Julich – the final starter, two minutes after Armstrong – was making his final preparations. Unlike the Texan, Julich chose to do his fast, wind-trainer warm-up at the end. He was wearing just a sleeveless T-shirt and rolled down bib shorts, and was sweating profusely until he dismounted, drank a gel-pack and some water, and went to dry off in his Cofidis team van exactly fifteen minutes before starting. Then, after his mechanic had removed, cleaned and refitted the wheels on his race bike – carrying it across the grass to the start – Julich pedalled his road bike the short distance to the road.

Once there, like stalking cats, he and Armstrong slowly pedalled their titanium race machines around a small barricaded-off section, awaiting their start call. Julich was straight-mouthed, his eyes expressionless, as he focused internally on the enormous task ahead. Armstrong's face was more lined, reflecting the huge pressure that had been on him for months, to be totally prepared for this moment. But he looked confident, and gave a split-second wink of recognition as I gave him a thumbs-up. Armstrong then climbed the steps of the start house, just as Crédit Agricole's Boardman sprinted away down the ramp. Armstrong was next … followed by world Time trial Champion Olano of once–Deutsche Bank … and then Julich.

As Armstrong set off, the controversial Richard Virenque – given a last-minute reprieve to ride the Tour by the Union Cycliste Internationale despite his part in the previous year's Festina team drug scandal – was about to finish his prologue ride. There were boos among the cheers coming from the tens of thousands behind the course's continuous line of metal barriers, with the Frenchman finishing with a very ordinary time of 8mins 53secs.

The fastest time was still the 8mins 20secs set almost three hours earlier by eighth starter Rik Verbrugghe – one of Belgium's promising young bloods. But a couple of riders behind Virenque came one of his former team-mates, Christophe Moreau, still with Festina after a six-month drug-related suspension, who blazed home in a time of 8mins 17secs.

Another caught up in the Festina affair, Alex Zülle, seemed to have the prologue sewn up when he arrived four minutes later, storming up the slight rise to the finish, to record an 8mins 9secs – three seconds faster than Induráin's course record. Zülle's ride looked all the more impressive when Boardman arrived next, with a time one second slower than Moreau's.

Meanwhile, Olano and Armstrong were waging a fierce battle out on the course. The Spaniard – looking immaculate in his white, rainbow-striped World Champion's jersey, and fresh from 400 kilometres of solo training in the Pyrenees – hurtled through the first 3.7kilometres at more than 56 kilometres per hour (35 mph). His intermediate time of 3mins 56secs was five seconds faster than the previous best, just set by Boardman, and eight seconds faster than Zülle.

This opening section was mainly downhill, including a couple of long curves, with a tight right turn through a roundabout on to a short hill, before levelling off and reaching the sharp right turn at the start of the Fossé climb. Armstrong reached the checkpoint second best, just three seconds slower than Olano, and ready to launch himself over the very difficult 3.1-kilometre finale.

This is where Armstrong experienced his only moments of doubt in an otherwise faultless, 50.788-k.p.h ride. 'At the last minute,' he said, 'I changed to the small ring [44], but I couldn't get it back to the big ring when the grade softened.' His crash at this point on the course the previous day probably contributed to his indecision.

To help him decide on that big ring-versus-small ring dilemma, Armstrong had quizzed each of his team-mates after they completed their rides; and he even did a lap in the team car, wanting to see how the course looked at true racing speeds, by following team-mate Tyler Hamilton 90 minutes before his own start. Hamilton used the small chainring on the climb for his 18th-place, 8mins 29secs ride. That was the same time obtained by Jonathan Vaughters, who never shifted from his big-ring, a 54. George Hincapie also rode the hill in the big-ring, to take 15th place in 8mins 28secs, while Tour rookie Christian Vande Velde, 14th in 8mins 27secs, shifted into his 44x19 for the climb. With such conflicting evidence, it was probably inevitable that Armstrong would make that last-minute decision change.

'My team-mates agreed that the race would be won on the last half of the hill to the finish,' Armstrong said later. By the top of that climb, angling across a grassy hillside, the American had taken command, three seconds faster than Zülle, with Olano in third, another three seconds back. Armstrong kept up the pressure on the next, mostly downhill two kilometres, smoothly negotiating three fast curves, before neatly rounding a slow-speed U-turn 400 metres from the line. By the finish, he had added four more seconds to his winning margin on Zülle, and another five seconds on Olano.

Behind, Julich was not having such a good time. He said, later, 'In order to hit the prologue right on, you have to be not only really fresh, but also very prepared ... to find the rhythm. I felt like I had the form, but not the rhythm.' As a result, from reaching the first check-point in eighth only six seconds slower than Armstrong, the Cofidis leader lost another eighteen seconds on the hill, and ended up in 22nd place, 28 seconds behind Armstrong.

For eight years we had waited for Greg LeMond to be joined by a second American in wearing the yellow jersey at the Tour de France. That wait came to an end late on that sunny July evening, when a smiling, resplendent Armstrong stepped on to the podium after winning the Puy de Fou prologue. It was an emotional moment for the 27-year-old Texan, and for all those American cycling fans who saw their hero slip on the hallowed golden garment. Friends and team-mates fought back tears, and thought back through the past two years and nine months since Armstrong was diagnosed with testicular cancer – and then fought back to health so bravely. Armstrong, also shedding tears, had become a shining beacon to the cancer community, and in his once-again powerful hands he not only held the key to winning the 1999 Tour de France, but the very future of the Tour de France. When, right after his prologue victory, he was asked about his feelings at the end of cycling's blackest year, Armstrong said, 'Remarks are made assuming we're all doped. That's bullshit. I'm here, and I hope the other 179 riders are here, to see cycling reassert itself and to reassure people that we are champions.'

Since his last appearance at the Tour, Armstrong had shed almost twenty pounds, due to the debilitating chemotherapy treatment he received in 1996 and '97, and also to his subsequent change in routine and a healthier lifestyle. His lighter weight had helped him become a different type of cyclist. As he said in Le Puy du Fou, 'I think I'm a better rider than I was before … certainly I'm a better person.'

Winning the prologue, of course, didn't ensure final victory in Paris, but given Armstrong's winning mind-set, his newly acquired climbing skills in the high mountains and his US Postal Service team's all-around excellence, the task ahead looked more than possible.

STAGE 7, 2001: STRASBOURG–COLMAR, 163kms.

Marguerite Lazell

Just in case the patriotic French public weren't sufficiently stirred at the sight of the Tour rolling by, Bastille Day – by happy coincidence – falls during the first half of the race. Pressure on the home riders shoots up an order of magnitude, as do the plaudits that rain upon the Frenchman who can capture the revolutionary spirit and reclaim a stage of his nation's race from the foreign riders who have dominated the event in recent years.

On 14th July, 2001 it was Laurent Jalabert who hoped to seize the hero's status, to take the stage to Colmar and confirm that his win three days earlier was no fluke. For an athlete who had spent most of the spring barely able to ride, let alone race competitively, it would be a sweet, sweet victory. At the end of the 2000 season Jalabert left the comfort of ONCE, in whose colours he had ridden since 1991, and took younger brother Nicholas to Bjarne Riis' CSC–Tiscali, with grand designs on the Tour of Flanders. He knew that to ensure the squad's selection for the Tour in July – ahead of Saeco, Mercatone Uno and the French-sponsored teams still looking for a place – they would need a solid set of early season results. He was the cornerstone of Riis' plans until a freakish domestic accident left the team with a seemingly impossible challenge. Jalabert fell from a step-ladder, breaking two vertebrae and plunging the team's Tour hopes to all but irretrievable depths. How could they garner sufficient UCI points to merit a wild-card Tour entry with their star player laid up in February without a race to his name?

Fortunately, the reality of Jalabert's recovery was not as slow as had been feared at the original prognosis. He made a tentative return to racing in April at the Flèche Wallone, a one-day semi-Classic organised by the Societé du Tour de France. It was a little sooner than he had planned, but with Tour director, Jean Marie Leblanc, riding in the lead commissaire's car, the race was an ideal opportunity to chalk up points in CSC's favour.

Jalabert's tenacious return to racing fitness, along with the inevitable kudos of having a former winner as a team manager, carried them into the Tour – no doubt helped by a timely sponsorship deal that saw CSC add its logo to the publicity caravan as well as the riders' jerseys. With a stage win secured in the opening week of the race, Jalabert had made good his promise to honour his place on the Tour start-sheet.

On the morning of 14th July, he was 3mins 19secs down on race leader Stuart O'Grady, and he knew that if he found himself in a break, he had a chance of taking the *maillot jaune* as well as the stage victory. The previous day's team trial had jammed the top of the general classification with riders from ONCE, US Postal, Telekom and Kelme, plus O'Grady's Crédit Agricole mob, who were in the enviable position of holding first and second spot. While CA would be monitoring every move made, they were unlikely to play the aggressor. It left Festina as the only French team in contention for the yellow jersey, but with their Christophe Moreau an outside threat to the final overall they could ill afford to send a minion ahead on the off chance of a Bastille Day win. There were no such long-term plans to constrain Jalabert – he was confident that the *parcours* suited him, and that the general classification contenders would sit tight on such a *moyenne montagne* stage. So, when a move went within a couple of kilometres of the steepest climb of the day – the Col de Fouchy – he made sure he was in the thick of it.

Fourteen men made the initial selection, and with Paolo Bettini (Mapei), Andreas Kloden (Telekom), Ivan Basso (Fasso Bortolo) and Jens Voigt (Crédit Agricole) amongst their number it was nothing so base as a publicity stunt. Voigt was acting as policeman for his team-mate O'Grady, but with only a 26-second deficit he had the added incentive of being virtual race leader within moments of the break going clear. His priority was to keep the jersey within the Crédit Agricole team camp – either for O'Grady or for himself – and, for today at least, a stage win itself was of less consequence.

Race organiser, Jean Marie Leblanc, had made a point of shortening Tour stages since 1998, in an effort to discourage doping within the peloton. The 162.5-kilometre run from Strasbourg to Colmar was a case in point, an exemplar of a sharp, technical, challenging stage that would generate plenty of excitement without decimating the riders' strength at a relatively early phase of the race. There was no danger of losing out to the time-cut, but anyone with designs on a good overall finish would have to be vigilant over the second-, and third-category climbs that punctuated the route profile. A simple enough sounding premise, but some riders were in trouble within 50 kilometres of leaving Strasbourg. While Jalabert was busying himself at the front end of the race, Britain's sole representative in the race, David Millar, was limping along in amongst the team cars. The young rider who had taken the yellow jersey in the previous year's Tour was discovering just what it meant to suffer in the biggest race on the planet. Having trailed in off the back of the main bunch almost every day since crashing in the prologue, Millar had tried to make a pre-emptive strike, attacking early on in the stage with Laurent Brochard (Jean Delatour) and Sergui Ivanov (Fassa Bortolo). After just thirteen kilometres of riding nose to the handlebars Millar and co. were hauled in; the lantern rouge was soon back where it belonged, illuminating the tail-end of the bunch.

Using the final intermediate sprint as a springboard, Ivan Basso jumped away from the leading bunch, stretching it out as the peloton behind tried in vain to retrieve them. Likewise Laurent Roux (Jean Delatour) – who had followed him across the line to take the minor points – used his sprinting momentum to open up the gap. Third-placed Inigo Cuesta (Cofidis) lost the wheel but was immediately up and chasing, as were Jalabert and Voigt. While the main bunch sat up, the pursuing trio were more tenacious. For several kilometres the deficit hovered at between ten and fifteen seconds – the kind of distance that is stingily far on the flat, but which translates to a much more manageable length of tarmac on a climb.

Once Basso and Roux started up the 9.7-kilometre Col d'Adelspach it was inevitable that they would be joined by their chasers. The five came together close to the summit and, showing for the first time in the race that he may have had designs on the climber's jersey, Jalabert shot passed the others to claim a maximum twenty points. The others may not have been interested in the polka-dot jersey *per se*, but the order over the summit – Jalabert was followed by Cuesta, Voigt, Roux and Basso – was the first indication of where the weaknesses in the group lay. It was these barely noticeable cracks that would split wide open in the final kilometres of the stage.

Jalabert was feeling good, and was not afraid to let his opponents know about it. He wasn't going to waste his time with showy little attacks from the group, but he was certainly doing his share of the work at the front. When it came to the climb he used his sprinting ability to speed past the others and snaffle the points without any undue waste of energy. Behind the quintet of leading riders, a straggle of dropped breakaways and would-be gap-crossers were isolated in between the front of the race and the head of the peloton. Unai Etxebarria (Euskatel), Steve Vermaut (Lotto), current mountains' leader Patrice Halgand (Jean Delatour), Christophe Agnulotto (Ag2r) and Vincente Garcia Acosta (iBanesto) floated in limbo for 20 kilometres before being picked off one by one by the peloton. Five riders were enough to satiate the Telekom and US Postal-driven bunch; it had no appetite for the men left out in front, and left them to fight it out for stage honours amongst themselves.

Almost three minutes behind Jens Voigt on general classification, Jalabert had only a minute chance of taking the yellow jersey. It was not a major objective for the Frenchman, but the threat of his presence was looming large in Voigt's peripheral vision. The German had come achingly close to glory in the Tour on several previous occasions, only to be brought back from the brink of victory in the final few hundred metres before the line. A deficit of five minutes could be negated by the peloton if it was so inclined, but Voigt knew that Jalabert presented a greater immediate hazard. In between the archetypal scrawny climbers and the muscular sprinters lie a disparity of physiques, and, of the two men, Jalabert was far better suited to the territory they were battling over. Voigt is a towering 1.92 metres tall and weighs in at almost 80 kilograms, and although he had proven his climbing ability with a spell in the polka-dot jersey in the 1998 Tour, he was visibly struggling to match the sinewy Frenchman over the nagging rises and short, steep climbs. But Jalabert needed Voigt. He needed someone to share the work with, and the German, always ready to drive himself into the tarmac, provided an ideal companion on the long road into Colmar. Of the five men in the lead group, Laurent Roux seemed to pose the most danger to Jalabert. Inconvenienced by a puncture, he was soon back and circling the break, watching Voigt slip from the back as they neared the top of the penultimate climb. Fortunately for the CA rider, the stage route brushed up close to the Franco–German border at the very time he needed support.

After more than eighteen kilometres of ascent Jalabert was first across the summit of the Col du Calvaire and still had the strength to salute the local fans as they applauded his effort. Voigt silently drew on the cheers of their neighbours to cling to the leading group. As the fivesome threaded its way down the descent from the Calvaire, the Telekom riders at the front of the bunch allowed incumbent King of the Mountains, Patrice Halgand (Jean Delatour) to take the six points on offer for sixth place on the climb – it was enough to keep him in the jersey for the next few kilometres at least. O'Grady was comfortable in yellow, tidily placed in the bunch with his stooge far, far up the road and the team's honour all but secure.

With just one third-category climb remaining, the latent reward of a stage win for one of the breakaways, and a yellow jersey for either Voigt or Jalabert was steadily transforming into something more tangible.

The Frenchman felt his way amongst the group, quietly assessing the value of each of his companions. He had to utilise their strength for his own benefit, without affording them the chance to attack and take 'his' stage win. The summit of the Collet du Linge was the final obstacle, and he decided to tackle it on his own. For a brief, beautiful moment the crowds watched in awe as their hero sprung from the front of the group, promising a glorious runaway victory. A reality check put things back in perspective – the prospect of half-an-hour alone in the drizzle, fighting to keep a baying group of chasers off his wheel was not a pleasant one.

Jalabert scurried back to the others, pleased at least that none of them had been confident enough to counter his move. He changed tack, taking a replacement bidon from the CSC–Tiscali team-car and doing his utmost to work with Roux, Voigt, Basso and Cuesto to make sure everything was in place for his new plan. Voigt was suffering under the cumulative strain of the previous four climbs and, in reality, his best efforts were only enough to hold on to the group; there was little left to contribute to its determined push to the top of the final col. But once he was latched on to them he was not going to let go – the yellow jersey was far too close. Across the summit of the Linge and his relief was palpable – only a crazy, downhill attack from Jalabert or a crash could keep him from taking the overall lead now.

The Frenchman had again claimed maximum points in the mountains classification – not quite enough for him to take the jersey from Halgand, but confirmation that he was serious in his bid for the polka dots. None of the other riders had contested the three last climbs of the stage. Either they were unconcerned with the King of the Mountain competition or, more likely, they were focused on the stage win, and wanted neither to waste their energy nor to expose their reserves for their rivals to see. So Jaja went unchallenged as he gathered the points – a harvest to be stored for later on in the Tour, while the realisation of a Bastille Day stage win would be the stuff of immediate feasting. Somewhat inappropriately for 14th July, he was hoping to have his cake and eat it.

A concerted effort by the US Postal and Telekom domestiques brought the bunch over the climb just under five minutes after the leaders. The rain began to fall more heavily and with it the inclination for any last-ditch bridging efforts from the peloton. There was no longer a threat to the breakaway's success, just a marshalling manoeuvre to keep the general classification within the bounds of the acceptable. In the final kilometres of a rolling stage like this one, when all the right preliminary moves have selected a strong, able combination of men to rise above the bunch, it is often an error that robs one of their number of his shot at victory. On this occasion it was Ivan Basso who lost his chance. He slipped turning a corner with just over ten kilometres to go, and although he was quickly righted and back on his bike and chasing, the impetus of a wet, muddied individual was never going to compete with the momentum of a quartet with its sights on the line, even though there was time enough to spare for them to sit up and wait for him.

For Jalabert, Basso's misfortune merely eliminated one of the dangers. He attacked again, and this time it worked. The remaining three danger-men were exhausted: Roux and Cuesta, who had worked so hard for the best part of the last 100 kilometres had simply run out of steam. All they could do was to hang on to Voigt's wheel, and he had only to finish within 2mins 53secs of Jalabert and the jersey was his; there was simply no one willing or able to bring the Frenchman back. As the final kilometres ticked away, Jalabert showed no signs of tiring. His lead was a slender, impenetrable barrier protecting him from the others. The certainty that he would reach the line alone spurred him on and, equally, deterred his competitors from countering. There was to be no dramatic twist to the finish of this stage, but Jalabert was taking nothing for granted. He continually checked over his shoulder lest a rejuvenated rider had launched a final attack. It was only in the last kilometre, when the lead cars had been diverted from the course and there was clear road all the way to the finish-line that he allowed the joy of deftly taken victory to wash over him.

His stage win a week earlier had elicited an urgent, air-punching celebration; this time he measured his response, opening his arms wide to the adoring crowd, welcoming the applause and offering his own tribute to the most important of French festivals. As an encore, Voigt won the sprint for second, and duly took the yellow jersey. Poetically, three of the four leaders' jerseys rested on German shoulders at the post-race press conference that night – points for Telekom's Erik Zabel, and best young rider's *maillot blanc* for ONCE's Jorg Jacksche. Jalabert had not quite toppled Patrice Halgand as King of the Mountains, but the foundations of his eventual triumph in the climbers' competition were laid on the road to Colmar.

To heap further poignancy onto an emotionally charged victory, it was the second time that 'Jaja' had come back from a career threatening accident to win a Bastille Day stage. In the 1994 Tour stage to Armentières, he and Wilfrid Nelissen were both seriously injured when an unthinking *gendarme* stepped out in front of the race to take a photo for a spectator.

The fans are separated from the race for good reason; the uniformed officers are briefed to ensure the safety of the riders and the crowds, and credited with the intelligence – or at least the sense of self preservation – to stay out of trouble themselves.

Unfortunately for Jalabert and Nelissen, when this particular *gendarme* took the lens he was transformed from level-headed law-keeper to snap-happy Tour fan. As he watched through the lens the peloton wound up for a sprint finish, spilling across the width of the road as all 150 riders fought to get near the front. Jalabert and Nelissen picked the wrong side of the road. Trapped between the barriers and the bunch, they collided head-on with the would-be photographer and crashed at 45 m.p.h. The damage was manifold: Jalabert suffered serious facial injuries and broken teeth, and had to have his jaw wired so it could heal in place. His bike was left in pieces, and his nerve for the sprint was irreparably broken. Nelissen was also hospitalised with multiple wounds to his head and one knee. As several other riders were left lying concussed on the tarmac Djamolidin Abduzhaparov – himself a veteran of a Tour finish-line crash three years previously – picked his way through the wreckage and sprinted to victory.

Twelve months later Jalabert buried his demons, winning the 14th July stage to Mende after a 200-kilometre-long break that left the normally serene Miguel Induráin on the verge of outright panic. The headline chosen to top the first Jalabert comeback story was so apt that the subeditors can almost be forgiven for reeling it out again in 2001: 'Jalabert storms the Bastille.'

FINAL STAGE, 2002: MELUN–PARIS, 144kms

David Harmon

It is remarkable how quickly the human ear can become attuned to the chorus of hums and whirrs that make up the fanfare of the arriving peloton. For nearly ten years I have clamped my hands to my head in an effort to protect my hearing from club-racers, then Le Mans racers and, finally, the banshee wail of the Formula 1 grid, but this dragonfly buzz of sound and colour feels like coming home. The time I had spent reporting and commentating on motor sports was, like so many people's careers, more accident than design. As a young sports reporter in London, still pedalling to and from work, and fresh from bike-racing, I had expressed an interest in four wheels as well as two. That passing remark sealed my fate for the next decade.

Here, in Paris, in 2002, I can hear the riders approaching on their first pass down the Champs-Élysées long before I can see them. To my left, commentators from across the globe begin standing up from their seats, craning their heads through the tiny windows of the commentary box to get the first view that satellites will instantly relay around the world. This hot, bright July day is hosting the final stage of what, to me, has always been the world's greatest single sporting event – the Tour de France. A circus of heroes and workers, back-room boys, sponsors' entourages, public relations, logistics, radio and television caravans that move around France like an army for three weeks. That now includes me, sandwiched on a flimsy, folding chair between Eurosport's legendary commentating duo of David Duffield and Sean Kelly. Short of riding alongside Armstrong, Beloki or Virenque you don't come much closer to the very heart of the Tour de France than in the commentary box. The Tour has wheeled its way into the twenty-first century as a big-business sport; its technology and following would have been unrecognisable to the riders of 100 years ago, but still it has retained its humanity, and the 2002 edition was as much a reflection of that as ever.

Three days earlier I had caught a flight to Geneva and, on arrival, a taxi for the trip across the border into France where I was to join David and Sean after the end of the stage into Cluses.

At the hotel being used by Eurosport, ahead of time, I retired to the bar with a beer, and waited. Journalists and TV crews arrived in a constant stream, calling to each other through the lobby, tying up the loose ends of another hot day shooting in the mountains. This is a world I know about and I pass my time wondering about the logistics of filming such a huge event when David Duffield's voice, instantly recognisable, cut through the chatter with the same verve and panache that has made him one of the great English-speaking sports commentators.

Duffield is tall, rangy, with kinked silver hair, and an open and generous face that meets you with a smile. We have never met, but the instant I offer my hand he takes it and exclaims, 'Welcome to the team!' Seldom have I encountered a person from whom such charming warmth exudes; it's easy to see why, as a commentator, his manner has won him an international following. I explain that, despite assurances from Eurosport, I have no room and there are none to be had in town such is the demand the Tour puts on hotel accommodation. David assures me that his room has a spare bed, and it is mine for the asking; it seems that I am, indeed, part of the team.

Back at the bar with David we are already deep in conversation about the remarkable comeback of the day's stage-winner, Dario Frigo, from a torrid and scandalised previous season when the unmistakable figure of Sean Kelly interrupts our flow. A multiple Classics-winner and four-times winner of the green jersey in the Tour's points competition, he still looks much as he did when he stepped off a bike in the mid nineties. Only a hint of greying at the temples gives the hint that his glittering professional career began in the 1970s, alongside the great Freddy Maertens. Kelly is as welcoming as Duffield. After years of marching up and down the paddocks and pitlanes of the motor-racing world, the presence of another legendary sportsman should have little effect on me, but motor-racing has been an adult career, while Kelly is a man of my teenage dreams. I feel a sudden panic about talking cycling lest I put my cleated foot so far down my mouth that I do untold damage to my fledging career in the world of pro-cycling.

Soon it's a blur, a whirl of names and faces and handshakes: Richard Virenque, the French heart-throb and climbing star of the 1990s; Santiago Botero, the Columbian all-rounder, looked upon earlier as a major threat to Armstrong's chances in the Tour, but now sadly out of the running; pony-tailed former World Champion, Laurent Brochard; and Axel Merckx, a man I have long admired for his determination to be himself and not live in the shadow of his father. I am introduced to each passing rider by

Kelly in a stream of languages, all laced with his trademark Irish accent that makes Flemish, especially, sound even more incomprehensible than it does naturally to the English speaker.

The talk continued to be about Frigo's two-second victory over talented Belgian Mario Aerts. Both are riders of great class but there are comments of general approval and admiration for the Italian who seems to have finally put his troubles behind him. Frigo was on the comeback trail after a six-month suspension since admitting possession of a banned substance during the previous year's Giro d'Italia and was riding for a new team, having lost his place at Fassa Bortolo. It was a popular victory for the blond man known on the continent as 'the refrigerator'.

x   x   x   x   x

Today, in Paris, the pack is making its fourth pass by the commentary position. Three riders are bidding to break away from the rest of the peloton in the hope of stealing victory in this showcase stage in front of tens of thousands of fans who have converged on the Champs-Élysées. The escapees have worked well and hold a twenty-second gap and continue to drive hard.

Breaks on the final day of the Tour are generally tolerated by the peloton. The entry *en masse* of the riders who have survived the exhausting hell of flat stages and the torture of the mountains is quite naturally celebratory, and there is no desire to chase down maverick men at the front. This relaxed atmosphere is, too, a mark of respect to those riders who have secured their place on the podium as one of the top three on overall classification, or for victory in the King of the Mountains or points competition.

It has become an iconic victory image of the *maillot jaune* posing for the cameras during the final morning's gentle run into Paris, spinning the pedals easily and sipping champagne. His picture will appear in the following day's newspapers around the globe. In 2002, as in the previous three years, the man holding the glass and smiling was the Texan, Lance Armstrong. Despite the best efforts of second-placed Joseba Beloki, and of his ONCE team, the gap between the two riders was over seven minutes. The little Spaniard who had done so much to improve his weakest areas so as to take the fight to Armstrong had again been forced to admit to himself, and to the world, that he simply could not take on the American.

The final podium step would be occupied by Raimondas Rumsas, the quiet Lithuanian, who would finish a minute behind Beloki. Rumsas, riding for the Italian Lampre squad, was a tough rider whose excellent time trialing abilities had kept him in touch with the leaders, and who had revealed himself as a good climber, to boot. Never launching an attack throughout the entire race, he had played a canny, watching game and had let the big names fight it out for the *maillot jaune*, sitting instead on the important wheels and content to follow. His strategy had worked and his trip to the podium was now assured as a gap of nearly five minutes separated him from fourth-placed Santiago Botero of the Spanish Kelme team.

Amongst the pundits there had been much talk of Lampre's new star: it was agreed by all that he was looking good. Stronger as the race progressed, he stood out from those around him in his quite distinctive blue and pink team clothing, and his shock of blond hair set off by his lean and well-tanned frame. So unexpected had been the rise of Rumsas as a contender that you could hear journalists asking each other just how did you pronounce his name correctly, or scrabbling to fill in the gaps in their knowledge about a man about to make history and step on to the podium in Paris.

This triumvirate, acknowledged by the peloton as the three strongest riders in the race, now entered the French capital, sheltered by their teams from any possibility of a crash. The general air of celebration surrounding the final stage of the 2002 Tour was further enhanced by it being widely known that it would be the final Tour-stage in the career of the great Laurent Jalabert.

'Ja Ja' had once been looked upon by the French public as a man to win the Tour, but he never was able to add a Tour victory to his glittering collection of laurels. Despite this, there was a love and respect for this down-to-earth, modest rider which was palpable among the thousands of fans lining the streets to cheer home the peloton. All the more so because Jalabert was finishing his career in the grand Tours in style: for the second year running he had secured the Mountains prize. Throughout the morning our commentary monitors had shown a steady stream of riders pulling alongside Jalabert to wish him well and shake his hand. The Frenchman, for his part, was as relaxed and smiling as we had ever seen him, on a bike repainted white with red spots to match his polka-dot jersey.

My mind slipped back to an encounter earlier in the morning, before the riders had entered Paris. Stepping out into the cooler air behind the commentary boxes, I was offered a cigarette by a large man with a lived-in hand. When I declined he shrugged, and lit his own. It was only then that I recognised him: the careworn expression on his face was a look I had seen many times before because Jean-François Bernard had also been championed as the great French Tour hope as the careers of Hinault and Fignon came to an end. Unlike Jalabert, however, this talented but highly strung man had suffered from the weight of expectation placed upon him, and the responsibilities of team leadership. The public, as quick to turn on a rider as they are to support him, had abandoned him. Now, we were both here – he with French television, and I with Eurosport – in a small moment of calm, both of us just slightly overweight TV commentators.

Whilst some cycling heroes, when their career is over, return to a very mundane existence, some cycling fans manage to become part of the carnival, itself. Ozzie was one of those. He had revealed himself to me on my second night on the Tour.

The day had been long and hot, and a cool beer was a welcome end to the day's work. The stage, a flat 176-kilometre stretch from Cluses to Bourg-en-Bresse, had been won by Norwegian strong-man Thor Hushovd who had rushed for the line in a three-up sprint with Frenchman Christophe Mengin and the unlucky Dane, Jakob Piil. The Danish CSC–Tiscali rider had watched his two fellow escapees like a hawk as they entered the final 500 metres and, in typical attacking style, had been the first to go hard for the finish-line. Then, on the very brink of the best win of his career, his desperate, lunging, failing legs pulled his shoe cleat from the pedal and, fighting to avoid crashing to the ground, he could only watch as Hushovd stole the win. The disconsolate Piil finished third, hammering his fists on his handlebars in frustration.

In the bar at the hotel I could sit alone and reflect on how I had coped with my first full day in the commentary booth, listening to Kelly and Duffield, and learning the skills with which they juggle split timings, gaps, poor conditions, questions, guests. And all this done with humour and panache. Suddenly, a wiry man in a Phonak team jersey came into the bar and walked straight up to me to ask if Richard had arrived yet. He was referring to Richard Virenque, the French climber, and when I informed him that I hadn't seen him arrive an expression of disappointment and slight annoyance spread over his face. He introduced himself as 'Ozzie', and said he had arranged to meet Virenque at the hotel to get a jersey signed for a charity. His tone of authority on matters relating to the whereabouts of the stars should have set me thinking: he certainly didn't look like a member of the Press or one of the teams. His weather-beaten face was topped with rough greying hair and sported a grizzled beard.

What really should have told me that this man was one of that rare breed of penniless, super devotees of the Tour was the gaping hole in one of his cycling shoes. His bike, too, as I later discovered, had seen much service following the sport round Europe and was made up of parts constantly replaced by sympathetic team-mechanics.

Having got his information from me he walked away, but within minutes his Antipodean tones could be heard from the reception desk in a crescendo of protest. Evidently the hotel had no record of Ozzie booking in for the night, and things were getting difficult. Inspired by David's generosity the previous night, but not listening to my better judgement, I offered the bewailing Ozzie the use of the spare bed in my room. The girl behind the desk asked me whom I was booked with, and I had replied, 'Eurosport'. Immediately the cat was out of the bag: Ozzie saw at once that I was the man who could glide him into the television compound, and move him even closer to the heart of a Tour de France that you already believed he was part of.

It was an interesting evening, and an even more interesting night in the constant company of this Australian who claimed that he got up at 5 a.m. every morning to cycle the stage-route in advance of peloton. But next morning he did not rise at 5 a.m.; instead, he joined me at the breakfast table where he ate enough for three people, all the time addressing a cheery 'Good morning' to riders, as if he had known them for ever. I made my excuses after breakfast and slipped into the television compound, and to freedom and safety.

Some two hours later English commentator, Phil Liggett, working for the US Outdoor Life Network came up to Sean Kelly, who was sitting next to me, clutching a familiar jersey covered in signatures. 'Just sign it, please Sean,' he pleaded. 'I've been Ozzied.'

x   x   x   x   x

Here, now, on this final stage, the escapees have gained 40 seconds over the cruising pack, but they have been reduced to two in number: one rider from Lampre, and one from FDJeux. Behind them the only action expected is the final sprint for the finish-line on the very last run down the Champs-Élysées, for it is this that will determine the outcome of the one unresolved issue in the 2002 Tour – the points competition. A head-to-head sprint between Erik Zabel of Germany who has won the green jersey six times, and the brash Australian, Robbie McEwen, will decide the outcome, and the focus of both Zabel's Telekom team and the Lotto outfit of McEwen is on controlling the pace of the peloton to set up their respective sprinters for this last, all important clash.

The gap to the remaining two men away off the front is now 42 seconds, but something is happening behind them. Beloki has moved up to the front and is looking anxiously around for help from his team-mates, but the ONCE team seems to be in disarray.

Suddenly we understand it: the Lampre rider away off the front is Raimondas Rumsas. He has not worn a helmet throughout the Tour, but now, hiding his trademark blond hair under a Lampre team helmet whose odd design turns the peak backwards to cover the neck, he has successfully concealed his identity and slipped the field. Panic spreads like fire through the ONCE squad: just eighteen seconds now separate Rumsas from Beloki, and if he makes up that difference, all their three weeks of toil will count for nothing.

But this is against the gentlemen's rules. The Lithuanian clearly intended to launch his attack when he knew all eyes would be elsewhere. Now, his legs whirling, he will have to hang out and increase his lead with seven circuits remaining, up and down the cobbles of the Champs-Élysées.

Six to go and still there is no co-ordination behind Rumsas: ONCE are moving in a strung-out mess towards the front to drag the peloton back to the breakaway. Lotto and Telekom, too, are casting glances about them. Neither team wants to miss the chance of a victory for McEwen or Zabel, but this is too early to wind up the chase. Every second of hesitancy plays into the hands of Rumsas.

With five laps to go the gap is steady at 30 seconds – enough to preserve second place for Beloki, but the ONCE riders are still nervous: this Lithuanian with little respect for the unwritten laws is obviously not a man to be taken lightly. With three to go the pace is so high that a lone rider has no chance of staying away from the now co-ordinated, speeding pack, but still he ploughs on. Finally, he is swept up by Lotto and Telekom.

The final run-in to the line is textbook, at least for Lotto, as McEwen takes the stage and the green jersey at the expense of Zabel who misses his clipping point on the final corner, and is forced to settle for seventh on the day and second in the points competition. It is a bitter blow for a man who has spent so long at the top, but already there is talk about the failing legs that come with age.

On the podium Armstrong and Beloki receive the applause. Rumsas, however, just looks tired: his attempt to improve his own destiny is over for this year. Yet, even as we all drank beer and reflected on the race in the early evening, the police had arrested his wife at the French border, her car boot loaded with banned substances. Rumsas, himself, had never tested positive for anything throughout the Tour, but his wife's detention served to extend the life of the 2002 Tour well into 2003 as she languished alone in a French jail. Her husband refused to return to France to visit her lest he be arrested too.

In the end, the Tour de France is the most extraordinary event I have ever been involved in – the human need to win borne out by the uncompromising behaviour of Rumsas; the human cost of not being able to do so reflected in the eyes of Jean-François Bernard. As a sporting event it is fuelled and buoyed up by the passion of millions who line the streets, and it infects all those who ever come into contact with it, myself included, with a sublime madness for cycle-racing. As one era slips into another, riders and teams come and go, and the world moves on about it.

STAGE 18, 2011: PINEROLO–COL du GALIBIER, 200.5kms.

Carlton Kirby

The morning of 21 July 2011 was a perfect day for cycling. Everything was in place. France had its annual Tour hero, Tommy Voeckler, still in yellow, the sun was shining, the light breeze was keeping temperatures in the valleys reasonable, and the 98th Tour de France was about to head into it's Queen stage. Everyone agreed stage 18 was potentially a day for heroics. Today, with three days of racing to go, we would find our champion. We knew who the protagonists were likely to be. Nobody knew the storyline. So it was that viewers in their millions settled down to be shown a tale of woe, drama, elation, endeavour, heartbreak and joy. Pure cycling magic.

Everybody had a view on what the result might be; just how we'd get there was about to be revealed. Time then to pick your favourite and begin shouting at the television screen. I had picked my hero some time earlier; 1998 to be precise. It was on a long loop out of Draguignan during the VTT (Mountain- bike) Tour de France that I had been blown away by the antics of a young Australian called Cadel Evans. He was impish, fragile, prickly, focussed, needy, tetchy, shy and of course he was magnificent. Here was the antithesis of the classic sporting hero. There were bigger, more magnetic personalities everywhere. Cadel is no magnet. He will repel attention and journalists' questions apparently at will. This, however, is not wilful. Cadel Evans has ultimate focus. He knows what he needs to do and he pours all his mental and physical attention to the task in hand, no matter how small. As a result, you almost wake Cadel up every time you talk to him and he buys time with his opening answers. It can be infuriating on live television.

'How was today?'

'Good, yeah'.

'What went wrong out there?'

'Oh you know, cycling is hard'.

Answers accompanied by the now familiar, apologetic, lop-sided smile and caught-in-the-headlights stare. Only when his full focus turns to the interviewer does the wall begin to come down and we get a glimpse into the man. The best question I ever asked him was simply: 'Tell me the story of your day.' He calmly re-booted and then told us everything. I like Cadel Evans a lot.

So what about the story of stage 18? What a magnificent tour chapter it turned out to be.

Seven riders with a real chance of winning the Tour de France battling over three enormous climbs, including the Galibier, the highest finish line in the history of the Tour at an altitude of 2,645m. We'd ridden higher, and would do in the early part of the day, but this finish line was special. This was the Tour to celebrate 100 years since the Alps were first used, and today was the pinnacle of this Alpine celebration. Back in 1911 Emile Georget had been the first man over the top. Today we would not be going down the other side. It was our destination, but not before two other huge tests: the Col d'Izoard at 2,360m was the penultimate peak. A mighty test on any other day but in this company simply an appetizer to the main course. The trial started early with the ascent of the Col Agnel. Mountains that form borders in the high Alps are usually dramatic enough to keep warring nations apart. So it was we crossed from Italy back into France on the vicious ramp of the opener.

The Agnel is a climb of 23.7 kilometres taking us to a remarkable 2,744m – that's over 9000 feet above sea level. This was the ceiling height of the 2011 tour. Aircraft operate well at this level and altitude sickness commonly kicks in at 8,000 feet. A dizzy start then.

On stage 18 the focus of the French public and press was on Tommy Voeckler. Despite overcooking it on a tricky decent the previous day, where he misjudged a corner and ended up in someone's barbecue area, the Europcar star remained in yellow ahead of Evans. Press speculation centred on the Schleck brothers and Ivan Basso, who had all done well to keep up on the same tricky downhill of stage 17, and, of course, on Alberto Contador. The defending champion was riding under appeal after testing positive for minute traces of Clenbuterol. He was still in the title hunt along with Samuel Sánchez and Damiano Cunego. So, seven riders and all with very realistic, but varying, chances of being crowned Tour Champion. For me I was watching and waiting for Cadel to affirm his Tour winning chance.

Evans started the day second, 1–18 behind Voeckler, but despite his credentials he was largely being ignored. Evans, let's not forget, had become World Champion in 2009. However, this was regarded by many as his crowning glory. He had taken that World title to general surprise after a lone attack in Mendrisio with five kilometres to go. Although not regarded as a fluke, there were qualified congratulations throughout the world, save for in Australia. Both I and colleague David Duffield, another Evans fan, were cock-a-hoop.

Cadel had always been an outsider. Success for a character like him can be a bitter pill for those around him to take. Bigger personalities with more bravado push to the fore and get credit where it is sometimes not due. It almost felt like every time Cadel came out on top some would think he hadn't really won it, but had somehow stolen it. How did he do that? He was even being talked about as the modern day Raymond Poulidor. Destined to be a bridesmaid. Poulidor had finished the Tour de France second on three occasions. Cadel likewise twice.

I reminded people that Cadel Evans is not a rocket, he smoulders; but from embers bush-fires start. Two years after the World's and with a chance of winning cycling's ultimate crown it was time to light it up again.

Crossing from Italy back into France, it was a quick start. The teams of the leaders, keen to have riders up front, had largely succeeded. Sixteen men finally made the break stick and were joined by three others as we hit the long ramp of the Agnel. The leading group were just over eight minutes clear with 108 kilometres to go. Hosting the chase at the front of the peloton were team Europcar of race leader Voeckler, the man most likely to suffer on a day such as this. Tommy is not a high-category climbing specialist, but the yellow jersey does things to a man. It engenders its own power. Some say that simple sunny colour on ones back is good for an extra ten per-cent. Well that percentage would be accounted for on some of the day's slopes. Hopes for the Frenchman were accompanied by prayers.

We headed into the first climb with nineteen riders out front. With that early break the pressure had eased a little. BMC, Leopard/Trek and Euskaltel had all managed to get two riders each in the lead group. Europcar and the yellow jersey for now seemingly content to sit on the chasers and save themselves for later. That was all about to change.

The calm was broken on the opening climb of the Col Agnel. With 98 kilometres to go there were waves of attacks off the front of the peloton. Notable efforts came from André Grivko and Philippe Gilbert, the opening stage winner who tried to bridge to the escapees along with Carlos Barredo. Di Gregorio, a very good climber, also gave it a go along with Levi Leipheimer. This forced a reaction from the peloton. Fear began to spread that should these guys make it, there would be too many good riders up the road, and the big favourites couldn't allow this. Big gaps are possible on days such as this and those at the top table in any sport do not like giving away slices of cake to anyone. Up went the pace to close down the upstarts. The GC stars turned it on and dreams crumbled.

Every change of pace in cycling has its casualties. On any one day riding too slow can for some be just as bad as riding too fast for others. It's part of the magic of the sport. Today's climbs took a mighty toll when the speed increased. As the favourites' teams upped the pace the quick men fell away. Hushovd and Cavendish now slowed dramatically with seven kilometres remaining to the top of only the first climb of the day. This opening test was torture for sprinters with over half of its distance covered, coupled with an incline of 10%. This was looking ominous. We fully expected massive gaps to appear in the overall standings, and here already those chasms were opening up.

So the bunch stretched out. A sinuous snake of the world's finest athletes in a struggle-chain. Pain for everyone, some pleasure for a few who were coping the best. Those few were destined to become a very select bunch today.

With 95 kilometres to go the gap was tumbling on the hopefuls up the road. Down to 5–20 and the hurt was on everybody. No one looked comfortable. Some days there is a game of false calm where pain is shrouded from those around you. Today was not like that. It was more than a game of bravado; this was about showing off. Nobody was hiding their pain, you couldn't, so we were treated to some contorted faces and manic acknowledgement of it as a badge of honour. It appeared almost, well, joyous: 'Yes pain, but I can take it. Agony? Pah! Man up, pedals down!'

In any box of fireworks there are small rockets. They promise a lot but offer only a short burst of entertainment that ultimately fizzles out with no explosive display. So it was that Arroyo, Lieu Westra and Di Gregorio went for it again … and just to keep an eye on them a potentially bigger banger, Basso, joined them for the tease.

It was a crazy, but great, opening climb of the day. Towards the back of the main peloton we found Contador. Whatever your opinion of the man, he is not burdened with a lack of self-belief. His head remains clear in extremis and he is therefore able to deliver on the most complicated of daily strategic plans. So just as we had asked questions about his visit to the medical centre in the morning where he complained of knee pain, we were now wondering if this was a little bit of bluffing or for real. He was certainly sitting back. We then wondered if a bike change may be in the offing. Too early for such a move at this point perhaps, but it's a strategy he had used before to good effect. A new bike with different gearing to cope with the punishing elements of the day? Just as with his integrity on this Tour, there were more questions than answers at this point.

As Contador lagged close to his team car, up front Voeckler was busy helping out. This was amazing. Voeckler was expected to hand over yellow on this day. His team had resigned themselves to what the Army call a 'one way mission' – fight to the death. The death of this fine run in yellow was, by all accounts, certain for the Frenchman. Nonetheless, here he was, whipping his team into shape while encouraging and cajoling himself as ever in a manic game of facial badminton. Each new expression hanging for a moment before another stroke would send his visage back into an alternative choice from the bad-clown lexicon of faces. Baf, agony, baf, joy, baf, quizzical, baf, baboon kissy-lips... the list was endless. Possessed of great talent or just plain possessed?

First man over the top with 93.2 kilometres to go was Maxim Iglinsky, followed by Hoogerland and Devenyns. Brave they were, but also spurred on by climb bonuses that had been added to the day to give the crowds a racing spectacle on each of the tests. Iglinsky took a few thousand Euros for his trouble. Worth a push then, despite the fact that this break was doomed.

As they all crested the mountain we had the usual fumble-fest as gillets went on. It was cold with little moisture in the air at the top. Not-for-reading newspapers were grabbed with gusto. Up went the chill factor taking some of the heat from overworked legs. Snow was visible in the area clinging in the hollows trying to bridge to winter. The chase group with Basso were now just 40 seconds clear of the main bunch. Bridgable for good descenders, but opportunities to gain ground were not that plentiful. Any catching up would have to be done on the two remaining climbs.

Wide open U-shaped valleys were the playground. Technical hairpins with long interludes opening into sweeping fast bends. With such glorious scenery and positions held for a few minutes the temptation as a commentator was also to take a break and simply shout: 'Weeeeee.' But we didn't.

So over the summit and back on French soil, some of which was tasted by Tony Martin who took a tumble trying to get back on. He remounted and continued chasing.

At the foot of the Angel there was precious little respite. A little kick at Château Ville Vieille levelled to provide the feed zone before we almost immediately hit the ascent of the Col d'Izoard. The pace slowed a little as heavy, filled musettes were taken with great care ensuring sustenance for the battles ahead.

The intermediate group were all but caught as the push up the Izoard began – 10% at its worst in the middle of the 14.1 kilometres, and hitting this percentage again after a brief downhill close to the top. *Hors Categorie* again with a total average of 7% and speculation starting about how many would fail to make the day's cut-off. The organisers were already thinking of percentages and of allowing all late comers to ride on to Paris.

Of those trying to stay off the front of the peloton, Philippe Gilbert and Jelle Vanendert were the most determined and, as if to show some verve and to remind everyone who was the boss, at the start of the day at least, Thomas Voeckler joined the remaining intermediates. But it was a margin counted on fingers.

With 71 kilometres to go the gap to the real escapees was five minutes. More than manageable. Speculation that Contador might go on this early climb instead of the last proved groundless, as he continued to chug towards the rear of the main group.

Out front the breakaway was falling apart. Both BMC boys, Brent Bookwalter and Marcus Burghardt, had fallen back towards the yellow jersey group which was itself thinning down. But Leopard/Treks' Bert Postuma pushed on with a view to thinning out the hopefuls while remaining on hand to help either of the Schleck brothers should they need him.

There are three 'zones of black' on the Izoard, proper testy areas where the going gets really tough. The first comes just over two kilometres in, and Frank Schleck was not enjoying himself. He got unnecessarily annoyed with a motorbike camera man and the world saw his mood. 'Cameras are part of the game, Frank,' we commented as if he could hear. We then wondered if he was in trouble or just playing with us as well as the other teams who get to see the live pictures in their supporting cars.

If Frank wasn't happy neither was Voeckler. He ripped out his earpiece as a gesture of defiance to those barking instructions to him. Sometimes encouragement is the last thing a man needs when he knows exactly what he has to do and, more importantly, what he is able to do. Direct links to the team are not always of benefit.

Other news filtered in from Australia. The nation expected glory even if the French press were focussed elsewhere. There were moves to declare a national holiday should Cadel win the Tour. Probably a good idea considering both the time difference and the level of celebrations the Aussies are capable of, following such sporting success.

But even in Australia they keep cycling on a shelf compared to the attention given to other sports. Cadel lived in a small town called Barwon Heads in Victoria. After he finished runner up in the Tour de France for the first time in 2007 there was a vote in his home town for the Sports Personality of the Year. Cadel came third, behind a swimmer and an Aussie rules player. It seemed things were changing Down Under.

With 62 kilometres to go there were some telling signs of team strategy. The further up the road you go on a day such as this your strategic options start to evaporate. There would be one game in town for most riders and that would be survival. As the end game approached teams began to show their hands. Voeckler was now being protected within the head of the peloton. He was lucky. At the back, the sprinters and other non-climbers were fighting to get into some sort of 'bus', hoping to come home together and make their group too big to be eliminated from the event. The trouble was that this was a difficult thing to organise. Such groups of stragglers usually form along the valley roads. Stage 18 had hardly any; it was mostly up or down. Down and potentially out were many big names. There was no thought of keeping something back for Alpe d'Huez the following day. It was all about getting in under the declared time limit.

Time then for someone to drop a bomb in the peloton. Leopard/ Treks' German star and team stalwart, Jens Voigt, increased the pace to thin out the yellow jersey pack. It worked. It also snuffed out any possibility of Alberto Contador springing something early here. He would have just one more chance on stage 19. Contador didn't, or couldn't respond.

Was the Voigt move a game opener? Oh yes. Just as we reached one of the very steepest slopes in a black zone a virtual starting pistol had been raised. BANG! Andy Schleck attacked. It was a magnificent piece of work. Frank remained on the shoulder of Voeckler. The reaction of the big names? They just kept their rhythm.

So, with 60.4 kilometres to go Andy Schleck began his mission to catch his two teammates up front. This was the start of a dramatic finale to this Queen stage.

It seemed to take everyone by surprise. They took time to gather their thoughts. Surely he had gone too early? *Directeur Sportifs* blurted garbled instructions into earpieces. Collectively the pace began to rise. This was no chase-down, but it was now becoming a very select group.

Contador's response was to pick his pace up. He went onto the wheel of Daniel Navarro. Evans remained solid. Voeckler still shoulder to shoulder with Frank Schleck. Samuel Sánchez and Ivan Basso were also in attendance.

The attrition rate grew as the contenders pushed on. Team Sky's Rigoberto Uran was suffering in the white young riders jersey. No game for youngsters this.

By the 59 kilometre to go mark, Andy Schleck was still looking good. His lone pace was extraordinary. So, with such majesty on display for all to see and with little effective response from the star group, help was being called for. Brent Bookwalter came within sight and was passed by Schleck. He was on his way back to help Cadel. How much assistance he could offer after the early efforts was a moot point. Schleck's gap on the yellow jersey group was now approaching a minute as Postuma came in range. Andy was eating up the escapees here.

The message had got through to the men up the road. Those without the burden of assisting anyone behind were free to go for it. Iglinsky took his chance. Pacing himself away from the rest of the escapees he had a 48 second lead as we hit 58 kilometres to go. Andy Schleck was three and a half minutes behind and closing.

The shakeout was beginning amongst the favourites. Contador dropped back off the main group of twenty or so riders. Was he holding off or suffering? Despite the neutral mask it was the latter.

At 56 kilometres to go Evans finally had a friend. Bookwalter was now at hand. But was it a helping hand? Evans rhythm was becoming everyone's rhythm and it quickly looked too much for his teammate. Such was the fear of the Australian that nobody was prepared to offer any assistance in the chase of Andy Schleck. Frank wasn't going to do it to his brother. Voeckler wasn't, probably couldn't, and didn't have to. Contador certainly had flat batteries and Sánchez had by now lost his two guardsmen and was out of sorts. So Cadel took up the mantle of Group Captain steering the chasing ship. It was a vessel full of passengers. He didn't like it.

Cadel Evans would make a lousy poker player. He has certain 'tells' that inform you of his level of discomfort. Under duress his complexion turns light grey. Under extreme exertion, particularly when climbing, his head turns to one side. I once pointed this out on air and was rebuked by him. He told me the head thing was due to a riding injury when he was a youngster of 14 and should not be ridiculed. Of course, no lack of respect was intended, but a useful observer's tool it certainly is at moments such as this. For now Cadel was still in the pink but getting paler. The head was solid, straight up. No problems yet then.

Andy Schleck crested the second peak with a gap of two minutes on the yellow group. His legs must have screamed relief to have some help from gravity at last. He was trying to bridge to Maxine Montfort. He found him on the descent busy eating and calmly waiting for his teammate and leader. Montfort is a good descender; Andy is not. He needed a guide.

As everyone was asking questions of the main contenders the forgotten man of the day, Maxim Iglinsky, was already heading to the bottom of the V that heralded the final climb of the day. The nearest men to him now were running close together: Schleck and Montfort along with the remnants of the escape –Nicolas Roche, Dries Devenyns and Egor Silin.

The favourites were splitting on the descent. Evans showing signs of stress berating Bookwalter who had earlier dropped back behind him.

At the bottom, just after Briançon, Contador went for the predicted bike change and then used Samuel Sánchez to get back on. Different teams maybe but as was proved in this instance very good friends.

And so it was, with 34.9 kilometres of this massive day remaining, we began the climb of the mighty Galibier. It may not be an ascent of startling gradient, but it is very long. Averaging between 5 and 6 percent for just over 23 of those kilometres, with a steadily increasing level of difficulty over its run and with two black sections of more than 10% in the last five kilometres, it is a climb without respite and is rightly feared even by the very best.

Iglinsky now led Andy Schleck's group by just 68 seconds at the foot of the climb. The favourites were almost four minutes down. We had begun the day with eight men in the frame for overall victory. The gap covering those riders in the standings was three minutes.

Despite his bike change, Contador was failing to make an impact and remained at the back of the yellow jersey group. Voeckler was shadowing Evans who was being forced to work in the absence of any other willing leader. By using Evans in this way Voeckler was cleverly resting his helpers for use later on, Pierre Rolland in particular. As the final bidons were taken Evans' frustration bubbled up. He began to weave across the road imploring the others to share the load. Not one offered.

With 30.7 kilometres to go the favourites began looking at each other, Frank Schleck the most relaxed of them. He was being towed and of these men was potentially the biggest gainer today after his brother. Andy Schleck had started the day with a deficit of 2–36; 29 kilometres from the finish he was comfortably the virtual leader as the five breakaways became six with the capture of Iglinsky.

Adding to the toil, a headwind began to develop. With 23 kilometres to go Voeckler suddenly looked like he'd been hit with hunger knock. Quickly his teammates offered bars, gels and liquid. He chewed and swallowed frantically to get the energy needed on board.

Some early protagonist were now falling out of the back door – Gilbert and Voigt looking for a bus ticket as Andy Schleck, buck toothed, sloppy chin-strap and praying mantis arms, continued to look every bit the day's winner.

The remnants of the original break were being led by Montfort who was sacrificing himself to the cause. The biggest questions were now being asked of Roche and Silin.

Behind was Contador, presumably hoping Andy Schleck would destroy himself today. I speculated he was thinking of Alpe d'Huez tomorrow, coupling that with the well known time trialing advantage he holds over Andy. If I was thinking it, he was certainly ahead of me.

With 17.5 kilometres to go Montfort blew up. Silin was suffering too. Andy Schleck was now one of four.

The *domestiques* were now beginning to crumble 16 kilometres from home. There was little place to hide. Frank Schleck dropped back for a last bidon and looked comfortable. Meanwhile Evans was starting to head into the grey-faced zone as his work-rate began to take its toll.

Up front just Schleck, Roche and Iglinsky remained, with the gap expanding to a remarkable 3–56 over Evans' group. This was getting critical. Over the next two kilometres a mini drama played out amongst the favourites. Evans turned to Voeckler and begged for assistance. Chin up in familiar pose Voeckler said, and offered nothing. Evans, now gesturing and swearing, began to weave across the road. The bunch came to a near standstill. Still nobody responded. Evans deliberately dropped back but the pace was tardy. Everyone was looking at each other. In exasperation Evans once again came to the fore and from that moment knew he had to do this thing alone. Basso rejoined the regrouping leaders.

Such was Andy Schleck's pace the little spat behind gave him a further boost. He now led by 4–17 seconds with 10.7 kilometres to go. This would stretch further to briefly nudge 4–50.

Montfort drifted back into the chasers and out the back door. Frank Schleck gave him a congratulatory nod. Cadel Evans head remained straight miraculously suggesting some reserves remained despite his efforts.

Into the final 10 kilometres and Nicolas Roche dropped off the leaders as Iglinsky and Andy Schleck pushed on. It felt like an attack from the bunch was imminent. So it was that when Sánchez stopped for a bike change, Evans decided to go for it. Sick of dragging everyone up the mountain he struck out. Voeckler's team-mate, Rolland, set off after him. Basso with fresh vigour responded but in so doing dragged Voeckler up as well. Back together they came.

Over the Col du Lauteret they went. A brief downhill on the mighty Galibier then again onwards and upwards.

Evans' attack had taken some time back off Andy Schleck. He and Iglinsky now led by 3–50. Cadel had personally trimmed a minute off the gap within a single kilometre. Remarkable, but with a price. With eight kilometres to go the head began to hang right and we knew Cadel was nearing the end of his considerable resources.

Then Andy Schleck re-ignited. It was as if he was damned if all that effort from 60 kilometres out was going to go to waste. He dropped Iglinsky with 7.7 kilometres to go. Two riders were delivering a master class in solo effort. Evans alone in a crowd; Andy Schleck on his own now up front. The gap was now 3–29.

Six kilometres to go, with glaciers behind them, the day's big losers started to show themselves. Sánchez drifted back ten bike lengths off the group and looked finished. Evans upped the pace to try and shake out some more.

The massive and excited crowd began to thicken, forming pinch-points at the hairpins. The riders were forced into the middle of the road away from the more comfortable lines through the turns. As is his habit, Contador moved up to Voeckler's shoulder and had a good look at him. Satisfied, he then moved on to Frank Schleck and did the same, his deep stare charting for weakness. He found none. Contador did not go to check on Evans face. If he had he would have seen an open-mouthed, bare-toothed head-tilter in full mountain-eating mode and to hell with everybody.

There were two men fighting here. It was a prize fight for the biggest crown in cycling. It's not that everyone else was incidental, but this was about Andy Schleck versus Cadel Evans. Voeckler was fighting the mountain and his personal demons and was getting a free ride. Frank was happy to play passenger for now. Contador? Well nobody knew what was happening inside his head but we were about to find out.

Eddy Merckx knows the Schlecks well and was in full car-banging mode, urging Andy on. Cadel seemed to have no supporters. The crowd's din was all aimed at Voeckler in yellow.

There were no more complaints from Evans as he struggled on, churning the big ring. He'd given up wasting his breath and now had that locked-on look we know about. No distractions from the task at hand.

With the gap stubbornly stuck, this was going to be a remarkable day for the Luxembourger. Not so for Alberto Contador. With 1.9 kilometres to go he said goodbye to his legs and to his ambitions for this year's Tour.

Andy Schleck went under the final kilometre kite with a gap of 2–44 seconds. The climb flattened for his run in and he took time to punch the air and roar his own approval. Alone and magnificent, Andy conquered the Queen stage and the highest ever finish line in the history of the Tour de France. A simply remarkable long distance effort planned and executed almost to perfection. Celebrations count for a lot, but they cost time too. The final margin of victory was 2 minutes and 7 seconds.

At whatever level you ride, cycle racing is ultimately about the clock. It began to tick ominously above the finish line as we looked back down the mountain. Over six hours in the saddle and still the battle raged. Finally the group fractured as reserves saved were used to good effect. Frank Schleck rounded both Evans and the final corner to make it a brotherly 1-2. As for Cadel, he had done more than enough work. For me he had 'won this bloody Tour', as any good Aussie would say. Not that you would have known it from the reaction of the crowd and the media throng. He finished third on the day thanks to a phenomenal effort and, of course, no thanks from those he dragged up the Galibier. Cadel came home with me beaming as I watched him. He'd done it. The remaining days were tailored for him. The time gaps to those ahead of him on the general classification were about to be eaten away. Firstly on Alpe d'Huez, where Voeckler would inevitably falter and new leader Andy Schleck would see his advantage cut to 57 seconds. The following day saw Evans blow the pretenders away taking the yellow jersey in the 42.5-kilometre Grenoble time trial. He finished second behind time trial specialist Tony Martin to carry a comfortable cushion of 1–34 overall into the final 'parade stage' to Paris.

For me, the 18th stage of the 2011 Tour de France was the day Cadel Evans really won the Tour and it seemed hardly anyone noticed. Few plaudits were offered to him at the Galibier finish line. As he came in the crowd were looking beyond his shoulders searching for Voeckler.

The Frenchman had met his nation's demand for a hero with fifth place behind Basso, to keep hold of the yellow jersey by the slender margin of 15 seconds ahead of Andy Schleck who was now second overall. So Voeckler, not a high-mountains specialist remember, had delivered for France on the Queen stage and the nation went predictably wild with adoration. In reality, Evans' endeavour had done much of the work for Voeckler. The cameras and security staff battled under a cacophony of sound for space around the Frenchman as he sat in the road exhausted. Quietly to stage left Cadel Evans was greeted by his BMC team who guided him away from the melée. The world would greet the Tour de France victor in three days time.

Cadel's journey had been a long one. From the stony pistes of Southern France where I first came across him in 1998, to the final run up the Champs-Elysées in 2011. As the Tour de France winner he had faced many challenges in the past, the sort of setbacks that might well have dimmed the light of his ambition. Often surrounded by 'doubtful sportsmanship' and Tour runner-up on two occasions, this man from Barwon Heads in Australia kept his own held high. He never gave up believing and, likewise, I held the faith. I knew in 1998 that this was a special rider and in 2011 he came to be crowned one of the most courageous Tour de France winners of the last few decades. Good on yer mate!

STAGE 19, 2011: MODANE–ALPE D'HUEZ, 109.5kms.

Lucy Fallon

It was July 2009, and the Boss was back. Like Norma Desmond, the ageing movie queen in *Sunset Boulevard**, Lance Armstrong had come out of retirement still feeling very much the star. No matter that his new team, Astana, already had a leader, the young Spaniard, Alberto Contador, winner of the 2007 Tour. The rookie would have to move over, willingly or otherwise.

At the end of the first week, as the peloton rolled out of Barcelona, heading for the Pyrenees, Armstrong was classified a mere second behind race leader Fabian Cancellara. Confident the yellow jersey was his for the taking, the winner of an incredible seven Tours de France was looking forward to a triumphant re-emergence in Andorra.

Steps had been taken to ensure the master plan. On the stage to Montpellier, Contador had found himself on the wrong side of the gap when the peloton was split by the wind. In the leading group, Astana were given orders to pull as hard as they could, Armstrong himself working harder than anyone. But to his intense frustration, in Andorra he had to watch the Spaniard break free, and instead of the yellow jersey, the American was left clutching thin air. Contador was six seconds short of claiming it for himself, having made his first move to overall victory.

In the post-stage interview, a stony-faced Armstrong, barely suppressing his anger, reflected: 'It wasn't really to the plan but I didn't expect him to go by the plan. It's no surprise. Like Norma Desmond, Armstrong had found that his come-back script was unworkable. Though he got to stand on the final podium in Paris, it was on the bottom step. The 37-year-old couldn't disguise his coveting of the trophy: the cameras closed in on a nakedly bitter face, with an oblivious Contador two steps above. It wouldn't be the last time that Contador shattered other riders' plans.

x x x x x

---

* 1950 Hollywood classic directed by Billy Wilder and starring Gloria Swansong.

Two years later, in the 2011 Tour de France, the last stage in the Alps was getting underway in the village of Modane. Under balconies festooned with yellow balloons, Tommy Voeckler, chin jutting proudly, led the peloton through the cheering crowds. He had the air of a heroic but doomed general at the head of his troops, determined to resist one more day against the odds. A beneficiary of the calamitous Saint Flour stage (when ten riders were injured in a series of horrendous crashes and forced to abandon), no one had expected him to still be in yellow ten days later, only three days from Paris.

Voeckler was riding in Europcar, the second smallest team in the race in terms of budget. He was the plucky underdog who thrives on attention, acting up to the cameras, tongue-waggling, dramatizing his suffering for all to see. The last time the French held the yellow jersey so far into the race was 1989 (when Lemond beat Fignon by eight seconds). No one saw Voeckler as the overall winner, but his tenacity was winning him respect.

Any semblance of hierarchy in the peloton, with its ensuing law and order, had been slow to materialise in the Tour that year, abetted by the decision to pack all the race-defining mountain stages into the second half. An enduring image of a particularly accident-prone race was of Johnny Hoogerland embedded on a barbed wire fence, after he and Juan Antonio Flecha were run off the road by a French TV car. So much for the relative safety of riding in a breakaway. Earlier that day Alexander Vinokourov had careered off a precipice and was stretchered away with a broken leg. Having skirted all the obstacles, the survivors of Voeckler's escape group arrived with an ample margin of over 5 minutes, which the Frenchman would go on to defend so assiduously.

In Modane, classified only 15 seconds behind Voeckler was Andy Schleck, fresh from his historical win the previous day on the first ever stage to finish on the 2,645m Col du Galibier. Leopard-Trek had prepared, and perfectly executed, a classic strategy. When Schleck attacked on the Izoard, with more than 60 kilometres to go, his rivals were complacent – there was valley to spare to round him up later. But with the help of opportunely escaped team-mates, Schleck kept his advantage to the foot of the Galibier, where he accelerated again, and rode solo to victory.

But his overall position was far from secure. He urgently needed to gain more time on Cadel Evans, who stood at 1min 12secs, to have any chance of surviving the following day's time trial. In principle, the terrain was in his favour. The unusually short stage (109-kilometre) would be taking the peloton up the Galibier again, this time by the more difficult Col du Télégraphe side, with a finish on Alpe d'Huez.

And what about Contador? In the pre-stage speculation there was little mention of his name. And he was completely excluded from any conjecture about the podium in Paris. The previous day, so magnificent for the Luxembourgers, had been a painful experience for the Spanish. They'd watched in dismay as, 2.5 kilometres from the finish, Contador cracked. He'd also ridden the Galibier alone, but struggling with overwhelming fatigue and knee pain. The champion was definitively vanquished. The organizers must have heaved a sigh of relief.

x x x x x

There'd been another incident in the dramatic Saint Flour stage, minor but symbolic, involving Contador. After his handlebars collided with the seat of the Russian giant, Vladimir Karpets, he was spat sideways out of the peloton. No one else was affected. At that moment the Spaniard cut a solitary, fragile figure, far from emanating the solid invincibility we've come to associate with grand tour champions, who seem entitled to more space in the pack.

The truth was, Contador was not wanted in France.* With a doping case hanging over his head, his very presence in the Tour was a headache for the organizers. A protracted legal battle was coming to an end, and Contador was facing a two-year ban, which, if confirmed, would strip him of the 2010 Tour victory and subsequent wins. Besides the vociferous booing of the French, he was also facing rivals who'd carefully tuned their performance to peak in July. Contador had already raced – and won – the Giro d'Italia, uncertain what the season had in store. Another handicap was losing over a minute on the very first stage in a pile-up. After his abrupt encounter with Karpets, Contador picked himself up, wincing with a sore knee, and found his place in the peloton without a patron.

x x x x x

Nearly two weeks later, after limping over the line on the Galibier, Contador had considered packing up and going home. Lying seventh at 4mins 44secs, his options were few. The idea of riding out what remained as mere peloton-filler was unbearable. But an alternative idea had begun to germinate.

---

* A minute trace of clenbuterol had been found in a urine sample of 2010 Tour.

225

Despite all these unpropitious circumstances, Contador had already left his mark on the race. Not in the Pyrenees, which after such a long, tense wait proved a dismal anti-climax. The main contenders, Andy and Frank Schleck, Cadel Evans and Ivan Basso spent much of the time warily watching each other, and were capable of only the most timid attacks. In Luz Ardiden, their sense of smell for a rival's weakness proved so poor that Contador successfully masked his low form and knee trouble, losing only nine seconds.

Disillusioned by the cautious racing, followers of the race had few expectations of stage 16 into Gap, a prelude to the Alps. Unsettling memories of cross-country riding and agonised screams on melting tarmac were briefly stirred and quickly forgotten on this wet, gloomy day.* Riders scowled into the rain, waterproofs billowed, and mist shrouded the hills. The commentators were laying bets on who in the escape group would win, when the cameras suddenly cut back to the main field, climbing the Col de Manse. Contador had attacked.

The Schlecks were quickly shepherded across by Fabian Cancellara, followed by Evans, yellow jersey Thomas Voeckler and Samuel Sánchez, Asturian climber extraordinaire, who immediately launched his own attack. Improbably, the fireworks expected in the Pyrenees were now exploding on a damp, unspectacular 2nd-category climb.

It was Andy Schleck's turn to accelerate, and when the main contenders regrouped, he signalled for someone else to take over at the front. He seemed keen to re-establish order. But when Saxobank's Dani Navarro moved up, you suspected the show wasn't over, not just yet.

On his second attack, Contador was more insistent. While Evans and Sánchez fought their way over, the Schlecks, astonishingly, were dropped. The finish in Gap was at the end of a long sinuous descent along country lanes, habitually battered by heavy farm machinery, the patchwork tarmac treacherously slick in the rain. Paralysed by nerves, Andy Schleck would lose over a minute to Contador. After the stage he complained loudly, 'We don't want to see riders taking risks. A finish like this should not be allowed.' Cycling fans, revitalised after the Pyrenean stupor, thrilled by the spectacle of dare-devil chasing, might chose to disagree.

x x x x x

---

* The crash of Joseba Beloki in the 2003 Tour de France, which Armstrong managed to avoid by riding over a field.

Just 15 kilometres out of Modane, with viewers barely settled on the sofa, and race commentators still warming up, few could believe their eyes when Contador boldly rode away from the peloton. Within minutes he had dynamited the field. The battle would rage all day.

Only Andy Schleck was able to match the Spaniard's second acceleration. Evans struggled with an inopportune mechanical, while Tommy Voeckler, the pride of France, found himself in no man's land. His instinct was to fight back to Contador, rather than drop to the group behind. That stubborn temperament, which fuelled his riding, would cost him dear.

The sheer guts of Contador's ambush sent expectations whirling. A wild variety of scenarios suddenly materialised. Would Cadel Evans lose a stack of minutes and Andy Schleck ride into Paris in yellow? Or perhaps Contador's knee was really better and he would storm through the time trial tomorrow? Although the Giro-Tour double is virtually unattainable in modern cycling, for a few heady moments anything seemed possible. The two climbers rapidly caught the escape group, and Contador, with a look of total concentration, remained at the front, never once looking over his shoulder. Over the Col du Télégraphe and onto the Galibier, by the time they were climbing out of the tree line, Schleck was collaborating. He had signed up for the adventure, for better or worse.

After two bike changes, Evans was two minutes behind, but fighting back with an organized team. Voeckler was still in limbo at 30 seconds. Logically, he should have been riding tucked securely behind the Australian to defend a podium position, but he preferred the doomed gesture, powered along by roaring compatriots. On the tight hairpins, the grimacing Voeckler looked up to see Contador swing buoyantly round the next curve. Not too far below, Cadel Evans was hunched over his bike, wrestling it forward in his strenuous but powerful style.

The steepest part of the climb comes in the final five kilometres, where the serrated peaks and barren scree loom close. The Tour, with all its pandemonium, shrinks on the majestic Galibier. The helicopters, convoy of vehicles, and spectators at the roadside are all reduced to insignificant figurines, and the cyclists are lost in their individual struggles. On the final stretch Alberto Contador was beginning to show the strain. Ahead still lay 60 kilometres, while strewn behind him was a peloton in turmoil – all his own doing. The measured pace up the Galibier many had hoped for had been transformed into a fight for survival.

The Contador/Schleck partnership would never exceed a two-minute advantage. Unable to withstand a united front of teams, each pursuing their own interests, they were hunted down in the interminable valley. Viewers, emotionally exhausted, were given a respite and some time to speculate on the unfathomable outcome of the stage.

Unlike the Galibier, the Alpe d'Huez is a humanized landscape, with its chalets, ski installations and general rowdiness. It's the Tour de France's most iconic climb: just look at the number of times it features in the contributions to this book. On the famous 21 curves the race turns into a carnival, 13.2 kilometres of sustained, barely controlled mayhem. People strip or don disguises, and pelt ritualistically alongside the riders. They never keep up for long though, testament to the power on display.

Tension was building as the re-grouped peloton, including Voeckler, hurtled to Bourg-d'Oisans. Evans was warily observing Frank Schleck, winner on the Alpe in 2006, who had enjoyed an easy ride so far. The Australian was also haunted by memories of losing the Tour to Carlos Sastre on the climb in 2008. In the scramble for position, the Schlecks got trapped behind a green bottleneck of Europcar riders, and on the first kilometre, agonizingly steep after so long on the flat, were already on the defensive as Evans powered away from them.

No sooner were the rivals together again, Contador decided to use up his last shot. In reality, when he sprinted away from the group, his reserves were running low, but a series of short, precise accelerations were enough to reach and overtake the two escapees, Ryder Hesjedal and Europcar's Pierre Rolland. Voeckler, resigned to his fate, had given his lieutenant free rein. Next to make a move, eight kilometres from the finish, was Samuel Sánchez, aiming to secure the mountains prize. Rolland coolly attached himself to the Asturian's wheel.

Though riding close to the limit, Contador settled into a rhythm, and continued the strange hallucinatory climb up the Alpe. A knight in a plumed helmet, someone in a silver top hat, a towering apparition in an electric blue body stocking, all flashed past in a delirium. A green-gowned medic came charging by, brandishing a stethoscope. Without missing a beat, Contador punched him out of the way, reconnecting with reality.

Back in the group, at 57 seconds, Andy Schleck was having to grit his teeth and work alone. His exhortations to Evans to lend a hand were drowned by the bellowing crowd. Three minutes down came Voeckler, podium lost, snarling into the wind.

In the end the two Spaniards were outwitted by a Frenchman. Sánchez steadily continued narrowing the gap to Contador, towing the silent enemy in his wake. You could see how this would end. At the precise moment they made contact, only two and a half kilometres from the line, Rolland made his move, and proved unreachable.

While the French were emotionally celebrating their first stage win in the race, Sánchez had the compensation of climbing onto the podium to receive the polka dot jersey, and Andy Schleck, visibly extenuated when he crossed the line, was the new race leader. Knowing the glory would be fleeting and would not survive the next day's time trial, his smile was rather wan.

At the margin of the celebrations, Alberto Contador unobtrusively melted away, work done. The organizers could be happy: without winning anything, he'd set the race alight, enthralling the spectators. Even some of the most cynical, for whom cycling has been reduced to a game of judging performance authenticity, were briefly caught up in the excitement. The eventual winner, Cadel Evans, could also be glad. He hadn't expected such a tough ride, having to fight back single-handed on the Galibier for a second day running. But it was the day his reputation as a wheel-sucker was buried for good.

In an age of conservative, radio-controlled racing, Contador was the one who took risks and was unafraid of failure. He came to the Tour under a cloud – 21st century professional cycling is perpetually enveloped in a storm cloud – but redeemed himself through courage and audacity. *El Pistolero*, the persona Contador adopts for his victory salute, hadn't materialized, but he'd be reappearing in a sequel. The ambush on the Télégraphe would turn out to be a dress rehearsal for the 2012 Vuelta, when Contador would take equally unexpected measures to dislodge the tenacious Purito Rodríguez from the top of the classification.

STAGE 17, 2012: BAGNERES DE LUCHON–PEYRAGUDES, 143 kms.

Paul Francis Cooper

Far away from the cols of the Alps and Pyrenees and fourteen years before the world had seen a British winner of the Tour de France, a group of promising young cyclists enjoyed the post-ride bonhomie that follows a good training session in the hills of North Wales. Youthful and optimistic, the lads chatted in the front sitting room of a semi-detached house in the Wirral Peninsula, near Liverpool. It was the family home of a young Steve Cummings, future Great Britain team pursuit World Champion and a powerhouse of the professional peloton, who was then a junior in the GB talent development programme. Standing close to him in the sitting room was his friend, another up-and-coming GB talent, and future winner of the 2012 Tour de France, Bradley Wiggins.

They had first met as junior riders competing in the National Junior Individual Pursuit Championship in 1997, Cummings the son of a Merseyside policeman, part of a family that loved sport, in a region that adores football, Wiggins, brought up in Kilburn by his mother, the son of an estranged father, who was a professional bike racer. Although different in personality, the two lads easily became friends, sharing an irreverent sense of humour, and, most importantly, a total commitment to a dream of a life in elite bike racing. As the youthful conversation drifted from a review of the Welsh ride to thoughts about the future, most of the lads wondered if they might ever become pro-riders. Cummings and Wiggins didn't wonder; they planned, and knew that one day they would realise their dreams.

Wind the clock forward to late in the afternoon on 19th July 2012, the two friends still sharing climbs. This time, though, high in the Pyrenees, and, their youthful self-confidence vindicated, they were competing for opposing World Tour teams, Wiggins in Sky, Cummings in BMC, in the seventeenth stage of the Tour de France. In a situation that mirrored the pattern of both riders' 2012 seasons, Wiggins was at the front of the peloton, on the brink of securing overall victory in *La Grande Boucle*, having already entered history as the only cyclist ever to have won Paris-

Nice, the Tour of Romandie and the Dauphiné in one season, while his friend, who had endured one of his most difficult seasons in racing, was some kilometres back, and facing very real trouble.

The seventeenth was the Tour's last stage in the mountains and Wiggins started the day, as the race's outstanding favourite, with a healthy two minutes and 23 seconds lead over his nearest general classification rival, Vincenzo Nibali. But, with only two fully competitive days to follow the difficult passage from Bagnères-de-Luchon to the summit finish at the ski resort of Peyragudes there was every incentive for a dramatic, last ditch, mountain attack by Nibali. And, with an attack by the challenger widely anticipated, the stage's five categorised climbs were strongly tipped as the setting for the race's big bang, final, general classification decider. But, despite the high expectations and the strong efforts of Nibali and his committed Italian Liquigas team, the pattern of the 2012 Tour continued and Sky's implacable dominance of the race prevailed.

The Peyresourde was the stage's penultimate climb and as the yellow jersey group, containing Wiggins and Nibali, approached the summit through the day's clearing mist, Nibali, started to crack. As he did, Wiggins' for the first time ever, allowed himself to believe that he was within touching distance of becoming the first British rider to win the Tour de France.

On the final ascent to Peyragudes, he glanced over his shoulder to see Nibali, his nearest challenger, slipping behind, and, with 2.5 kilometres to go, Wiggins, a paragon of self-discipline throughout the Tour, momentarily succumbed to his emotions. His team-mate, Chris Froome, forfeiting his chance of catching the stage's eventual winner, Alejandro Valverde, stayed nearby directing and encouraging his leader safely to the finish line. It was vital for Sky that he did, because, for a few perilous seconds, his team leader's mind had slipped from the final ascent of the Tour and the race's few remaining kilometres in the Pyrenees, leaving him vulnerable to an attack by a weakened, but still capable, Nibali.

Later that day, a deeply contented and appreciative Wiggins told the world's media how his team-mate had looked after him, when he fleetingly lost his race concentration. Emotionally overcome by the magnitude of what he was about to achieve, his mind had drifted to recall all that he had done, and the people who had helped him, to reach that moment when the prize, which had eluded him in his two previous Tours, was, at last, practically within his grasp.

But, just as the page turned in the history of British cycling, and Wiggins allowed himself those few seconds of sweet reflection, his long-standing friend, Cummings, was far from satisfying ambition and experiencing anything but a dream. Instead, in a situation that resonated miserably with much of what had gone before in his 2012 season, he was facing, what he later described as one of the lowest points in his professional racing career.

Seven months previously, his year had started with such promise. After two years with Sky, the hardworking and resourceful Merseysider had made the move to BMC in January, looking forward to developing his career with the ambitious and big spending outfit.

A good friend of Max Sciandri, BMC's *directeur sportif*, he was a natural fit for the comradely atmosphere of the stellar cast team, in which, recruited for his strength, and race savvy, his programme was to include major support roles in the Spring Classics and the Grand Tours, as well as opportunities to chase individual stage wins in his own right. And, following a good winter's training in the Montalbano Hills, near his home in Tuscany, the spring of 2012 saw him making a strong impression in the team's pre-season training camps, relaxed, fit and confident.

His optimism, though, was to be rewarded with an early season of almost relentless bad luck. In February he received a painful fracture to his pelvis when another rider clipped his handlebars on a descent in the third stage of the Tour of the Algarve. Racing again in April's infamously tough and mountainous Tour of the Basque Country, his bike slipped in tricky, wet conditions, and he fell and broke his wrist. Six weeks later he was one of a group of six riders ensnared in a pile-up close to the finish of the second stage in the Tour of California. He came away with some ugly cuts to his knee, which required several stitches, and suffered yet more debilitating injury by falling awkwardly on the wrist that had broken six weeks earlier.

A focused professional, Cummings met each painful and frustrating setback with a disciplined commitment and a resolve to overcome the disheartening effects of the recurring misfortunes that could have broken the will of many riders. His reward, a chance to re-establish his inevitably bruised confidence and put the worst of the season behind him, was a place with BMC in the Tour de France – a place, which was particularly hard earned as Cummings' opportunities for race conditioning had been significantly reduced by time spent recovering from injuries. But, if being in the race's starting line-up, in Liège on 30th June, held out promise for the future, events during the race were soon to undermine it.

The first blow came a few days later on 4th July, the day of the Tour's 4th stage, from Abbeville to Rouen in Northern France. The fourth longest stage of the Tour ended in dramatic style with a perfectly executed sprint to victory by German dynamo Andé Griepel (Lotto Belisol) with Switzerland's Fabian Cancellara (RadioShack-Nissan) retaining overall lead ahead of Bradley Wiggins. But, the news of the moment for Cummings came, not from the stage's closing events in Normandy's historic capital, but from across the English Channel, where, in London, the Merseysider was the surprise omission in the British Cycling and British Olympic Association announcement of riders selected to compete in the British Olympic road race team on the streets of the British capital on 28th July.

'I am very disappointed, of course,' he said publicly. 'It's everyone's dream to be selected for the Olympics.* But I hope the guys do well and bring back a gold medal.' Privately he was bitterly upset at having been initially named in the six-man road race line up, only to miss the final cut.

And, apparently unintentionally driving home the compounded effect of Cummings' season of bad luck, David Brailsford, GB Team Performance Director, offered the following rationale. 'It was a tough decision,' Brailsford said. 'Steve's been going well, but he's had a few crashes and injuries that set him back a little bit.'

Cummings response was to focus on the here and now of the Tour, commenting. 'Being here with Cadel makes up for it. Especially after everything that I've been through this year. The race has been going well so far. I've managed to stay out of trouble, although I am braking a lot more and I'm still pretty nervous, but I've been getting through safely.'

Until the seventeenth stage, that is exactly what he did. By that time Cadel Evans, BMC team leader and 2011 Tour winner, was out of the reckoning for a second Tour victory, but was still chasing a top-ten finish. His lieutenant, Tejay van Garderen, was pushing hard for the best young rider's white jersey, and Cummings, with his renowned big-engined capacity for endurance, was consistently tireless in support of both. But, about 15 kilometres before the start of the ascent of the Port de Bales, the stage's fourth major climb, the personal ill fortune that had dogged the season and, which Cummings had hoped to have left behind him in California, made its haunting reappearance.

It was at the feed zone ahead of the Port de Bales that a crash brought a number of riders down. The reigning road race World Champion, Mark Cavendish, and his Sky team-mate, Bernie Eisel, were amongst them, and

---

* It would have been Steve's third consecutive Olympics, having already won a track Silver medal in 2004 in the team pursuit.

233

shots of them anxiously remounting featured in the stage's TV coverage. Unobserved by the motorbike cameramen, Cummings was also amongst the fallers. He avoided injury, but picked up some damage to his rear wheel and derailleur mechanism when another rider collided with him.

Keen to regain a good position at the front of the peloton for the forthcoming 19-kilometre climb, he moved off before fully checking his machine. He struggled with ineffective gears as he tried to move through the field and, with BMC mechanics way ahead in team cars near Cadel Evans and Tejay Van Garderen, he was unable to make the relative safety of the front end of the bunch.

At the top of the climb, which is regularly rendered impassable by snow in the winter, and often shrouded in mist in the summer, Cummings grabbed the chance to slip on his rain jacket before accelerating into the twisting and turning road that winds from the broad open summit towards the green pasture land below. But, as the pace of his tricky descent quickened to more than 60 kilometres an hour, a race motorbike crossed his line. Forced to brake, he made his correction, but his damaged back wheel locked, pitching machine and rider helplessly towards the right side of the road, which, as a barrier to descending mountain water, is bounded by a deep concrete drainage gully that is backed by a high kerbstone. Powerless to prevent the high-speed, rear-end skid, he entered the gully, back first. His body hit the gully basin and bounced against its wall, before being thrown upwards for its final high velocity pounding as the base of his back hit the sharp kerb edge.

Dazed and shaken, Cummings was experiencing extreme difficulty in breathing due to the excruciating pain in his back, his leg was hurting, and he had lost a lot of skin in extensive lacerations to both sides of his body. In his own words he was 'in a mess'. But, although he would later describe the crash as the worst in a very difficult season, he was utterly determined to continue in the race.

His concerned *directeur sportif*, Fabio Baldato, was close by and was anxious for Cummings to abandon. But, for Cummings, who had shown such determination to make the BMC Tour team, leaving the race was not an option that he was prepared to consider. Speaking later he said. 'In every other race, I would have got into the ambulance. Fabio wanted me to stop, but there was no way I was stopping. I fought so hard to get to the Tour, I wasn't going to stop unless I physically couldn't go on.'

Driven by the need to move quickly to keep within the stage's time limit, which was being relentlessly set further ahead, in the superb breakaway ride of stage winner Alejandro Valverde, Cummings, helped by Baldato, painfully mounted the spare bike and cautiously set off down the mountain. 'I didn't have a decision,' he said later. 'I think bike riders crash and immediately look for their bike and try to start again. Only if you physically can't go on, do you stop. If I had stopped, I would have lived to regret not trying.'

Now, riding alone on the descent, and anxious about making the stage's finishing time limit, Cummings received support from a sympathetic Baldato, who, following in a team car, encouraged, cajoled and calmed his injured rider. Cummings recalls. 'Once I got going, Baldato was amazing. He knew what it was like for me. I know he had been in my situation before.' And, as the worried pair edged their way to the relative security of the *gruettpo*, the race ambulance crew administered urgently needed first aid.

First riders to make contact were Tyler Farrar (Garmin-Sharp-Barracuda) and Sebastian Langeveld (Orica GreenEDGE) as they brought up the rear of the race. In their own pursuit of the *grupetto* they had caught the steadfast, but struggling, Cummings, and, despite their own concerns over the time limit, rather than pass him, they took care and time to ensure that he was able to hold on to their newly formed *lanterne rouge* trio. A grateful Cummings describes the riders as 'absolute gentlemen'. Once with the *grupetto*, further help and support was at hand from team-mate Manuel Quinziato and his old friend and GB team-mate, Mark Cavendish.

At Peyragudes, 30–57 behind the stage winner, alongside Quinziato, Langeveld and Farrar, with Mark Cavendish trailing fractionally behind, Cummings arrived safely within the cut-off time in the company of the comrades of the peloton whose help had been so critical in his struggle to survive in the race.

Once there, like Wiggins, who had effectively won the Tour a little over thirty minutes earlier, Cummings was emotionally overwhelmed by the physical and psychological strain of the day, and, 200 metres beyond the finish line, lay helpless on the road until the team doctor made a space in the *soigneur*'s car for their descent to the team bus. Reaching the finish line came at a huge price, but, for the determined and professional Cummings, intent on redeeming his season, it was a price that had to be paid.

Cummings has a favourite saying, which may well have crossed his mind as he sat dejected in the car on its descent from the finish line. 'The victory is not reaching the top of the mountain,' he says. 'It's picking yourself up every time you fall on your way.' And, summing up his experience that day, he said later. 'The Port de Bales was the lowest point of my season. I had reached rock bottom. But I've learnt in my career that, no matter what happens, if you always try your best, that's all you can do. It's a very simple philosophy; life is not fair, but you can only play the cards you have.'

Supported by team-mates and BMC medical staff, Cummings, continued to play his difficult hand through to a very welcome end of the Tour, three days later, in Paris. Wiggins, as yellow jersey winner, finished in style. Playing an unusual lead-out role for the Tour's winner on the last day of the race, he helped Mark Cavendish to a classic sprinter's stage win on the Champs-Elysées, before going on, ten days later, to take the gold medal in the time trial at the London Olympics.

x x x x x

But the Tour isn't everything. In its aftermath Steve's suffering and determination paid off. He went home to Tuscany, making little comment, even to close associates, about his experiences. Just as it had been earlier in his season, his focus was exclusively on recovery and regaining the opportunity to perform well in subsequent races. And, continuing to try his best, he went on to defy the season's bad luck with even greater determination than ever.

With a strong and tactically astute win in the thirteenth stage of September's Vuelta a España – 172 kilometres from Santiago de Compostela to Ferrol – he joined Chris Froome, Mark Cavendish, David Millar and Bradley Wiggins as British 2012 Grand Tour stage winners. Part of a six-rider, day-long break, he seized the perfect moment to drop his rivals at four kilometres from the finish, turning his previously soul-destroying season around with his first-ever, Grand Tour stage win. After the race, he described the remarkable context for his victory, making specific reference to his crash in the Tour, saying. 'It's been a long, hard year, and I crashed really badly in the Tour de France so I wasn't sure of my condition when I came here. But I knew if I got through the first week alright things could start to get better. When I was a kid I always watched the Giro d'Italia, Tour of France and the Vuelta and dreamed of taking a stage in one of them.'

And, further emphasising that steadfast determination to chase a dream, even in the face of setbacks, really does bring results, he wrapped up his year with a flourish in one of the season's most dramatic race finishes. Almost unconsciously mocking his misfortune in stage seventeen of the Tour de France, Cummings escaped a twelve-man breakaway to join that year's Giro d'Italia winner, Canadian star Ryder Hesjedal, on Sizuo Lou, the 5.4-kilometre final climb in the Tour of Beijing's ultimate stage, from Chang Ping Stadium to Ping Gu Centenary Square.

From the start of the rapid and treacherous descent from the summit of Sizuo Lou, Cummings, and Hesjedal, were very hotly pursued by a twenty-eight rider chasing group and at one time looked practically certain to be caught, until the duo put down the gas yet again. Cummings easily out-sprinted the Canadian to cross the finish line in Ping Gu, two seconds clear, and seventeen seconds ahead of the chasing bunch. After the race, Cummings closed his tumultuous season with the comment: 'It sure is nice to win this way.' Steve was the only British stage winner of the race that year; however, British riders had won stages in all three Grand Tours in 2012.

Could the young riders in the Wirral sitting room have imagined a season like 2012, or envisaged events like those they experienced in that Tour stage from Bagnères-de-Luchon to Peyragudes? Probably not. But as intelligent students of their sport they will have been aware of the qualities that competitive cycling, at its best, idealises and celebrates in races made golden by their presence. Back then, on their ride in Wales, they would already have known the qualities of teamwork, loyalty, camaraderie, determination, resilience and courage as part of the sport's continuing story and the foundations of their youthful dreams of success. And, with their team-mates and fellow riders in the peloton, on that seventeenth stage of the 2012 Tour, they added to that story, demonstrating these qualities, and inspiring yet more youthful dreams.

Bradley Wiggins and Steve Cummings, at the Surrey League Revolutions 5-Day in 2002 where they each won a stage.

Emma Felton

Steve says, 'No!'
Steve Cummings refuses to get into the ambulance after falling heavily during the tough, mountainous 17th stage in 2012
(emmafeltonphotography.co.uk)

Bradley Wiggins during the final time trial of the 2012 Tour,
from an original painting reproduced by kind permission of Jeff Platten

EPILOGUE

That's the second time she's walked past the window. This time she checks her stride, pulls up the collar of her coat against the wind that whips up the walk and looks about her. Is she waiting for someone to join her in one of the comfortable bar booths I find myself in? Thinking back a decade or more she would have only been a vague shadow behind the frost and scroll of the etched Victorian glass, but a lot has changed in ten years here in 'the office', and in life.

'The Flask' public house, Hampstead, North West London, commonly known as 'the office' used to radiate the warm, lived-in atmosphere slowly disappearing in city pubs. It was a the boozer of choice for born and bred Hampsteadites, a discrete watering hole for arty types, for old locals, off duty policemen, artists, for sports agent Richard Allchin, young and aspiring Olympian Bradley Wiggins and at some later date, lost now in a comfortable alcoholic haze, for me.

The etched glass window disappeared one Boxing Day night when an over-lubricated drinker, put out onto the street by the jovial but strict Irish landlord John, registered his displeasure by hurling a chair through it and attempted to climb back in. There then ensued a punch up in the finest traditions of the pub brawl as Richard, myself and my brother, enjoying a social rather than 'office' time, waded in. It was a real James Joyce fist fight culminating in a single blow from Rich landing the now astonished drunkard on his back, my brother hurling his weight on the drunk's equally drunk companion, pinning him to the floor until the police came to cart them away. I was never sure whether Rich was more annoyed with the assault on John, the tears of barmaid Angela, or that the Christmas peace of his beloved 'office' had be disturbed.

Gone too is the flowered wallpaper, the chipped wooden tables, the predictable but generous pub grub and John, replaced by tones of sage green, sanded wooden boards, half a dozen student bar staff and a gastro menu to match every other pub in the genteel Hampstead drinking quarter.

One thing has remained constant in this sea of hostelry change. Between us sits a bottle of red wine, now two thirds empty. It sits there in silent expectation that it will soon be joined by another bottle, cradling as it does too much for one glass yet not enough for two.

Richard Allchin half stares into the distance and his lower lip relaxes, arms resting across his large frame and a look of inner contentment slides gently across his face.

'What did I tell you when we first came here Dave?' he drawls to me without shifting his gaze from the middle distance.

'I don't know, what did you tell me when we first came here?'

'I told you he could do it, I told you Brad could win the Tour. Brad didn't really believe me; he was more interested in the Olympics. See, I was right'

It was true, he did tell me that. He had told me that Wiggins could win the Tour. He had told me that over a decade ago. He knows I haven't forgotten, but he tells me again anyway and I let him. Happiness spreads over his face and he breaks into a wide gap toothed grin looking every inch the aging pub pugilist.

Who am I to deny him the pleasure of knowing he was right? Richard had given his heart and soul but mostly his heart to the protection and nurturing of the teenager from Kilburn and when, inevitably, Wiggins' ambitions as an athlete outstripped his long friendship with his agent and he had moved on to pastures new, Richard had been heartbroken. Both passionate, both with qualities and flaws, each more of an artist than an artisan, they were both fiercely loyal and then fiercely at odds in the way only men in friendships can be. In truth I've never been sure how Richard's other colleagues, Adrian Bell and Mick Clark, have ever put up with his temperament for so long. I'm not sure how I have but Wiggins, too, must have felt the tugging of regret at leaving, but the young man was growing, evolving in Britain's greatest and most compete bike rider. His needs were bigger, greater than his friend could fulfill for him.

'I had a lovely phone call from Brad you know, Dave. After everything he still called me his best pal,' he went on beaming at me. 'Funny isn't it after all this time, and I always told you he would do it.'

In truth, I hadn't believed him ten years ago but so much in the world has changed. Riding a bicycle everyday is no longer freakery but fashionable, the country not a backwater but the breakneck conquers of the road and Wiggins the ruler of a very British Empire.

An Olympics in London in our lifetime? A boy from London a winner of the Tour de France? This was madness a decade ago and yet here we sit, older, more bruised by life and probably none the wiser, and all these things have come to pass.

'So what do we do now then Rich? Nothing more to achieve is there?' I asked.

A sudden fiercely aggrieved expression came over him.

'What do you mean? It never stops, Dave. We just do our bit, whatever we can do. I'm just glad we are all pals again. Look after your friends, Dave.' The grin spread slowly back across his broad face again as he lifted his glass, 'and next time I tell you something maybe you'll believe me.'

David Harmon
Eurosport TV's leading cycle racing commentator

NOTES ON CONTRIBUTORS

Alex Bannister was Group Managing Editor and Cycling Correspondent of the *Daily Express* before taking his present position as Managing Editor at the *Daily Mail*. After graduating from Cambridge, where he studied Classics, he was a runner-up in the *Guardian* sports-writing competition and became a freelance sports journalist before joining Express Newspapers. Alex's love of cycling grew from watching the Channel 4 Tour de France coverage in the 1980s and his enthusiasm continues to the present day. A fine club-rider, he finished l'Etape du Tour at his first attempt, despite damaging his gear mechanism early on! Alex continues with his demanding position at the *Daily Mail* and still competes l'Etape du Tour which he continues to finish when time permits and he is able to ride the event.

Keith Bingham is a former second-category roadman from Merseyside and recently retired from *Cycling Weekly* after 40 years of continuous service, a record which looks like standing for a very long time. His past assignments have included several Tours de France, the Classics and many World Championships. The 1982 Tour was his first as chief reporter for the weekly, and the success of Sean Kelly that year has always been very close to his heart. Keith continues to freelance and is still supportive of many initiatives which 'try to make cycling safer and more enjoyable for everybody who loves his cycling for whatever reason.'

Michael Breckon has been a cycling addict since first seeing the Tour of Britain in 1952. A successful racer, he was a member of the Yorkshire Road Club's winning team in the British Best All-Rounder in 1958. He emigrated to Canada in the early 1960s where as a volunteer, whilst working in marketing, he established the national cycling team and managed it at World Championships, Commonwealth and Olympic Games, later becoming 'the voice' of cycling on Canadian TV. He returned to the U.K. in 1988 to work for Raleigh and has been writing about cycling for various publications on both sides of the Atlantic for fifty five years.

Paul Cooper's career is as varied as it is long, but with one constant throughout, his love of cycling. He has worked as a gardener, probation officer, university lecturer, and as a Head of Management Development and Training in the British police. He now works freelance as a management trainer and cycling writer and photographer. Based in his hometown of Liverpool, he is the cycling correspondent for the *Liverpool Echo* and writer and photographer with North West England's digital cycling magazine Spincyclemag.com. He is currently researching a book with Richard Allchin of Sport and Publicity/ Mousehold Press on the career of Merseyside's cycling star World Tour rider Steve Cummings, provisionally entitled *Soldier of the Peloton*.

John Deering is a freelance writer who has contributed to *Procycling*, the *Official Tour de France guide* and *Ride Cycling* review. He has, amongst other jobs worked for Sigma Sport and he was Press-Officer for the ill-fated Linda McCartney Professional Cycling Team. His experience of the strange and chequered history of that team spawned the book *Team on the Run* (Mainstream Publishing 2002). Last year *Bradley Wiggins: Tour de Force* (Birlinn 2012) brought John back into the limelight and he's just completed his latest work with Sean Yates, *12 months in the Saddle* (Carlton 2013). Away from cycling, John's other love is football: he supports Chelsea FC for his sins!

Luke Edwardes-Evans is a renowned journalist and is former editor of Winning : Bicycle Racing Illustrated and past editor of *Cycle Sport*. He has also freelanced for World Service Radio and compiled (with Phil Liggett) *The Complete Book of Performance Cycling*. He often works as a motor-bike pilot for one of the best known cycling photographers Graham Watson at many top Continental races. Recent books include *The Official Treasures of the Tour de France* (Carlton 2007) and *The Advanced Cyclist's Training Manual* (AC & Black 2010). He was editor of *Land Rover World* for a time but jumped at the chance to return to cycling and is currently deputy editor at *Cycling Active* magazine and editor of *Tour, the Tour de France preview magazine*.

When **Lucy Fallon** moved to Spain she found a country gone completely mad on cycling: it was the time when Perico Delgado and Miguel Indurain were reigning in France, when a female cyclist could expect to receive encouraging shouts of 'Venga, Induraina!' from passers-by. Infected with the fever, she co-authored *Viva la Vuelta!* a history of the national race set against the turbulent events of 20th century Spain. She continues to observe the ups and downs of Spanish professional cycling with keen interest.

Graeme Fife is a prolific English writer and broadcaster whose has written and directed plays for stage & radio. He was educated at schools in London and Durham University, where he gained a General Arts degree with first class honours in Greek language and literature. He is one of the few cycling writers who can honestly claim to have ridden over all the Tour's major climbs, and has written about them in his books: *Tour de France; the history, the legend, the riders* (Mainstream Publishing 1999/revised 2012) and *Inside the Peloton; riding, winning and losing the Tour de France* (Mainstream Publishing 2001). More recent titles include *Great Road Climbs of the Southern Alps* (Rapha 2010), the acclaimed *Brian Robinson, Pioneer* (Mousehold Press 2010) and *Great Road Climbs of the Northern Alps* (Rapha 2011).

David Harmon, a former Westminster Abbey choirboy, discovered cycling at Sheffield University where he studied archaeology, and was an early mountain biker in the 1980s. After a knee injury forced him off the bike following the 1993 National MTB Championships he became a sports journalist with Channel One TV – a job which he discovered to his horror, included an 18-hour solo commentary at the Le Mans 24-hour race. Five years spent commentating on sports as varied as motor-racing and equestrian eventing, he finally returned to his first love, with a cycling commentary debut in the 2002 Tour of Spain on British Eurosport. David has cemented his reputation as cycling's leading English speaking 'voice' at Eurosport and his partnership with co-commentator and Irish legend Sean Kelly during the racing season has elevated them to being leaders of the pack. He now devotes much of his time to his P.R.and production business (www.spokesmen.co.uk) and successfully worked hard to bring the Tour de France to Yorkshire for next year's *Grand Départ*.

Graham Healy is an Irish author whose first title was *Shay Elliott - The Life and Death of Ireland's First Yellow Jersey* (Mousehold Press, 2011). He has just published his latest book, entitled, *The Curse of the Rainbow Jersey* (Breakaway Books, 2013). He is also a regular contributor to the Sticky Bottle website.

Carlton Kirby began broadcasting at the BBC over 25 years ago. Moving to ITV and then Eurosport he has become one of the most recognisable voices in sports commentary, covering cycling and motorsports with equal aplomb. Whether it's live from the roadside or ably assisting fellow commentators at the Grand Tours, Carlton's enthusiasm for the task in-hand goes without question. Anecdotes collected from a lifetime of worldwide travel stretching from Timbuktu to Tuvalu, where he ran the local radio station. Keeping the nine island nation together right on the International Date Line to his favourite hobby of pistol-shooting, a skill handed-down from his Father, a 'cross-rifle' badged sharp-shooter (sniper) in Korea. Carlton helps to keep an audience entertained through the quieter moments of the longest stages of the Tour de France with his historic knowledge and his foodie and vino expertise of the regions the race is passing though. This contrasts with his ability to call the action throughout the many races he covers for Eurosport as lead commentator. Schooled at Tapton Comprehensive in Sheffield as was Lord Coe and half of the Def Leppard line-up at the then Lancaster University where he captained the 1st rowing eight, Carlton is fast becoming a national treasure and for some reason the house-wife's favourite!

Marguerite Lazell has physics degrees from Sheffield University and Imperial College, but rejected a science career to pursue her love of cycling, and worked for *Cycling Weekly* and *Cycle Sport* for five years. She covered five Tour de Frances, two Olympic Games, many one-day Classics and stages races, and World Championships on the road, track and cyclo-cross. Her book, *Tour de France – the Complete Illustrated History*, published by Carlton Books, is currently in its ninth edition. Talented as an editor and proof-reader as well as being a fine freelance journalist, she is based in Sussex and watches as much cycling on television as her two small children will allow. Cycle racing is, of course, still one of her major passions and she hopes to cement that love of the sport in the coming years in her professional career.

John Pierce was the first British photographer at the Tour de France in 1967 and has covered every Tour since. He is a former Great Britain International speed-skater and racing cyclist and was coach/consultant to the US Women's Olympic cycling team throughout the 1980s. In 1989 he won the award for Sports Action Photographer of the Decade and currently owns the largest and oldest independent cycling picture library in the world.

Matt Rendell is a prolific cycling writer, linguist, historian and former jazz musician. He survived Hodgkin's Disease and lectured at British and Lavian universities before entering journalism. He has written for television documentaries (including the British coverage of the Tour de France) and for *Procycling*. He is the author of a very well received Channel 4 documentary about cycling in Colombia and his book *Kings* *of the Mountains: how Colombia's cycling heroes changed their nation's history* (Aurum Press 2002) won him the National Sports Book Publishing Award for best new writer. Matt's has been a prolific writer in the last decade: *A Significant Other: Riding the cententary Tour de France with Lance Armstrong* (Phoenix 2005), *The Death of Marco Pantani* (Phoenix 2007), *Blazing Saddles: the cruel and unusual history of the Tour de France* (Quercus 2007), *Olympic Gangster: The legend of Jose Beyaert* (Mainstream 2011) and *Salsa for people who shouldn't do it* (Mainstream 2011) and for the past few seasons has worked on Channel 4 Tour de France coverage and many other broadcasters.

Chris Sidwells is a top cycling journalist and author who was born in Harworth and is the nephew of the great British rider Tom Simpson. He has in the past been a detective, which we claims helps him to understand cyclists better, he is now a prolific cycling-writer contributing regularly to *Cycle Sport, ProCycling, Cycling Weekly* and *Cycling Plus*. His book *Mr Tom : the true story of Tom Simpson* (Mousehold Press / Sport & Publicity 2000) is the finest account of Simpson's racing career. His published range covers road racing: *A Race for Madman* (Collins 2011), leisure cycling: *Best 100-mile Bike Rides* (Harpersport 2013) and Tour Climbs: *The Complete Guide to every Mountain stage of the Tour de France* (Collins 2009), maintenance books: *The Complete Bike Book* (Dorling Kindersley 2003) and *Bike Repair Manual* (Dorling Kindersley 2011) plus sportive preparation: *Cyclosportive: Preparing for and taking part in long distance cycling challenges* (A&C Black 2011).

Herbie Sykes is a cycling journalist and historian. He lives in Turin and has written extensively about the Giro d'Italia and Italian cycling and is a regular contributor to a number of cycling journals, amongst them *ProCycling* and *Rouleur*, where is historic articles are held in such high regard. His first book *The Eagle of the Canavese*, was a biography of Franco Balmamion, twice a Giro winner in the early sixties. Published by Mousehold Press and Sport & Publicity in 2008, it achieved widespread critical acclaim. *Cycling Weekly* called it 'a gem of a book'. Sykes's second book, *Maglia Rosa* (Bloomsbury Sport 2011) was an illustrated history of the Giro which won the Podiumcafe.com book of the year award. Herbie's latest work *Coppi* (Bloomsbury Sport 2012) is a beautiful photographic evocation of the great *campionissimo*. Herbie's writing is some of the very finest around and his knowledge of Italian and historic cycle racing is second to none.

Rik Van Walleghem was born in Wevelgem and is one of Europe's most accomplished cycling journalists working today. He has written for most of the top newspapers and cycling magazines in Belgium and his work frequently appears in translation in journals throughout the Continent. His book *Eddy Merckx: the greatest cyclist of the 20th Century* (Penguin Productions 1993), is acknowledged as one of the finest books written about cycle-racing's greatest champion: it also stands as a model for a sports biography. Apart from all that, Rik is the curator of the splendid Tour of Flanders museum in Oudenaarde in the heart of Flanders and is where this great classic race now finishes. Visitors to the museum will be welcomed by the legendry Flandrian and twice World Road Champion Freddy Maertens working on reception.

John Wilcockson is a British sports journalist and author who has covered professional cycling for over 40 years. He raced for Redhill CC as a first-category roadman in the 1960s and spent two seasons completing in France. Trained as a civil engineer at London University, he gave up that career when invited by Jock Wadley to join the staff of *International Cycle Sport* in 1968. He has been a professional writer ever since and was cycling correspondent for *The Times* before moving America in 1987. To-date he has written 12 books including *Marco Pantani: The Legend of a Tragic Champion* (Velopress 2005) and *Tour de France 2007* (Velopress 2007). He has also received two awards from the Tour de France organisers: the Medaille de la Reconnaissance and the Plaque de la Reconnaissance. John now lives in Boulder, Colorado where he works freelance and is currently concentrating on producing E-Books.

Les Woodland, with nearly 30 publications to his name, is a long-established cycling author and long-time member of the Westerley RC. He has been writing and broadcasting about the sport ever since he ignored his Mother who told him writing about bicycles wasn't a proper job and joined the staff at *Cycling Weekly* in the 1970s. Les admits he has spent all his life unearthing strange stories and personalities behind the world's greatest and oddest sport. *The Inside Story: All the bumps of cycling's cobbled classic* is his latest offering about the punishing Paris-Roubaix race. He lives near Toulouse in South West France, just twenty kilometres from the route of the 1903 Tour de France.

Charlie Woods discovered the glories of Continental cycle racing as a teenager in the mid-fifties through the sepia images of the French sporting journals. His dream of becoming the Louison Bobet of the South of

England never materialised, however. A librarian by profession, Charlie lives in West London and has written for many cycling magazines. His autobiographical book *Bikie: a love affair with the racing bicycle* was published by Mainstream in 2002 and he's been involved until recently with the highly successful Riverside cycling film-shows at Hammersmith.

Richard Yates was a wonderful and passionate cycling historian who rode with the Southern Velo and VC Sacchi in Great Britain but lived in France for the last twenty years. He described himself as *un collectioneur* – a collector of old cycling books, magazines and memorabilia. He had written numerous historical articles for journals and distinguished himself with *Master Jacques : the Enigma of Jacques Anquetil* (Mousehold Press/ Sport & Publicity 2001). His other works included *Ascent: the Mountains of the Tour de France* (Midpoint Trade Books Inc. 2007). Very sadly Richard passed away in June 2011 aged 73.